GREAT SINGERS OF TODAY

By the same Author

SOPRANOS OF TODAY

TWO CENTURIES OF OPERA AT
COVENT GARDEN

THE CONCISE OXFORD DICTIONARY
OF OPERA (with John Warrack) published
in 1964

Also Editor of OPERA ANNUALS 1–9
    „   OPERA MAGAZINE

MARIA CALLAS

GREAT SINGERS OF TODAY

HAROLD ROSENTHAL

CALDER AND BOYARS LTD. · LONDON

FIRST PUBLISHED IN GREAT BRITAIN IN 1966
BY CALDER AND BOYARS LTD.
18 BREWER STREET, LONDON, W.1

© Copyright Harold Rosenthal, 1966

All Rights Reserved

SET IN 11/14 pt. MONOTYPE BEMBO
AND PRINTED IN IRELAND BY
HELY THOM LTD. DUBLIN

CONTENTS

Name	Page	Name	Page
LICIA ALBANESE	17	CHRISTEL GOLTZ	68
LUCINE AMARA	18	RITA GORR	77
SALVATORE BACCALONI	19	JOSEF GREINDL	78
FEDORA BARBIERI	20	ELISABETH GRÜMMER	78
ETTORE BASTIANINI	21	HILDE GUEDEN	79
TERESA BERGANZA	21	JOAN HAMMOND	80
CARLO BERGONZI	22	MARGARET HARSHAW	81
JUSSI BJOERLING	23	JEROME HINES	82
KURT BÖHME	24	ELISABETH HOENGEN	83
INGE BORKH	29	GRACE HOFFMAN	84
OWEN BRANNIGAN	30	HANS HOTTER	93
GRÉ BROUWENSTIJN	31	JAMES JOHNSTON	94
MARIA CALLAS	32	SENA JURINAC	95
ROSANNA CARTERI	34	PETER KLEIN	96
BORIS CHRISTOFF	34	OTAKAR KRAUS	97
FRANCO CORELLI	35	ERICH KUNZ	98
FERNANDO CORENA	36	BENNO KUSCHE	98
RÉGINE CRESPIN	45	GERDA LAMMERS	99
LISA DELLA CASA	46	ADÈLE LEIGH	100
MARIO DEL MONACO	47	RICHARD LEWIS	109
VICTORIA DE LOS ANGELES	49	WILMA LIPP	110
GIUSEPPE DI STEFANO	50	GEORGE LONDON	111
MATTIWILDA DOBBS	51	JEAN MADEIRA	112
OTTO EDELMANN	52	ROBERT MERRILL	113
GERAINT EVANS	61	NAN MERRIMAN	114
DIETRICH FISCHER-DIESKAU	62	ZINKA MILANOV	114
SYLVIA FISHER	62	MARTHA MÖDL	116
GOTTLOB FRICK	64	GEORGINE VON MILINKOVIC	116
NICOLAI GEDDA	65	ELSIE MORISON	125
HOWELL GLYNNE	66	BIRGIT NILSSON	126
TITO GOBBI	66	PETER PEARS	127

	Page		Page
JAMES PEASE	128	ANTONIETTA STELLA	163
JAN PEERCE	129	RISË STEVENS	164
ROBERTA PETERS	130	TERESA STICH-RANDALL	173
CLARA PETRELLA	131	EBE STIGNANI	174
ANNA POLLAK	131	RITA STREICH	176
REGINA RESNIK	132	JOAN SUTHERLAND	177
ELENA RIZZIERI	141	SET SVANHOLM	178
NICOLA ROSSI-LEMENI	142	FERRUCCIO TAGLIAVINI	193
LEONIE RYSANEK	143	RENATA TEBALDI	194
PAUL SCHOEFFLER	144	BLANCHE THEBOM	196
ELISABETH SCHWARZKOPF	145	RICHARD TUCKER	197
GRAZIELLA SCIUTTI	146	HERMANN UHDE	198
IRMGARD SEEFRIED	147	CESARE VALLETTI	199
AMY SHUARD	148	ASTRID VARNAY	200
CONSTANCE SHACKLOCK	158	JON VICKERS	205
CESARE SIEPI	159	RAMON VINAY	207
GIULIETTA SIMIONATO	160	LEONARD WARREN	208
LEOPOLD SIMONEAU	160	WOLFGANG WINDGASSEN	210
ELEANOR STEBER	162	VIRGINIA ZEANI	211

ACKNOWLEDGMENTS

The author wishes to acknowledge his gratitude to the following photographers who have granted him permission to reproduce their work:

DEREK ALLEN	MARCHIORI
ERICH AUERBACH	CAROLYN MASON-JONES
RUDOLF BETZ	ANGUS McBEAN
BOSIO	LOUIS MELANÇON
M. CAMUZZI	WILFRID NEWTON
RENZO CINTI	PARTICAM
ANTHONY CRICKMAY	ERIO PICCAGLIANI
HANS DIETRICH	CLAUDE POIRIER
DINAMI	REALE
DELIRVA	F. RICHTER
ELLINGER	HOUSTON ROGERS
GÜNTHER ENHENT	ENAR MERKEL RYDBERG
HENRY ELY	OSCAR SAVIO
FAYER	SCAFIDI
FOTO FILM	GUSTAV SCHIKOLA
GIESSNER	HELGA SHARLAND
GUY GRAVETT	DAVID SIM
ENGBERT GÜNTER	NANCY SORENSEN
ROBERT HARPER	DONALD SOUTHERN
NANCY HOLMES	LISELOTTE STRELOW
ROBERT LACKERBACH	THE TIMES
SEDGE LEBLANG	SABINE TOEPFFER
LEVI	A. VILLAIN & FIGLI
LOCCHI	HANS WILD
A. MADNER	ROGER WOOD

as *Madama Butterfly*

as *Violetta* in 'La Traviata'

LICIA ALBANESE

LUCINE AMARA

as *Tatiana* in 'Eugene Onegin'

as *Donna Elvira* in 'Don Giovanni'

as *the Sacristan* in 'Tosca'

SALVATORE BACCALONI

as *Leporello* in 'Don Giovanni'

as *Geronte* in 'Manon Lescaut'

FEDORA BARBIERI

as *Amneris* in 'Aida'

as *Carmen*

ETTORE BASTIANINI

as *Ernesto* in 'Il Pirata'

as *Gérard* in 'Andrea Chénier' as *Posa* in 'Don Carlos'

as *Cherubino* in 'Le Nozze di Figaro'

TERESA BERGANZA

as *Rosina* in 'Il Barbiere di Siviglia'

as herself

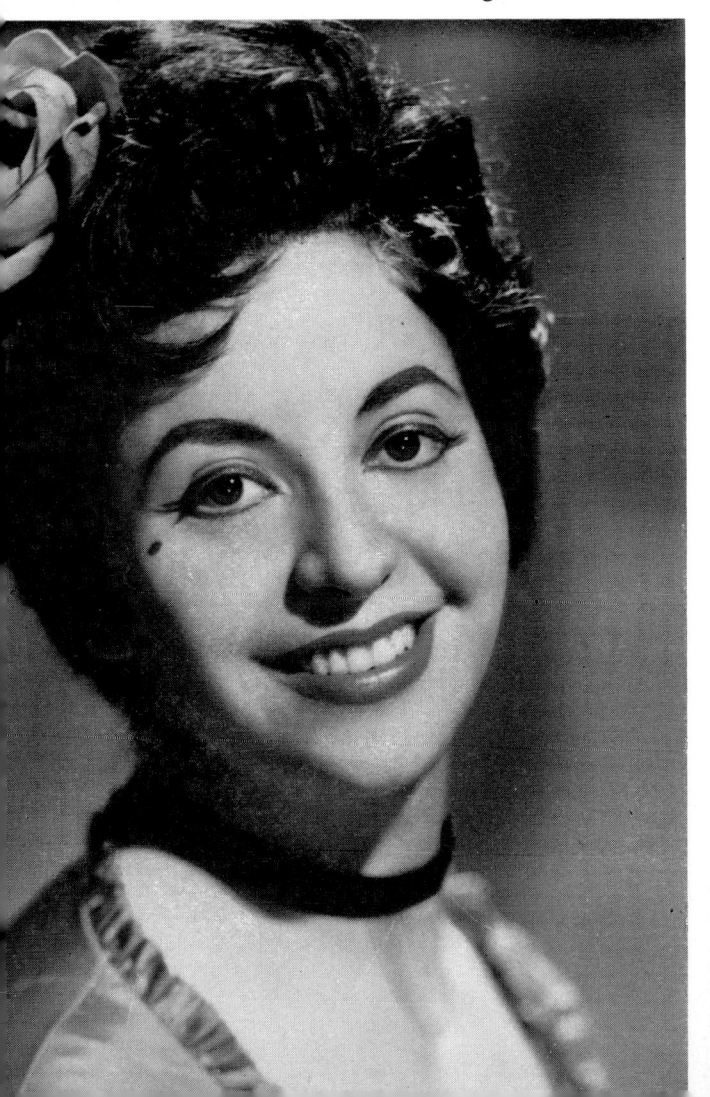

CARLO BERGONZI

as *Radames* in 'Aida'

as *Canio* in 'Pagliacci'

as *Alvaro* in 'La Forza del Destino'

JUSSI BJÖRLING

as *Rodolfo* in 'La Bohème'

as *Des Grieux* in 'Manon Lescaut'

GREAT SINGERS

LICIA ALBANESE

At the end of the 1962-63 opera season at the Metropolitan, Licia Albanese completed her twenty-fourth season with the company. Although she is now an American citizen, married to a New York stock-broker, and has only sung in Italy two or three times since the war, she is still essentially an Italian prima donna—without however the flamboyance and temperamental outbursts that mark so many Italian-born singers.

Licia Albanese was born in Bari on July 22, 1913. Her family was musical, and she was originally destined to become a professional pianist. She soon discovered however that she had a voice, and went to Milan to study singing with Giuseppina Baldassare-Tedeschi. In 1935 she entered for a singing competition organised by the Italian government and was awarded first prize over 300 rivals, the conductor Gino Marinuzzi specially singling her out for praise. As a result she was engaged for the Reggio in Parma where she made her début in June that year in the title-role of *Madama Butterfly*. That was her official début, but in actual fact she had sung the same role a few months earlier at the Teatro Lirico in Milan, when she was summoned from the audience by the manager to replace another soprano who had fallen ill half-way through the first act. The soprano always looks on her success on this occasion as the foundation of her 'luck' in the future.

During the next few years she quickly established herself as one of the most promising young Italian sopranos. She sang Lauretta (*Schicchi*), Suzel (*L'Amico Fritz*), Micaela, and Mimi at La Scala; Monica (*La Fiamma*), Sophie (*Werther*), Vivetta (*L'Arlesiana*), Pamina, Inez (*L'Africana*), Liù and other roles in Rome; and Butterfly, and Nannetta at other leading Italian theatres.

In 1937 she was engaged to sing Liù and Nannetta during the Coronation season at Covent Garden. 'Her voice was fresh and steady, and she carried her appeals to Calaf and the princess to their climaxes with a fine sense of phrase and tone' wrote *The Times* critic, following her Covent Garden début. Her Nannetta was also singled out for special praise in an otherwise not particularly distinguished performance of *Falstaff*.

Another success soon followed, she was engaged to record Mimi opposite Gigli in the His Master's Voice recording of *La Bohème*; and it was her voice that was heard singing when the Vatican Radio Station was opened in 1937.

When war came to Europe in 1939, Albanese continued to sing in Italy for a little longer, but when an invitation came to her to join the Metropolitan in New York for the 1939-40 season, she eagerly accepted it, making her début there on February 9, 1940 as Butterfly, and following it with Mimi a fortnight later. Of her performance in the latter role, *Musical America* wrote: 'Mme. Albanese seemed much at home in the part, singing with notable grace and generally exquisite tonal quality. Histrionically her performance was unaffected and sympathetic'.

Those kind of words were to be repeated often throughout her American career. As her dramatic insight into roles deepened, and her voice grew in size, she enlarged her repertory, which by 1952 included Violetta, Giorgetta (*Il Tabarro*), Manon Lescaut and Tosca. Violetta is probably her most successful role, and certainly the one in which she will always be remembered. Toscanini chose her to sing it in his broadcast performances for the N.B.C. in 1946, and the performances have been preserved on gramophone record, as has also the *La Bohème*, in which Albanese sang Mimi.

In San Francisco, Chicago and Cincinatti Albanese is a great favourite, and she has sung in addition in many of the smaller American operatic centres. Her repertory further includes Lady Harriet (*Martha*), Norina, Zerlina, Susanna, Suor Angelica, Giulietta (*Hoffmann*), Madeleine de Coigny (*Andrea Chénier*) and Nedda.

Albanese's approach to opera is highly serious, and she studies and analyses her roles thoroughly when she is

17

preparing them. 'In presenting an operatic portrayal', she said in an interview in America, 'even the smallest things are important, for everything must be part of the final characterization. For example, in the first act love duet, the white veil that Butterfly wears over her head is a sign of her youthful purity. As night falls on her wedding day and she and Pinkerton enter their little Japanese house, I let the veil fall and remain on the steps: a little thing, but effective'.

Albanese is also painstakingly careful over her stage make-up; for she says, popular misconceptions can be disproved by careful research. And to quote from *Butterfly* again: 'I do not slant my eyes way up high as is often thought to be authentically Japanese. Actually the eyes of the Japanese are slanted directly to the side'.

This care and serious approach to her art, allied to a voice, both beautiful and well-schooled, combine to make her a most satisfying artist.

LUCINE AMARA

ONLY a very few American sopranos have sung a leading role in a new production on an opening night of a Metropolitan opera season in New York. But this honour fell to Lucine Amara in November 1957, when she sang Tatiana in *Eugene Onegin*, thus consolidating a position she had been slowly building up as one of the Metropolitan's leading sopranos.

Lucine Amara was born of humble Armenian parents (her real name is Armaganian) in Hartford, Connecticut on March 1, 1927. When she was six she began to have piano lessons, and then when she was eleven and had moved with her family to San Francisco, she began to study the violin, with the intention of becoming a teacher of that instrument. She even played in a local orchestra at the time, and although she sang in a church choir, had no thought of becoming a singer.

When she was eighteen, she was encouraged to study singing by Stella Eisner-Eyn, who has been her only teacher. During the 1945-46 season she sang with the San Francisco Opera chorus at night, earning her living during the day working in a bank. In 1947 she was heard in San Francisco by the Metropolitan conductor Paul Breisach on whose suggestion she went to New York to audition; she was then only twenty and was told that her voice had not yet matured. In the summer of 1947 she made her San Francisco début in a solo recital, and the following month was awarded a scholarship to the Music Academy at Santa Barbara. The next year she won a nation-wide singing contest called the Arwater Kent award valued at $2,000, gaining the prize from 1,500 other singers. Part of her award was an appearance in the Hollywood Bowl under Eugene Ormandy.

This concert brought her to the attention of Carl Ebert, head of the opera department of the University of California, where she was awarded a scholarship. While studying with Ebert she sang in his productions of *Ariadne auf Naxos* and *Albert Herring*. In January 1950 she appeared in San Francisco in Honegger's *Roi David* under Rodzinski; and in March of the same year had an audition at the Metropolitan, and was engaged by Rudolf Bing for the 1950-1 season.

Amara's New York début was as the Celestial Voice, an unseen role, in *Don Carlos*, which also marked the opening night of Bing's régime as general manager of the Metropolitan. The late Cecil Smith wrote 'Miss Amara, confined to the few phrases of the off-stage Celestial Voice in the auto-da-fé scene, sang brightly and prettily, and reached the high Bs without the slightest apparent difficulty'. During her first season she only sang small roles—Wellgunde, The First Lady (*Magic Flute*), Kate Pinkerton, and Inez (*Trovatore*). The following year she repeated these parts adding to them the Countess Ceprano, the Priestess in *Aida*, the Fourth Maid in *Elektra*, the First Flower Maiden in *Parsifal* and her first major role, Nedda in *Pagliacci*.

By February 1954 she had added Micaela, Mimi and Donna Elvira to her repertory; and *Musical America* writing about her Elvira commented: 'Watching Miss Amara mature steadily as an artist and singer since her début at the Metropolitan three years ago, in a tiny off-stage part in *Don Carlos*, has been a heart-warming experience. Her voice has become even better focused and more gleaming, and at this performance it seemed debatable that Donna Elvira's music had ever sounded so meltingly lovely. Miss Amara met the challenge of the coloratura passages with almost complete ease, and she brought to the role an appealing temperament—more than she had previously displayed'.

In the summer of 1954 Amara went to Glyndebourne to sing Ariadne, a role she has repeated there on a number of occasions since. In New York she has further added to her stature by singing Countess Almaviva, Desdemona, Antonia (*Hoffmann*), Eva, Pamina, Eurydice, the Tatiana mentioned at the very beginning of this biography, and the title role in *Aida*. This last role she has also sung in Italy at the Terme di Caracalla and at the Vienna State Opera. Still in her thirties, Amara can look ahead to a long and successful career.

SALVATORE BACCALONI

It is probably no exaggeration to say that Salvatore Baccaloni is the greatest buffo bass since the immortal Lablache, the creator of Don Pasquale, and admired singer in the days of Queen Victoria, to whom he gave singing lessons.

Baccaloni was born in Rome on April 14, 1900. When he was seven he sang as a boy-soprano in the Sistine Chapel Choir; but when his voice broke, he gave up thoughts of singing and studied to become an architect. Yet he had a natural love for the theatre, and indulged in amateur theatricals whenever he had time to spare. He sometimes participated in musical evenings, and on one such occasion he was approached by an old gentleman who asked him why he was studying to be an architect when he possessed such magnificent vocal material. The old man was the famous baritone Giuseppe Kaschmann, who became Baccaloni's teacher.

After two years study Baccaloni made his début at the Teatro Adriano in Rome in 1922 as Bartolo in *Il Barbiere di Siviglia*. In 1926 he was engaged by Toscanini for La Scala, where for three seasons he sang mostly straight bass roles, including The King in *Aida*, Timur in *Turandot*, Angelotti and Geronte. It was in such small bass roles that he made his first London appearances at Covent Garden in 1928 and 1929, but he had begun to display his comic talents even then as the Sacristan in *Tosca* and Varlaam in *Boris Godunov*, which he sang in the Chaliapin performances.

It was Toscanini who urged Baccaloni to concentrate on the buffo repertory. He began with Bartolo in *Figaro* and he was soon singing such parts as Dulcamara (*L'Elisir d'Amore*), Pasquale, Fra Melitone, Geronimo (*Il Matrimonio Segreto*), and roles in the comic operas of Wolf-Ferrari.

In the summer of 1936 he was engaged for the Glyndebourne Festival where he made his début on the opening night of the season as Leporello in *Don Giovanni*; 'a capital rustic Leporello, a genuine buffo character, but not exaggerated', wrote the *Daily Telegraph*; and later that season he enacted a wonderfully ripe Bartolo. The following summer he repeated these roles, and was heard as Alfonso in *Così fan tutte*. 'It is conceivable that Mr. Baccaloni has an equal in buffo roles. It is impossible to believe that he has a superior', wrote one of London's leading critics. When, in 1938, he sang Don Pasquale at Glyndebourne with the unsurpassed Mariano Stabile as Malatesta, the critics ran out of superlatives. The late Bonavia thought 'his performance left no loophole for adverse criticism'.

In December 1940 Baccaloni made his début at the Metropolitan, New York, and has been a member of the company ever since. His European triumphs were repeated in America; *Don Pasquale* and *La Fille du Régiment* were both revived for him in his initial season. And as the years went by he added Dulcamara, Leporello, Gianni Schicchi, Uberto (*La Serva Padrona*), as well as the roles he had already sung in Europe, to his repertory.

San Francisco and Chicago, Buenos Aires and Mexico, and other cities throughout the American continent have enjoyed Baccaloni's art during the last twenty or more years. Only perhaps his Falstaff, which he sang at San Francisco, did not meet with universal approval. In recent years he has become even more widely known through the medium of the cinema.

An enormous man, he weighs more than 320 pounds, he enjoys life and especially food. He tells that the saddest day in his life was when the doctor placed him on a fruit and vegetable diet; and the happiest day of his life, the day he gave it up. Baccaloni recalls that on that occasion, he went off on an eating spree, beginning with four pizzas, and then a three-meat meal, and finally a half-a-pound of

Italian desert cheese. Yet Baccaloni, like all great clowns, has a serious side to his art, and that is why his greatest role, Pasquale, is tinged with wistfulness, and always enlists the audience's sympathy at the moment when Norina slaps his face, and leaves him alone and dejected. We certainly have not seen his equal in our time.

FEDORA BARBIERI

ONE can think of very few opera singers who have been the subject of a feature article, complete with two photographs, in the sedate columns of the London *Times*. Yet this privilege was accorded the Italian mezzo-soprano Fedora Barbieri, when she came to London in the summer of 1958 to sing the role of Eboli in the Covent Garden centenary production of Verdi's *Don Carlos*.

Fedora Barbieri was born in Trieste on June 4, 1920, and from her early childhood always wanted to be a singer. She began to study in her teens with Luigi Toffolo, and in 1940 won a scholarship to the famous Centro Lirico Sperimantale at Florence, where she studied with Mario Labrocca and Giulia Tess. She made her début there in November, 1940, as Fidalma in Cimarosa's *Il Matrimonio Segreto*, following it the next night with Azucena. A further period of study followed, and in May, 1941, she sang at the Florence Festival in a revised version of Alfano's *Don Juan de Manara* opposite Gigli, and in Gluck's *Armide*. She opened the 1941-2 season at the Rome Opera in the Alfano work, and then after further appearances in Rome and Florence, made her La Scala début during the 1942-3 season as Meg in *Falstaff* under Victor de Sabata.

During the next four years she added several roles to her repertory, including Preziosilla, Ulrica, Mistress Quickly, Carmen, Eboli, Laura (*Gioconda*), Princess of Bouillon (*Adrianna Lecouvreur*), and Leonora in *La Favorita*.

In 1947 Barbieri made her first appearances outside Europe, at the Teatro Colon Buenos Aires, where she was heard as Amneris, Adalgisa and Preziosilla. She has returned to Buenos Aires on several occasions since, and has also been heard in other South American cities.

In the autumn of 1950 Barbieri was heard in London with the Scala Company when she sang Mistress Quickly and the Verdi *Requiem* at Covent Garden. Shortly after that she went to New York to inaugurate the Bing régime at the Metropolitan, by singing Eboli in the new production there of *Don Carlos*. Cecil Smith wrote: 'Her voice, like those of many other Italian mezzo-sopranos, possesses a vehement chest register, which she uses with force and abandon. She vocalizes skilfully across the break into the middle voice, retaining an adequate volume, and when she is lucky she is able to reach a secure B flat. .... As an actress she was at ease volatile, and sensible, and even when her singing was not at its best, it was enhanced by her personal dynamism'.

During her first Metropolitan season she was also heard as Azucena. Then between 1951 and 1954 she added Amneris, Laura, Santuzza, Carmen and Adalgisa to her New York roles; and she returned again to the Metropolitan for the 1956-7 season to partner Callas in *Norma*. She has also been heard in San Francisco and other American cities.

La Scala and other Italian houses hear her regularly and she has in recent seasons sung Orfeo (Gluck), Marfa (*Khovanshchina*), Delilah and the Princess in *Suor Angelica*. It was not until 1957 that she returned to London, when she sang an emotional Azucena and an exciting Amneris. Her Eboli in *Don Carlos* in 1958 taxed her vocal resources at the top, and her interpretation was less 'refined' than some people expected; but once again her dramatic intensity made a great impression.

As a recording artist, Barbieri must be one of the busiest of our time. She participated in the war-time *Ballo* recording with Gigli; and she has sung in two recorded performances of *Aida* and *Trovatore*, a further *Ballo*, a *Requiem* under Toscanini, *Falstaff*, *La Gioconda*, *La Favorita*, *Linda di Chamounix*, and *Suor Angelica*.

Off-stage Barbieri is a simple and charming person. Full of fun, and a lover of good company and food. She is married to Luigi Barzoletti, also a musician, and they have a farm in the hills not far from Florence, where they spend what spare time they have with their two sons, Ugo and Franco.

ETTORE BASTIANINI

One of the leading Italian baritones of the post-war era, Ettore Bastianini, began his operatic career as a bass. He was born in Siena on September 24, 1922, and like many Italian boys, first sang in public as a local choir-boy. When he was in his teens he began his vocal studies with Fatima Amanati in Siena, and then a general music course at the Cherubini Conservatory. After two and a half years of military service, he continued his study at Florence under Flaminio Contini, and made his début at Florence in November, 1945 as Colline.

During the next five years Bastianini sang leading bass roles throughout the Italian provinces. While preparing the role of Padre Guardiano in *La Forza del Destino* with his teacher, he suddenly began to sing the tenor music in the last act. His teacher suggested to him that he thought he was not a bass at all; and so Bastianini stopped singing for six months and then began to study the baritone repertory. He made his second début, this time as Germont in *La Traviata* at Bologna on New Year's Eve, 1951.

He soon established himself as one of the leading Italian singers of the day. Besides singing the standard Verdi-Puccini repertory, his beautifully schooled voice is specially suited to Russian roles, and he has been heard as Prince Yeletzky in *The Queen of Spades* at Florence in December 1952, Prince Andrei in the world première of Prokofiev's *War and Peace* at the Florence Festival in 1953, the title-role in Tchaikovsky's *Mazeppa*, also at the Florence Festival in 1954, and as Eugene Onegin at La Scala the same year.

It was as Onegin that Bastianini made his Scala début, and his interpretation was hailed by Claudio Sartori, one of Italy's leading critics, as being 'particularly notable for its stylishness'. The same critic continued 'He showed himself the possessor of a supple voice, possessing some beautiful collorations and a warm tone'.

Bastianini has returned to the Scala regularly since—indeed one might say that he has become the theatre's leading baritone. He has sung there in most of the Verdi repertory and has also been heard in many leading roles of the bel-canto operas: Belcore in *L'Elisir d'Amore*, Ernesto in Bellini's *Il Pirata*, Severo in Donizetti's *Poliuto*, Lica in Handel's *Hercules*, and Riccardo in *I Puritani*. To all these he brings a well-schooled, warm and beautiful baritone voice, and a finished style, which suit him no less in parts like Gérard in *Andrea Chénier*, and Michele in *Il Tabarro*.

The baritone's American début was at the Metropolitan in December 1953 as Germont, and he was accorded a great ovation after his singing of 'Di Provenza'. In New York he also sang Amonasro, Posa, Enrico, Marcello, Di Luna, Gérard, Rigoletto, Escamillo and Carlo in *Forza*. He has also appeared with the Chicago Lyric Opera.

In the summer of 1958 Bastianini scored a great success as Posa in *Don Carlos* at Salzburg under Karajan, and he is also immensely popular in Vienna, where he made his début the same year in the title role of *Rigoletto*. He made a highly successful London début early in 1962 as Renato in *Un Ballo in Maschera*.

TERESA BERGANZA

One of the most amazing careers of recent years has been that of the young Spanish mezzo-soprano, Teresa Berganza, who in 1957 was virtually unknown, and who, by 1960 was in demand in the world's leading opera houses. Berganza was born in Madrid in 1934, and studied the piano at the Madrid Conservatory. There, as her second musical subject, she decided to study singing. Her teacher was Lola Rodriguez Aragon, who herself was a pupil of Elisabeth Schumann.

In 1954 Berganza carried off the first prize for singing at the Conservatory, and the following year made her début, in concert, at the Ateneo in Madrid. In 1957 she won the Isabel Castello prize, and was heard by that great discoverer of voices, Gabriel Dusurget, director of the Aix-en-Provence Festival, who engaged her for that summer. She made her début as Dorabella in *Così fan tutte*, scoring a great success both with her rich creamy mezzo-voice, and her enchanting stage personality. Her singing of the usually cut aria 'E amore un ladroncello' was one of the great moments of the *Così* performance.

The 1957-8 season found her at La Scala, where she was heard as Isolier in *Le Comte Ory*. 'Her warm, mellow singing was a joy to hear' wrote Claudio Sartori in *Opera*. An appearance at the San Carlo in Naples, as Dorabella, followed and then during the summer came her English début at Glyndebourne as Cherubino, an appearance at Cannes and Aix as Rosina. Writing about her Aix appearances, Andrew Porter said 'As Rosina she was outstanding, and offered some of the most perfectly accomplished singing I have ever heard. The voice runs more evenly than Supervia's. The basic colour is dark and glowing, but not at all dense. It can be bright and brilliant at the top, and it runs down to the low G without taking on any exaggeratedly chesty quality . . . . Her singing is marvellously fleet and flexible, encompassing runs, roulades and turns with precision . . . . She knows how to use words, how to colour phrases individually so that we may be constantly delighted, surprised, and engrossed'.

In the autumn of 1958 Berganza sang Cenerentola at the charming Teatro di Corte in Naples, and then made a highly successful American début as Isabella in *L'Italiana in Algeri* at Dallas. There too she was heard as Neris in *Medea* opposite Callas, and should have sung the same role at Covent Garden in the summer of 1959, but was prevented from so doing as she was expecting her first baby. She had married Felix Lavilla, a young Spanish composer, who had accompanied her in some of her recitals, the previous summer.

Other memorable events in the autumn of 1958 were Berganza's two concerts at the Leeds Festival, the first of which was attended by the Queen, the Duke of Edinburgh and the Queen Mother. The latter was so impressed that she attended her second concert too.

During the 1958-9 season, Berganza sang *L'Italiana* at Naples, Cherubino at the Vienna State Opera, Rosina at Genoa, and Cenerentola at Glyndebourne. Then came the birth of her first baby, and with it a natural curtailment of her activities for most of the 1959-60 season. By the spring of 1960 however, she had resumed her career. Covent Garden heard her Rosina, and Aix her Dido (Purcell) and her Cherubino.

During the 1960-61 season she continued to show an even deeper musical understanding of all she did. Her Cherubino at the Holland Festival in the summer of 1961 was as completely a satisfying a performance as one could wish for. It was exquisitely sung, and in the 'Non so più' one suddenly fully understood Cherubino's adolescent heart-pangs. This was one of the rare moments in an opera house when conductor, soloist and audience are magically at one with each other, and because the conductor on this occasion was Carlo Maria Giulini, a conductor who has often worked with and has the greatest admiration for Berganza, the spell that they cast was complete and binding.

Berganza's continued artistic growth is also to be heard in her concerts and recordings of Spanish songs. It is obvious that the future holds great things for this young artist, still in her early thirties.

CARLO BERGONZI

LIKE Bastianini, whose biography appears elsewhere in this volume, Carlo Bergonzi has had two singing careers, the first as a baritone from 1948 to 1951, and the second as a tenor since that date. He was born in Parma and trained at the local conservatory. He made his début as a baritone at Lecce in 1948, as Figaro in *Il Barbiere di Siviglia*. For the next three years he sang in the Italian provinces with fair success as Germont, Rigoletto, Marcello, Sharpless and in other baritone roles. Then in 1951 he found his voice changing, and after a further period of study made his second début at the Teatro Petruzzelli, Bari, as Andrea Chénier.

He very quickly established himself as one of Italy's leading dramatic tenors, and his brilliant upper register, his fine phrasing, and general musicianship, quickly earned him engagements all over Italy. The Italian Radio engaged him to sing a number of Verdi's roles during the Verdi Celebrations of 1951, namely, Gabriele Adorno, Alvaro, and Carlo VII in *Giovanna d'Arco*; and he appeared with success at La Scala and the San Carlo, Naples.

In 1953 he made his London début in a season of Italian opera at the Stoll Theatre, when he was heard as Alvaro in *La Forza del Destino*. *Opera* noted that his singing was reminiscent of Lauri-Volpi, and that he offered some of the best Italian singing since the war. When Bergonzi returned to London in 1962, this time to Covent Garden, again as Alvaro, he earned a well-deserved ovation after his singing of 'O tu che in seno agli' angeli'.

Two years later Bergonzi went to Chicago, where he

was heard as Turiddu and Luigi (*Tabarro*); and then he was engaged for the 1956-7 season at the Metropolitan, New York, where he made his début early in the season as Radames, following it with Manrico. During his second New York season he had a lot of work, and was heard as Cavaradossi, Don José, Alvaro, Chénier, Edgardo and Pinkerton, in addition to Radames; and he received consistently good notices from the critics, at least as far as his vocal efforts were concerned; as his partners included Callas, De Los Angeles, Milanov and Stella, this was no mean feat.

The *New York Times* writing about his Chénier said, 'He sings with taste and his intonation is impeccable'; while of his Rodolfo the same paper wrote that it was 'intelligent in action, more humorous than most Rodolfos know how to be, yet tender and passionate as the mood demanded. Mr. Bergonzi does not have a block-buster voice, but what a pleasure it is to hear the role sung for the music that is in it, without stentorian plays for the galleries'. And the *Herald-Tribune* commented of his Cavaradossi that 'his singing was consistently limpid and lovely'.

All this would suggest that Bergonzi is that rare thing, a cultivated and refined Italian tenor. He was engaged for the 1959-60 Metropolitan season, which opened in a new production of *Il Trovatore* with Stella and Simionato. Indeed his singing of Manrico's 'Ah si ben mio' on the Decca LP recital that he has made, complete with grace notes, is one of the most accomplished pieces of tenor singing to be heard today. He now sings regularly at the Metropolitan, New York and at the Vienna State Opera, and he has a repertory of more than fifty operas. Wisely he has decided not to sing Otello until much later in his career.

JUSSI BJOERLING

THE death on September 9, 1960, of Jussi Bjoerling, robbed the operatic stage of one of the greatest tenors of our day. He was forty-nine when he died, and he had spent almost as many years singing before the public, for he was not ten when he made his début!

He was born in Stora Tuna, in the province of Dalarna in Sweden. His father, Karl David Bjoerling had been trained as a singer in Vienna, and had appeared in America. When Jussi was eight years old his mother died, and his father decided to return to America with his three sons— Jussi, Gösta and Olle, all of whom had sung in a church choir. They joined their father in the 'Bjoerling Quartet' —all of them tenors. They toured America and then eventually returned to Sweden, and continued to appear there. The Quartet was heard by John Forsell, the famous Swedish baritone and director of the Stockholm Opera, who singled out Jussi and took him as his pupil in 1928. In 1930 he joined the school attached to the Royal Opera, and the same year he made his début as Ottavio in *Don Giovanni*.

For five years he sang with success in Stockholm, building up a repertory of some twenty operas (eventually it numbered more than fifty). Then gradually he began to make appearances abroad; first in Scandinavia—Copenhagen, Oslo, Helsingfors and Riga; then in 1936 he appeared as a guest in Prague and Vienna. 'In him at last the long-sought for lyric-heroic tenor in the grand style has been found', wrote a leading Viennese critic in March, 1936; while in Prague he was hailed as 'a real tenor with a God-given voice, who conquered a sold-out house in one stroke'.

His American début was made at the Chicago Opera in December, 1937 as the Duke in *Rigoletto*; and just a year later he made his New York opera début at the Metropolitan as Rodolfo following it with Manrico. 'Not in a long time has anything more lovely than his performance of 'Ah si ben mio' been heard on the Metropolitan stage', wrote *Musical America*. London heard him as Manrico the following summer, when his singing earned the highest praise.

During the 1939-40 and 1940-41 seasons at the Metropolitan, he was heard as Faust, the Duke in *Rigoletto*, and Riccardo in *Un Ballo in Maschera*, as well as Manrico and Rodolfo. Few singers have been the recipients of the kind of critiques that invariably came his way. What tenor would not give his right hand to read this about his performance in *Rigoletto*?

'Of Mr. Bjoerling's singing throughout the performance nothing but the highest praise can be said. Not only did the voice itself sound lovely in every moment but the exquisite flawless production, especially of the high register, was something for which to give thanks. One does not often hear such perfect singing. From 'Questa o quella' to 'La Donna è Mobille' it was a wonderful experience.'

During the war years Bjoerling remained in Sweden, singing at the Royal Opera in Stockholm. But in November, 1945, he returned to the Metropolitan, 'his perfectly lovely voice as delightful as ever, and its perfectly even scale a lesson for all tenors'. In January, 1947, he sang his first Roméo in New York, a role always associated with Jean de Reszke, and one which the Swedish tenor invested with 'youthful fervour and musicianship'. Three years later Bjoerling sang his first Des Grieux in *Manon Lescaut* at the Metropolitan and exhibited 'exemplary plasticity of phrasing and sensitivity of nuance'.

Bjoerling also appeared regularly with the San Francisco Opera Company and occasionally in Chicago; but the great European houses rarely heard him. He sang in a summer season organized by La Scala at the Palazzo del Sport in Milan in 1946, when his Duke of Mantua was acclaimed, but it was not until 1951 that he appeared at La Scala, when he sang Riccardo in *Un Ballo in Maschera* during the Verdi Celebrations. By this time the Bing régime at the Metropolitan had begun, and Bjoerling was as valuable a member of the company as he had been under the Edward Johnson management and indeed was chosen to inaugurate the Bing era by singing the title role in *Don Carlos* on the opening night of the 1950-1 season. He was absent from New York for the 1954-5 season, made only a few appearances between 1955 and 1957, and was again absent from 1957 to 1959; but he returned for the 1959-60 season, when his appearances elicited the warmest praise from the New York critics.

These long periods of absence from the New York stage did not mean idleness on Bjoerling's part, for he spent much time on the concert platform and the recording studio. And he also found time for appearances with the San Francisco and Chicago Operas, where he sang his first Radames in America in the autumn of 1958.

Finally in the winter of 1960 Bjoerling returned to Covent Garden to sing Rodolfo in *La Bohème* opposite Rosanna Carteri. The ease, style and beauty of his singing came as a revelation to many, and even if some of the more exacting of his critics took him to task for walking through the role and barely attempting to act, there was no denying that such finished singing is rarely heard on the operatic stage today.

When Bjoerling first began to be known in the late 1930s there was much talk about a second Caruso; but the Swedish tenor's voice did not possess that baritonal quality which characterised the great Italian singer. Bjoerling's voice however had something of a mediterranean warmth about it, and his many recordings bear testimony to one of the finest singers Sweden has ever produced.

KURT BÖHME

KURT BÖHME is a well-known figure to visitors to Munich and Vienna, and he divides most of his time between these two cities. He does find however opportunities to sing in other European centres, and always manages to return to his native Dresden two or three times a year to appear as Baron Ochs and Pogner.

Böhme was born in Dresden, and hearing a performance of *Carmen* at the local opera house decided to become a singer. He studied in Dresden with Dr. Kluge and made his début as Caspar in Der Freischütz. From 1933 to 1950 he was a permanent member of the Dresden ensemble, and it was with that company that he first came to London in 1936 singing Bartolo (Mozart), the Commendatore in *Don Giovanni*, the Notary in *Rosenkavalier* and A Lackey in *Ariadne auf Naxos*.

By the early 1940s however he was singing leading roles—Rocco and Baron Ochs at Florence, Gurnemanz in Vienna, Sarastro and Pogner in Dresden. During the war years in Dresden he created a number of roles, including Montague in Sutermeister's *Romeo und Julia*, Prospero in the same composer's *Die Zauberinsel* and La Roche in the first Dresden performance of Strauss's *Capriccio*.

In 1950 he sang Tarquinius in the Salzburg production of Britten's *The Rape of Lucretia* and in 1955 Tiger in the première of Egk's *Irische Legend*. Other modern works in which he has appeared include Orff's *Die Kluge*, *Trionfi d'Afrodite* and *Antigonae*.

KURT BOEHME

as *La Roche* in 'Capriccio'

as *Osmin* in 'Die Entführung aus dem Serail'

as *Baron Ochs*

INGE BORKH

as *Elektra*

as *Sieglinde* in 'Die Walküre'

OWEN BRANNIGAN

as *Noah* in 'Noye's Fludde'

as *Swallow* in 'Peter Grimes'

GRÉ BROUWENSTIJN

as herself

as *Leonore* in 'Fidelio'

Böhme made his American début at the Metropolitan as Pogner in November 1954, a role he has also sung at Bayreuth, and was also heard as the First Nazarene in *Salome*; during the 1956-7 New York season he sang Fasolt, Hunding, Fafner, and Hagen. It was also in the *Ring* that he returned to Covent Garden in 1956.

Perhaps his best role is Baron Ochs, which he sings regularly at the Munich summer festival, and which he presents in a decidedly racy manner; his rich bass voice can deal more than adequately with it from the musical point of view. Londoners heard him at last in this role in the revival of *Der Rosenkavalier* at Covent Garden in December 1960. This was the performance that introduced Georg Solti to London as an opera conductor (Solti of course is now Covent Garden's musical director), and also brought Elisabeth Schwarzkopf back to the opera house as the Marschallin, and Sena Jurinac as Octavian. 'Vocally the evening belonged without question to Kurt Böhme' wrote Martin Cooper in the *Daily Telegraph*; 'it was a triumph of musico-dramatic characterization. Like the great Richard Mayr he succeeded in holding the balance nicely between the boor and the nobleman...' Similar sentiments were expressed by other leading critics. Since then Böhme has sung the part in San Francisco and has added another role to his gallery of buffo characterizations, that of Don Pasquale in a new production of Donizetti's opera at Munich.

INGE BORKH

THE German approach to art being far more serious and thorough than elsewhere, it is hardly surprising that so many operatic artists who receive their training in Germany are as fine actors as they are singers. Indeed the careers of a number of outstanding German operatic personalities began, if not on the legitimate stage, at least with it in mind. Inge Borkh, for example, is a product of the Max Reinhardt School. She was born in Mannheim on May 26, 1917, the daughter of a Swiss diplomat and an Austrian soprano, and in 1936 went to Vienna to study at the Reinhardt Seminary, which was attached to the Burgtheater. Only then did she discover that she had a natural singing voice, and she was advised to go to Italy to study.

After a period of vocal and musical study in Florence, Milan and at the Mozarteum in Salzburg, she was engaged by the Stadttheater in Lucerne, where she made her début in 1940 as Cipra in *Der Zigeunerbaron*. All the war years were spent in Switzerland, and her engagement at Lucerne was followed by appearances at Berne, Basle and Zurich. Her roles at this time included Leonore (*Fidelio*), Aida, and Marie in *Wozzeck*.

In 1951 her performance as Magda Sorel in the first performance in German of *The Consul* at Basle created a sensation. This was a role which suited Inge Borkh's temperament and natural dramatic instinct, and it was not very long before the news of her success had spread into Germany, and brought her an invitation to sing as a guest artist at the Munich Opera, where her first performances were in the roles of Salome, and Senta in *Der Fliegende Holländer*. Munich, with its Richard Strauss tradition and history of great performers in the title role of Salome, quickly surrendered to this new young interpreter of the part of the Princess of Judaea.

At the Berlin Städtische Oper Inge Borkh's name soon appeared on the programmes, and to the parts she had already sung with success in Switzerland and Munich she added the title-roles of *Tosca*, *Mona Lisa* by Schillings and *Elektra*. In the summer of 1952 she sang Freia and Sieglinde at Bayreuth. Her vocal performances in these two operas were of a high order, but the Reinhardt-trained young actress found it very difficult to adapt her dramatic talents to the new Wagner production techniques. A few weeks after the Bayreuth Festival was over, Inge Borkh made her British début at the Edinburgh Festival, singing Leonore as a guest artist with the Hamburg ensemble. She was heard again at Edinburgh in the summer of 1956 when she sang some performances of Salome, and in 1958 when she sang Eglantine in a revival of Weber's rarely performed *Euryanthe*.

Borkh's American début was at San Francisco in the autumn of 1953 as Elektra, followed a little later by Turandot; she returned to San Francisco in 1954 and 1955. In the latter year she had a sensational success as Lady Macbeth in Verdi's opera which was having its first American performance for close on a century. In 1958 she made her Metropolitan Opera début as Salome, and was also heard as Sieglinde. She returned to the Metropolitan two years later to sing Elektra.

In Italy too Borkh is a familiar figure; and has sung the title role in Respighi's *La Fiamma* at La Scala and Rome; and has appeared as Turandot in Trieste and elsewhere.

At Salzburg in 1955 she created the role of Cathleen in the première of Egk's *Irische Legende*; and she has also sung Elektra there more recently. It was in this role that she made her London début with the Stuttgart Company in 1955, dividing the critics both professional and amateur. Some thought her lightish Italianate voice would have been more suited to the part of Chrysothemis; others found her visually too mannered; but all agreed that she sang the role with a rare freshness and purity of voice.

Borkh is not attached permanently to any one opera house; though she does spend a good deal of her time at Stuttgart, where her husband, Alexander Welitsch, was for many years one of the company's leading baritones. It must be an odd experience to sing John the Baptist or Orestes opposite one's own wife!

OWEN BRANNIGAN

ALTHOUGH Owen Brannigan sings such roles as Sarastro and Sparafucile in opera, and is heard regularly in oratorio, it is as a buffo that he has earned special distinction for himself in post-war British opera. Indeed it is safe to say that he has few rivals in this sphere in England today.

He was born on March 10, 1908, at Annitsford in Northumberland, and comes of Irish ancestry. His father was an organist in a local church and Brannigan sang in the choir; as a boy he also learned the piano, and accompanied for various school functions. When he was nineteen he became a member of two male voice choirs. Two years later he left Northumberland and went south in search of employment—those were the days of industrial depression and Brannigan was a skilled joiner. He found employment in Slough and soon joined the Windsor Operatic Society where his bass voice attracted attention and he was advised to have it trained professionally.

Accordingly he began to take lessons with William Barrand, a member of the Eton College Choir.

Soon he began to study at the Guildhall School of Music in London, where he worked in the evenings from 1934 to 1942 with Walter Hyde, and Ethel Atwood. In 1942 he won the School's Gold Medal, and the following year that of the Worshipful Company of Musicians. During this period of study he was a member of the choir of Westminster Cathedral, and in 1939 he took part in a B.B.C. studio production of *Hugh the Drover*.

In 1943 he was offered a contract with the Sadler's Wells Company making his début on tour as Sarastro and following it with Colline. It was not until 1944 however that he really established himself as a buffo, when he was heard as Don Alfonso in the wonderful production of *Così fan tutte* with Joan Cross, Margaret Ritchie, Rose Hill, Peter Pears and John Hargreaves, and then as Kecal in *The Bartered Bride*.

In 1946 when the Company moved back to its home in Rosebery Avenue, and opened a new chapter in British operatic history with the world première of *Peter Grimes*, Brannigan created the role of Swallow—a part he has sung at subsequent revivals at the Royal Opera House, and which he recorded for Decca in 1958. The following summer at Glyndebourne he created the part of Collatinus in Britten's *The Rape of Lucretia*. His association with Britten continued in 1958 when he created the title role in *Noye's Fludde* at Aldeburgh, and in 1960, also at Aldeburgh, when he sang Bottom in *A Midsummer Night's Dream*.

When the Edinburgh International Festival was launched in 1947, he was invited to sing with the Glyndebourne Company there as Bartolo and Banquo in Verdi's *Macbeth*; and in 1951 he was heard as Melitone and Leporello.

Meanwhile Brannigan's Sadler's Wells career continued and although he appeared there only as a guest artist between 1949 and 1953, he rejoined the company for its 1953-4 season, remaining with them until the end of the 1956-7 season. In November 1953 he scored a great success in the title-role of *Don Pasquale*, singing the role, according to *The Times*, 'With ripe delivery and firm vocal line'. A little later he sang his first Sadler's Wells Leporello and was also heard as Osmin, a role he had sung at the Bath Assembly several years previously. In June,

1954, he sang Dikoy in the revival of Janáček's *Katya Kabanova* under Kubelik, an interpretation that Desmond Shawe-Taylor found 'splendidly irascible'. Two other new roles he sang at the Wells during this period were Rocco in *Fidelio* and Dr. Coutras in John Gardner's *The Moon and Sixpence*.

Owen Brannigan possesses a fruity bass voice ranging from bottom C to top F. His diction is admirable, and his singing of Mozart especially is as convincing an argument for opera in English as any that can be advanced. Indeed this seems to have been recognised by the recording companies, for His Master's Voice have, in recent years, released a number of finely sung discs by Brannigan of Mozart and Handel arias sung in English.

GRÉ BROUWENSTIJN

HOLLAND, rather like the U.S.A. and Great Britain has no native operatic tradition, and it is only in the last ten years or so that a Dutch National Opera has been established. Like Britain too, Dutch singers in the past have been more renowned as lieder and oratorio artists. There were of course exceptions, and such artists as Elisabeth Ohms, Jacques Urlus and Anton van Rooy had world-wide reputations as Wagnerian singers earlier this century. With the establishment of a national opera, Holland is producing singers, a number of whom are already taking their places on the opera stages of the world. Such an artist is Gré Brouwenstijn.

She was born in Den Helder in North Holland on August 26, 1915, and started to take singing lessons when she was sixteen, attending classes at the Amsterdam Musik Lyceum. Her singing career started with appearances with the Dutch Broadcasting Company, when the Dutch critics looked on her as 'one of the most promising of our native artists'. In 1946 the Nederlandsche Opera was founded, and shortly after Gré Brouwenstijn joined the company. Her first leading role was Tosca in 1947, followed by Santuzza. Her roles with the company have included Elisabeth de Valois (*Don Carlos*), Leonora (*Trovatore*), Reiza (*Oberon*), the title-role in *Jenufa*, the Countess (*Figaro*), Amelia, and Tatiana (*Eugene Onegin*).

This singer's first appearances outside Holland were in Dublin, where she sang Tosca and Leonora in 1950. The B.B.C. was quick to recognise the potentialities of this talented young artist, and invited her to sing Jaroslavna (*Prince Igor*) and the title roles in *Iphigénie en Aulide*, *Rusalka* and *Jenufa*. She made her Covent Garden début as Aida under Barbirolli in October, 1951, and during the same season she was also heard as Leonora in *Il Trovatore*. She has been a constant visitor to London ever since, and her Amelia in Rennert's production of *Un Ballo in Maschera* will be gratefully remembered by many opera-goers.

The performances of *Rusalka* and *Jenufa* that Brouwenstijn sang for the B.B.C. were conducted by Rafael Kubelik, and conductor and singer developed a mutual admiration for each other's work. It was therefore appropriate that she was chosen to sing the part of Desdemona in the production of *Otello* at Covent Garden in October, 1955, which marked the beginning of Kubelik's régime as Musical Director of that theatre. Her Desdemona was probably the most moving interpretation of that role heard in London since the one unforgettable performance of the part by the Norwegian soprano, Eidé Norena, in 1937. When Brouwenstijn returned to repeat the role in the autumn of 1957, one of the most demanding of London's younger critics, wrote, 'Gré Brouwenstijn, was the tall, dignified, sweetly gentle and infinitely touching Desdemona'.

At the Holland Festival of 1957 she sang the soprano part in the Verdi *Requiem* under Carlo Maria Giulini, who was so impressed by her singing that he asked for her as Elisabeth de Valois in the Covent Garden Centenary production of *Don Carlos*, in May 1958. His confidence was amply justified, for Brouwenstijn sang the role with great feeling and displayed a beauty of voice that she had rarely shown in London before.

Brouwenstijn's sincere approach to music and her dramatic ability had already attracted the attention of Wieland Wagner at Bayreuth. She was asked by him to sing Elisabeth (*Tannhäuser*) in the 1954 Festival, and reappeared there in 1955 and 1956 as Sieglinde, Gutrune, and Eva. So quickly did she adapt herself to the new production methods of Wieland Wagner, that when he was asked by the Stuttgart Opera to produce *Fidelio*, he insisted that Brouwenstijn should sing the role of Leonore. His highly controversial production of *Fidelio* has also been seen in Paris and London and in both cities the Dutch artist scored a great personal success.

In the summer of 1958 she made her South American début at the Teatro Colon in the same role, in an unforgettable performance conducted by Beecham. She was hailed as the finest Leonore since Lotte Lehmann; a verdict that has been endorsed by several Viennese critics. She is now a regular member of the Vienna State Opera.

What are the secrets of Brouwenstijn's success? A beautiful voice; a natural musical intelligence; a graceful and attractive stage presence; and above all a great sincerity in all she does. And this is an attribute that British audiences especially appreciate in operatic artists.

MARIA CALLAS

WHATEVER one thinks of Maria Callas as an operatic artist there can be no denying that she has contributed more to Italian opera in our day than anyone else. Her name, like those of the legendary figures of opera from Catalani to Pasta, Pasta to Grisi, Grisi to Patti, is known to the man in the street. In Italy she has been the cause of the revival of long-neglected works by Bellini, Donizetti, Cherubini, Spontini and others—and her interpretations of the more familiar works in the repertory arouse fierce controversy. She is a sincere and highly intelligent artist; she demands the highest standards from her colleagues and from the opera houses that engage her; she is an untiring worker and seeker after perfection and a highly professional performer. All this has meant that the art of opera, especially Italian opera, has benefited.

She was born of Greek parents in New York on December 4, 1923, and it was in America that she spent her childhood. She went to Greece when she was thirteen and received her musical training at the Athens Conservatory, where her teacher was Elvira de Hidalgo, a Spanish coloratura soprano, who had sung at the Scala, the Metropolitan and at Covent Garden in the 1920's, strangely enough with the British National Opera Company.

Callas's début was made at the Athens Opera in the part of Martha in d'Albert's *Tiefland*, and she also sang Fiammetta in Suppé's *Boccaccio*. In 1945 she returned to America and in 1947 was heard by the famous tenor Zenatello, who recommended her to the Arena of Verona, where he had originated the open-air opera seasons as far back as 1913. It was at Verona therefore that she made her Italian début in the title-role of *La Gioconda* in August, 1947. The conductor of that performance was Tullio Serafin, who saw the immense potentialities of Callas, and it was with that great conductor that she studied many of her now famous roles. Serafin took the young soprano to Venice for the 1947-48 season, where she sang Isolde and Turandot. This latter role she repeated at Verona the following summer.

The turning point in her career came during the 1948-9 season at the Fenice Theatre in Venice, where she had been engaged to sing Brünnhilde in *Die Walküre*. The next opera due for production was Bellini's *I Puritani* with Margherita Carosio as Elvira. Carosio fell ill, and Serafin suggested that Callas should sing the role. It was unbelievable that an Isolde, Turandot and Brünnhilde should sing the 'delicate' part of Elvira, but Callas did; and she triumphed. For the first time for many years there was a dramatic soprano capable of singing florid roles. And why not? After all Lilli Lehmann sang Constanze, the Queen of Night, Norma, Violetta, Brünnhilde and Isolde! A week after the Venice *Puritani*, Callas was off to Rome to sing Kundry in *Parsifal*.

After the success of *Puritani*, Callas gradually gave up her heavier roles and concentrated on the Rossini-Bellini-Donizetti repertory. Operas not heard in Italy for more than a century were revived especially for her; works like Rossini's *Armida* and *Il Turco in Italia*; Cherubini's *Medée*, Spontini's *La Vestale*, Donizetti's *Anna Bolena* and Bellini's *Il Pirata*. Her Medea has been hailed as the greatest operatic interpretation to be seen and heard on the stage in our day; while of her Anna Bolena, Desmond Shawe-Taylor wrote, 'The final scene in the Tower of London, is the greatest thing in the opera, and it also showed Madame Callas at the height of her powers both as a singer and a tragic actress . . . . . Interpreted by such an artist as Maria Callas and directed with perfect taste by Visconti, this was a scene of high tragedy'.

Callas's London début was in November, 1952, when

she sang *Norma* at Covent Garden opposite the classic Adalgisa of Stignani. The late Cecil Smith wrote of this performance: 'Essentially, Miss Callas sings with two voices. Her chest voice and her upper voice are open and clean, with a splendid cutting edge that makes for exactness of pitch. In the middle register her tone is heavily covered. Each time I heard her (I attended four of the five performances) the "Casta diva" disappointed me a bit, for she sounded rather as if she were singing into a bottle—until she moved above the passaggio to F and the notes beyond. By some mystifying alchemy, however, these two voices coalesced into one as the evening progressed. In the scene and duet with Adalgisa at the beginning of the second act ('Io fui cosi rapita') her middle-register production suddenly ceased to be mannered at all; and she proved herself capable of a dozen wonderfully expressive colorations, none of which ever threw her singing out of joint.

'Her fioriture were fabulous. The chromatic glissandi held no terrors for her in the cadenza at the end of "Casta diva" and in the duet of which I have just spoken. Nor, in the second-act trio "Oh non tremare", did the superhuman leap from middle F to a forte high C. One of her most stunning moments came at the end of the stretto to this trio, when she held for twelve beats a stupendous, free high D. Among dramatic sopranos in my experience, I have heard this tone equalled only by Rosa Raisa. From this point onward, Miss Callas held her audience in abject slavery. She rewarded them by never letting them down, and by reaching a peak of eloquence in the infinitely moving closing scene of the opera.'

In the summer of 1953, she repeated her Norma at Covent Garden, and also sang Aida and the *Trovatore* Leonora. It was not until February 1957 that London heard her again when she returned as a much slimmer and more glamorous personality, to sing two more Normas, again with Stignani. Again there were divided opinions about the purely vocal side of her performance; but about her creative genius and personal magnetism there was little argument. In the summer of 1957 she sang Amina in *La Sonnambula* with the Piccola Scala Company at Edinburgh, a role that hardly suited her imperious and tragic personality.

By this time Callas had made herself known to American audiences. She first sang with the Chicago Opera in 1954 as Norma, Lucia and Violetta; and the following year as Elvira (*Puritani*), Leonora (*Trovatore*) and Butterfly. Between 1956 and 1958 she sang at the Metropolitan, New York, as Norma, Lucia, Violetta and Tosca. She cancelled her scheduled appearances as Lady Macbeth for the 1958-9 season, as she did not wish to sing this role and Violetta at the same period. Having also had differences of opinion with the San Francisco and Chicago companies, Dallas was the only American city where she appeared in opera in 1959 and 1960.

In the summer of 1958 Callas took part in the Covent Garden Centenary Gala before Queen Elizabeth and Prince Philip, and sang the Mad Scene from *I Puritani*. A week or so later she sang the first of five Violettas in which she gave ample demonstration of her great gifts as a singing actress. Each performance was better than its predecessor vocally, and each differed dramatically. In other words, Callas tries to vary and improve each performance, and although some of the inflections and nuances remain constant, because the artist has found the right tone for a certain phrase, others assume new significance as the drama unfolds.

That Callas has a serious approach to her art is generally accepted. She is a great believer in tradition and studies her roles and her scores with a thoroughness that puts to shame many of her contemporaries. Even if one does not agree with the way she interprets a role, she has her own very valid reasons for what she does, which she will go to the trouble of explaining at great length.

She is also a prolific recording artist, and is featured in no less than eighteen complete operas. In 1961 Callas astonished her admirers and confounded her critics by recording a recital of French arias. Half of these were of mezzo-soprano roles—Carmen, Delilah, Orfeo, and as usual with a Callas performance, one had the impression that one was listening to them for the first time.

Of course she has her detractors: what great artist has not? 'The voice is ugly'; 'She has three voices'; are criticisms one often hears levelled against her. In reply her admirers would suggest that there is a certain quality inherent in the voice that is capable of moving her listeners to tears; and her dramatic ability enables her to recreate an operatic character in such a way that the listener feels he is hearing the role for the first time. She is truly one of the greatest of present-day operatic artists and is assured of a place in operatic history as one of the finest singing actresses of all time.

ROSANNA CARTERI

JUST over thirty, Rosanna Carteri is one of the most sought after sopranos of today. She was born in Verona in 1930 and she began to study there, when she was only ten, with Maestro Cusinati. When she was fifteen she sang in her first concert at Schio opposite the great tenor, Aureliano Pertile. After further appearances in the Italian provinces she entered a vocal contest organized by Radio Italiana in 1948 and won first prize. Her first stage appearance was at the Terme di Caracalla, Rome, in July 1949 as Elsa in *Lohengrin*. This was followed by appearances during the 1949-50 season at Trieste (Micaela), Rome (Liù and Suor Angelica) and Bologna (Nannetta).

In the 1950-51 season Carteri made her Scala début as La Cecchina in Piccinni's *La Buona Figliuola*, since when she has sung there regularly. Her Scala roles have included Mimi, Manon, Gilda, Zerlina, Micaela, Adina, Lucieta (*Quatro Rustighi*) and Liù.

In 1952 she was chosen by Furtwängler to sing Desdemona at Salzburg opposite Vinay. Donald Mitchell, writing in *Opera* said, 'Desdemona, sung by the youthful Carteri could hardly have been better. Tenderness, purity, innocence, were all combined in a performance of real poignancy. For Desdemona Carteri has neither too ample nor too slight a voice, and its essential "whiteness" strangely reflected, established and emphasized the dreadful fate of this unhappy character'. This opinion seems to sum up more than adequately Carteri's vocal qualities. Visually, as can be seen from the photographs published in this book, she is most attractive, and has a most winning and pleasant stage personality.

Carteri's vocal and histrionic gifts have commended themselves to several composers and conductors who have been in search of a soprano to create new roles. Thus she was chosen by Rodzinski to sing Natasha in the première of Prokofiev's *War and Peace* at the 1953 Florence Festival; by Pizzetti to create the title role in his *Ifigenia* at Florence in 1951; by Castro to sing Flavia in the world première of *Proserpina e lo Straniero* at La Scala in 1952; and by Mannino to create his *Vivì* at Naples in 1957. In complete contrast, the Florence Festival authorities chose her to sing Elena in a revival of Rossini's *La Donna del Lago* in 1958.

Carteri's American début was with the San Francisco Opera in the autumn of 1954, when she sang Mimi, Manon, Susanna and Donna Gabriella in Cherubini's *L'Osteria Portoghese*. A leading American critic wrote, 'She scored a wild success .... she is a lyric soprano rather like Lucrezia Bori; she is also a superlative actress and her gifts of personality more than compensate for her vocal shortcomings; an occasional hardness of tone and choppiness of phrase'. Carteri returned to San Francisco in 1955 to sing Zerlina, and Marguerite in *Faust* in which role 'she brought forth new and unexpected resources of poetic and tragic expression.'

It was not until the summer of 1957 that Carteri sang in Great Britain, when she came with the Piccola Scala Company to the Edinburgh Festival, and she was heard as Adina in *L'Elisir d'Amore*. Some people found her voice too heavy and dark for the role; but no one could have failed but to have found her an extremely vivacious and beautiful Adina.

BORIS CHRISTOFF

ONE of the most picturesque and vital figures among contemporary singers is the bass Boris Christoff. Not only does he bring a fine voice, a keen intelligence and commanding presence to his interpretations, but his fiery temperament and powerful personality bring back an echo of the by-gone days of Chaliapin.

Christoff was born in Sofia on May 18, 1918. His mother was of Russian origin, his father a Bulgarian schoolmaster and also something of an amateur musician. The young Christoff however was destined for the legal profession, but he had a great love for music and singing; and when at university he applied and got a place in the famous Gusla Choir which was directed by Assen Dmitrov, one of the conductors at the Sofia Opera. Although he had never had a singing lesson in his life, he was given many solo parts, and soon was a member of the cathedral choir.

In January 1942 on Bulgaria's National Day, the choir was singing in the Square outside the royal palace; the temperature was below freezing and the choir was invited into the palace by the king. Christoff sang an old folk-song, and was congratulated by the king personally, who told him that he should give up law and concentrate on a singing career. A week later Christoff received a letter from the Royal Chancellery awarding him a scholarship.

Soon after Christoff left for Rome where he studied with the famous baritone Riccardo Stracciari. Eighteen months later when Italy was invaded, he escaped to Austria, where he studied for several months at Salzburg; his studies were interrupted however by the Nazis who sent him to a concentration camp, from which he was released by the French in 1945. He returned to Italy, quite penniless, and continued his studies with Stracciari, who refused to take any payment whatsoever.

On December 30, 1945, Christoff made his début in a concert, and the following March he made his stage début at the Fenice, in Venice, singing Colline in *La Bohème* and gaining an encore for the Coat Song. In the 1946-7 season he sang Pimen at Rome, and was engaged to sing the same role for his Scala début the following autumn—the *Boris* cast on that occasion included Rossi-Lemeni as Varlaam and Tancredi Pasero as Boris. Appearances soon followed all over Italy, and he was heard in such roles as Rocco, Heinrich (*Lohengrin*), Hagen, King Marke, the Landgrave, Oroveso, Procida (*Vespri Siciliani*), Mefistofele, Padre Guardiano, King Philip, Fiesco, Mosè, Caspar and of course in the Russian repertory—Boris, Dositeus (*Khovanshchina*), Galitzky (*Prince Igor*), and Kociubei (*Mazeppa*).

Christoff's Covent Garden début was on November 19, 1950, when he sang the first Boris of his career, without the benefit of either an orchestral or full stage rehearsal. 'Christoff is a singer and actor in the great tradition', wrote the Earl of Harewood in *Opera*, 'the voice is not huge, but it is of fine penetrating quality, absolutely smooth, and round, and under perfect control, and his singing was musical from the first note of the Coronation scene to the last of the death scene.... Apart from anything else it was a rare joy to hear a male singer sing softly for much of his role and remain clearly audible throughout the evening'.

He has lived up to this initial criticism, and his finely spun pianissimi are always as effective and as musical as the most powerful climaxes. When he returned to London to sing King Philip in the Covent Garden centenary production of *Don Carlos* in 1958, he offered an enthralling study of that unhappy monarch. He was, on that occasion, singing with his brother-in-law, Tito Gobbi; and it was fascinating to watch them both through the opera glasses when they were *not* singing, for they remained completely in character and reacted to what was going on around them. They were no stars hogging the lime-light, but complete singing actors. Christoff's great aria in Act 3, became the expression of a personal grief and not just a show piece for a bass. Later that year he returned to sing Boris in Russian, and offered an even more detailed and penetrating study of the role than when he had sung it last in London seven years previously.

Christoff's American début took place at San Francisco in 1956 as Boris and he returned there in 1957, when he was heard as Fiesco. He sang with the Chicago Opera in 1958, then returned to La Scala to sing the title role in *Mosè*. More recently he sang in Boito's Mefistofele, Galitzky and Khan Kontchak in *Prince Igor* at Chicago, Don Basilio with the Covent Garden Company in Edinburgh, and the title role in Verdi's *Atilla* in Florence.

Christoff's musicianship and scholarship are amply demonstrated in the complete recording he undertook of all the songs of Mussorgsky. Christoff spent three years collecting, arranging and annotating them, and the result is little short of magnificent. Yet 'off-duty' he is excellent company, fond of good food, good wine and talking operatic shop.

FRANCO CORELLI

THE Centro Sperimentale Lirico at Spoleto has, since the war, produced a number of singers who have established themselves in international opera. One of these is the young tenor, Franco Corelli, who not only possesses a thrilling vibrant voice, but is blessed with good looks above the average, and a natural acting ability.

Corelli was born at Ancona where he spent the first few years of his life. His family then moved to Milan, where he went to school and then the University. He then embarked on a business career, but after a few months of office routine, began to study singing. In 1950 he entered for a Singing Contest organised at Florence, which he won, and the following year went to Spoleto, where he made his début as Don José.

Ottavio Ziino the conductor, who taught at Spoleto, took Corelli with him to Rome the following year, where he made his début at the Teatro dell'Opera as Romeo in Zandonai's *Giulietta e Romeo*. He has sung at Rome regularly ever since, and has been heard there as Dmitri (*Boris*), Turrus in Liviabella's *Antigone*, Don Carlos, Sesto (*Giulio Cesare*), Radames and Pollione. At the Terme de Caracalla during the summer seasons, he is a popular figure as José, Cavaradossi, and Andrea Chénier.

In a period when dramatic tenor voices are few and far between, Corelli soon found himself in great demand. At La Scala he opened the 1954-5 season as Licinio in *La Vestale* opposite Callas; he has also sung with her there in subsequent seasons as Loris in *Fedora* and in *Il Pirata*. His other Scala roles have included Canio, Sesto, Dick Johnson, Calaf, Illo in Handel's *Hercules*, the title-role in Donizetti's *Poliuto*, and Manrico.

He has appeared regularly at the San Carlo in Naples, where he has sung most of his famous roles, including Alvaro in *La Forza del Destino* opposite Tebaldi. Trieste, Bologna, Venice, the Verona Arena and Florence know him well and at the 1954 Florence Festival he sang in the rarely performed *Agnese di Hohenstaufen*.

Corelli's first appearances outside Italy were made at Lisbon where he sang in 1956. The following year he was heard at the Vienna State Opera, Eghien-les-Bains and Covent Garden where he sang Cavaradossi opposite Milanov. In the same performance the baritone, Giangiacomo Guelfi, sang Scarpia. Guelfi and Corelli are very close friends, and have made a number of records together for Cetra.

In the winter of 1961 Corelli made his Metropolitan début as Manrico in *Il Trovatore*, creating a sensation with his high C's and handsome stage presence. He won an even greater success with his Calaf in the new Turandot production a few weeks later.

Corelli has a considerable 'fan' following in Italy and America, especially among the young teen-agers. He cannot walk alone in the street without being besieged by youngsters asking for his autograph or to be allowed to photograph him. In these days of the 'Rock and Roll' singer, it is quite a change for an opera singer to be so fêted.

FERNANDO CORENA

This young Italian bass was born in Geneva of a Turkish father and an Italian mother—his name was originally spelt Korena. His Swiss childhood training when he spoke three languages (French, German and Italian) was to stand him in good stead for his operatic career. He was originally destined however for the priesthood, and with this end in view he studied at the University of Fribourg. Quite fond of music he persuaded his mother to take him to the local operetta theatre, where he proceeded to fall in love with the leading soprano! Learning that she gave singing lessons he accordingly went to her to study, and in the process discovered he possessed a promising voice. He then entered for a local contest at Geneva and won first prize. The conductor, Vittorio Gui, then encouraged him to undertake a serious career, and he went to Milan to study with Enrico Romano.

In 1947 he was ready to make his début which took place at Trieste as Varlaam in *Boris Godunov*. Appearances followed in the Italian provinces, and soon he was established as a young character bass, singing such roles as Pimen, Geronimo (*Matrimonio Segreto*), Bartolo and Melitone. In Zurich he was heard as Daland, in Lyons as Kecal and in Brussels as Pasquale.

Corena's Scala début took place in the 1948-9 season when he sang Cannizares in the first performance of Petrassi's *Il Cordovano*. The following season he was heard as Il Cavalier Astolfi (*Il Campiello*), Semplicio in Malipiero's *L'Allegra Brigata* and Don Pasquale; in the 1951-2 season he sang Uberto (*La Serva Padrona*), Rodrigo (*L'Osteria Portoghese*) and again Pasquale. Subsequently he

ROSANNA CARTERI

as herself

as *Elena* in 'La Donna del Lago'

as herself

as *Anna Bolena*

MARIA CALLAS

as *Medea*

BORIS CHRISTOFF

as *Moses* in 'Mosè in Egitto'

as *Attila*

as *Giulio Cesare* in 'Handel's Opera'

FRANCO CORELLI

as *Dick Johnson* in 'La Fanciulla del West'

'as *Calaf* in Turandot'

as *Manrico* in 'Il Trovatore'

FERNANDO CORENA

as *Dulcamara* in 'L'Elisir d'Amore'

as *Bartolo* in 'Il Barbiere di Siviglia'

as *Don Pasquale*

RÉGINE CRESPIN

as *Kundry* in 'Parsifal'

as *Giulia* in 'La Vestale'

as *The Marschallin* in 'Der Rosenkavalier'

as *Cleopatra*

LISA DELLA CASA

as *Arabella*

as *Salome*

MARIO DEL MONACO

as *Radames* in 'Aida'

as himself

has appeared at La Scala as Dotter Bombasto (*Arlecchino*), and Dulcamara.

He has also been heard often at the Florence Festival, where he has sung Prince Bolkonsky in *War and Peace*, King Balthasar in Menotti's *Amahl and the Night Visitors*, Il Padre in Malipiero's *Il Figliuol Prodigo* and Melchiorre in the same composer's *Venere Prigioniera*.

Corena's Metropolitan début was made in February 1954 as Leporello. *Musical America* reported 'Mr. Corena would seem to be a most valuable addition to the number of singing actors in the house . . . . His voice is an excellent one, securely produced, flexible if of no great richness'. A few days later he scored a notable success as Bartolo in a new production of *Il Barbiere di Siviglia*. When *Don Pasquale* was revived in December 1955, Corena was given the title-role, and has also sung the title-role in *Gianni Schicchi*.

In the summer of 1955 he made his British début with the Glyndebourne company at the Edinburgh Festival in the title role in *Falstaff*, when he was generally regarded as a worthy successor to Stabile in that role. He returned to Edinburgh with the Piccola Scala two years later in another Stabile part, that of Prosdicimo, the poet in *Il Turco in Italia*, and then as Dulcamara, a 'creation of the highest order, sung and acted with extreme good taste'.

Corena's Bartolo in *Il Barbiere di Siviglia* at Covent Garden in 1960 was generally considered one of the most amusing ever seen or heard in London. His facial expressions and often unrehearsed 'business' were at times as amusing to his colleagues as to the audience. It is rare too to find a buffo bass blessed with so fine a voice as is Corena.

RÉGINE CRESPIN

ONE of the discoveries of recent years has been the French soprano Régine Crespin. Not that she was unknown in her native France, where she has been singing since 1950 but it was only with her Bayreuth début in 1958, followed by her Glyndebourne appearances in 1959, and her success at La Scala, Milan, that her name has become known to international audiences.

Crespin was born at Marseilles in 1927 of a French father and Italian mother. In 1933 her family moved to Nimes, where her father owned a shop. The young Régine originally intended to become a chemist. One day her professor overheard her singing, and suggested she might have her voice trained. An audition was arranged with a singing teacher, who was not particularly impressed with what he heard, telling the young soprano that her voice was too small. However she persevered, and began to study the soprano roles in *Lakmé* and *Lucia di Lammermoor*. Her voice began to develop and when she was nineteen (in 1946), she entered for a contest organized by the now defunct French weekly *Opéra* to discover 'Les plus belles voix de France'. She won all the preliminary rounds, and was awarded first place in the soprano group in the final contest at the Gâité Lyrique in Paris. In 1947, despite parental opposition—her father still wanted her to become a chemist!—she entered the Paris Conservatory, where she studied singing with Mme. Cesbron-Viseu and Georges Jouatte, and stage work with Paul Cabanel. She remained at the Conservatory for three years, winning three first prizes, but was not engaged by the Opéra straight away. Instead she spent the first year of her career in the provinces, making her début at Mulhouse in 1950 as Elsa in *Lohengrin*. Engagements followed in Strasbourg, Vichy, Lyons, and Marseilles where she sang Marguerite, Tosca, Marina and other roles.

Crespin's Paris début took place at the Opéra-Comique in the summer of 1951 as Tosca, soon followed by Santuzza. Then in October 1951 she was engaged by Georges Hirsch for the Opéra, where her début role was again Elsa. During the 1951-2 season in Paris she sang Vita in a revival of D'Indy's *L'Etranger*, Desdemona, Marguerite, and Helmwige in *Die Walküre*. Hirsch left the Opéra the following season, and his successor, Maurice Lehmann did not re-engage Crespin, who spent the next three seasons in the French provinces. She also understudied the role of Danae in Strauss's *Der Liebe der Danae* at La Scala, Milan, where she had successfully auditioned for Victor de Sabata. During this period too she prepared the role of the Marschallin in *Rosenkavalier* which she sang for the first time at Marseilles.

In the summer of 1956 Crespin appeared at the Bordeau Festival, creating the part of Vannina in Henri Tomasi's *Sampiero Corso*. Then, a few months later she returned to the Opéra, where once again Hirsch was General Administrator. Besides singing her old roles of Elsa, Marguerite and Desdemona, she was the Sieglinde in a revival of *Die Walküre*, and also sang Reiza in *Oberon*. Then came Donna Anna, her first Paris Marschallin, La Nouvelle Prière in Poulenc's *Dialogues des Carmélites*, Elisabeth in *Tannhäuser*, and Amelia in *Un Ballo in Maschera*.

The summer of 1958 brought her two great triumphs—Dido in *Les Troyens* in the Arena at Lyons, and Kundry at Bayreuth, where she was the first French soprano since Germain Lubin, to be engaged. Lubin helped her to prepare the role, and was present in the audience at her Bayreuth début. Wieland Wagner has declared that Crespin is the Kundry he has long sought. He also wanted her to sing Isolde, but wisely the soprano felt that this role was not for her for another four or five years.

The following year, Crespin was engaged to sing the Marschallin in Carl Ebert's first production of this opera at Glyndebourne, and his last work there as Artistic Director. She proved to be one of the greatest of present day artists, endowed with the capacity to move the listener by the warmth and sincerity of her performance. Her voice, capable of every shade of vocal colour and inflection, moved one to tears at the end of the first act; and she knew how to move and hold the stage. Six months later she triumphed at La Scala, Milan, as Fedra in Pizzetti's opera of that name. Covent Garden heard her Marschallin and Tosca during the 1960-61 season, after which she sang Sieglinde at Bayreuth, the Marschallin and Kundry in Buenos Aires, and Dido in the first Paris revival of *Les Troyens* for many years.

Crespin's first season in the United States, 1962-3, was enormously successful: Tosca in Chicago, the Marschallin, Senta, Amelia, and *La Vestale* in New York. The soprano then came to London to sing Elsa in the new Covent Garden production of *Lohengrin*, conducted by Otto Klemperer.

The future must hold many exciting things for this artist. Isolde of course will come, and she herself has expressed the wish to sing Fidelio, Alceste, and Fauré's Penelope. When asked however what her favourite role is, she replied 'I prefer to give you the same answer as Claude Nollier did to the same question—"The next one I undertake".'

LISA DELLA CASA

THE legend of the stout and ugly prima donna dies hard; but as readers of this book can see for themselves, female opera singers of the 1960's are as attractive to the eye as they are beguiling to the ear. One of the most charming of all contemporary singers is the Swiss soprano, Lisa Della Casa. She was born on February 2, 1919, in Burgdorf near Berne, the daughter of an Italian-Swiss doctor and his Bavarian wife. When she was fifteen she went to Zurich to study with Dr. Margarete Haeser, who has been her only teacher. Her first engagement was at Solothurn-Biel, during the early years of the war. There she made her début in the title-role of *Madama Butterfly*, following it soon after with an appearance as Antonia in *Les Contes d'Hoffmann*. In 1943 she was engaged by the Stadttheater in Zurich, where she made her first appearance as Mimi. She remained a member of the Zurich ensemble until 1947, singing most of the light soprano roles.

In 1947 she made her first appearance at the Salzburg Festival as Zdenka in Strauss's *Arabella*, when her exquisite young silvery voice was heard for the first time, not only by the many visitors to Salzburg, but by radio listeners all over Europe. Many of those who heard her then must have wondered why the possessor of such a voice was not better known. It was not very long before she was.

Following her Salzburg appearances, she was engaged in Vienna, where her roles included Nedda in *Pagliacci* and Zerlina in *Fra Diavolo*. She returned to Salzburg in 1948 to sing Marzelline in *Fidelio*, and the following summer, when she sang the role of the Countess in Richard Strauss's *Capriccio*. This was really the turning point of her career, for so great was her success that she found herself famous all over Europe, and invitations to sing in the leading opera houses of the world poured in. The year 1949 was important for another and more personal reason: in that year she married Dragan Debeljevic, a Jugoslavian.

In 1951 she came to Great Britain for the first time, making her début as the Countess (*Figaro*) at Glyndebourne. Appearances followed during that year in Munich, where she was heard as Sophie (*Der Rosenkavalier*) and in the title-role of Richard Strauss's *Arabella*. It is as Arabella that Lisa Della Casa has perhaps enjoyed her greatest successes, and having first sung the role of Zdenka in the same opera she seems to have a really deep feeling and understanding for this role. Arabella's scenes with her younger sister are intensely moving in Miss Della Casa's hands.

London heard her Arabella at Covent Garden in September, 1953, when she appeared on the opening night of the Munich Opera's short season there. 'Miss Della Casa looked enchanting, sang impeccably and made the young lady, a less ingenuous Sophie vivacious and real', wrote one London critic. New York first heard her Arabella in 1957 when she sang the role for the first time in English. Just as she has sung the two leading roles in *Arabella*, so in another Richard Strauss opera, *Der Rosenkavalier*, she has graduated from the part of Sophie to that of the Marschallin, singing Octavian on the way. Other than Lotte Lehmann, few artists can claim this distinction. In the summer of 1961, she faced another Strauss challenge, the title role in *Salome* at Munich.

Della Casa's New York début had actually taken place during the 1953-4 season, when she sang the Countess and Donna Elvira. During ensuing seasons she has added Eva, the Marschallin, Cio-Cio-San and Elsa to her roles at the Metropolitan.

Singing the music Strauss has written for the female voice must be one of the most gratifying experiences for a soprano, and it is as a Strauss singer that Lisa Della Casa is pre-eminent today. In addition to the Strauss parts already mentioned she has sung Ariadne at Salzburg and Munich, and has specialised in singing the 'Four Last Songs' of that composer at concerts. After Strauss perhaps her favourite composer is Mozart. Donna Elvira, Donna Anna, the Countess and Pamina are among her most often-sung roles. Another classical composer whose music Della Casa sings particularly well is Handel. In his *Giulio Cesare* she sings the part of Cleopatra, and her appearance in this role is one of the great features of the annual Munich Summer Festival. Modern opera, too has attractions for this singer, and besides appearing as Die junge Frau in the première of Willy Burkhard's *Die Schwarze Spinne*, she has also created the roles of Fräulein Bürstner, Die Frau des Gerichtsdieners and Leni in Einem's *Der Prozess*.

When she is not singing in New York or Vienna and can find time to leave the recording studio and concert platform, she and her husband, together with their daughter Wesna, pass their time in Schloss Gottlieben an old castle which they have bought near Thurgau. This castle has several historical connections. One of its towers housed Jan Hus before his arrest in 1515; and Napoleon III spent some time there when fleeing from France.

But to return to this singer's vocal attainments. Perhaps they are best summed up in what Desmond Shawe-Taylor wrote in *Opera* about her Arabella: 'Having hugely enjoyed Della Casa's Salzburg broadcasts, I was curious to see and hear her in reality. She does not disappoint expectation; a charming and graceful actress, she spins out Strauss's soaring vocal line with smooth legato and exquisite taste'.

MARIO DEL MONACO

ITALY's finest dramatic tenor since the days of Pertile and Lauri-Volpi is undoubtedly Mario Del Monaco. He is adored by audiences the world over, less admired by the serious critics, and like Callas, the subject of fierce controversy.

Del Monaco was born in Florence on July 27, 1915. His father was an important member of the Pesaro City Council, and it was in that city that Del Monaco was brought up. The family appears to have been a musical one, his mother was a soprano of some talent, but did not make a professional career; and the tenor tells how as a child he knew many operatic arias, and dreamed of the day he would make music his life.

His education was at the Conservatory of Pesaro, where he studied music (piano, harmony, theory and history of music); his early teachers included Luisa Melai-Palazzini and Maestro Arturo Melocchi. He also spent much of his time at the Art Academy of Pesaro, where he studied sculpture and painting.

When Del Monaco was thirteen, he sang (non-professionally) on the stage for the first time; this was at the Teatro Beniamino Gigli at Mondalfo, where he appeared in Massenet's cantata for voice and orchestra, *Narcisse*.

When Del Monaco was twenty, he was invited by Tullio Serafin to enter for a competition for a place in the

Studio attached to the Teatro dell'Opera, Rome, and gained the place from eighty competitors. The tenor has never been too happy studying with coaches and teachers, and after six months he decided to have no other teacher but himself—and to this day Del Monaco relies on personal study and listening to records of the great artists of the past, in order to prepare himself for new roles.

For six and a half years he was in the Italian army, occasionally singing. His appearances included Turiddu at the Teatro di Cagli, Pesaro, in 1939, and what he regards as his professional début, Pinkerton at the Teatro Puccini, Milan, on January 1, 1941. During the 1943-4 season, the Scala was performing at Como, and Del Monaco sang Rodolfo in *La Bohème*.

His first really big season was that of 1945-6, when his appearances included Radames at the first post-war season at the open-air arena of Verona, Andrea Chénier at Trieste with the young Tebaldi, and Pinkerton at the Teatro Lirico with the Scala Milan Company. In the autumn of the same year he came to Covent Garden with the San Carlo Company, although he had not at that time been particularly associated with that company. He displayed a rather metallic voice, but one that clearly gave promise of future development. Desmond Shawe-Taylor wrote of his début in the *New Statesman*: 'The performance of *Tosca* was saved from nullity by Mario Del Monaco, a young tenor who is probably the most handsome and romantic Cavaradossi ever seen at Covent Garden. I fear that Hollywood will snap him up, and this would be a pity, because he has a good deal of voice, still a little on the raw side, but powerful, ringing and heroic'.

While at Covent Garden, Del Monaco was also heard as Canio (the first he had ever sung), Pinkerton and Rodolfo. There then followed four seasons in the leading opera houses of Italy and South America, as well as guest appearances in Egypt, Portugal, Spain, Sweden and Switzerland, during which period Del Monaco's repertory was further increased to include, besides the roles already mentioned, Manrico, Alvaro, Riccardo (*Ballo*), Enzo (*Gioconda*), Loris (*Fedora*), des Grieux (*Manon Lescaut*), Dick Johnson (*Fanciulla del West*), Calaf and Don José.

It was in the summer of 1950 that Del Monaco sang his first Otello, this was at the Teatro Colon, Buenos Aires. 'An impersonation of dramatic intensity, pathos and tenderness which was acclaimed by the audience', wrote one of Buenos Aires' leading critics.

In the autumn of the same year, he made his North American début at San Francisco, opening the season as Radames with Tebaldi, and also appearing in the title-role of *Andrea Chénier* with Licia Albanese. Rudolf Bing journeyed specially from New York to hear him and invited him to join the Metropolitan; Del Monaco was unable to do this for the 1950-51 season, but broke his journey back to Europe to appear there in one performance of *Manon Lescaut*. He was however able to join the company for the 1951-2 season and again sang at the Metropolitan 1952-3, 1954-5, 1956-9. His New York roles have included Radames, Turiddu, Otello, Edgardo, Don José, Alvaro, Cavaradossi, Canio, Pollione, Ernani, Samson and Chénier.

During his first season in New York, he was strongly criticised for singing too loudly, for his lack of taste, and for acting in a 'provincial' manner—that he had a thrilling and magnificent vocal organ was never denied—it was the way that he used it that was open to criticism. Not until half-way through the 1952-3 season, when he sang Don Alvaro in *La Forza del Destino*, did he receive a really good Press. One critic wrote: 'His performance was in every respect one of the best he has given this year. The young tenor made the aria "O, tu che in seno agli'angeli" a marvel of vocal colouring and interpretation, and he maintained the same high level of execution in what followed. Mr. Del Monaco revealed, above all, a most remarkable stylistic affinity to the vivid drama of Verdi's music and to the severe emotional demands of the role'.

Since then he worked to refine his art; and his interpretations of Otello and Samson have been especially praised for their sincerity and feeling, as well as for sheer vocal splendour.

In 1957 he sang his first Wagner role, Lohengrin, at La Scala, and he has ambitions to tackle other *heldentenor* parts like Siegmund. Of this seriousness of purpose there is no doubt, and a series of performances at the Bolshoi in Moscow in 1959, which included his first appearance as Herman in *The Queen of Spades*, induced him to learn the latter role in Russian.

This sincerity coupled with his unabounding admiration for the great Pertile, whom he considers 'the greatest interpreter of them all', and of course his superb natural voice, can yet combine to make Del Monaco into the greatest dramatic tenor of our time.

VICTORIA DE LOS ANGELES

SPAIN has given us many great opera singers during the last hundred years or so; Bori, Barrientos, Conchita Supervia are names that every opera-goer knows, and in our time Victoria de los Angeles has quickly taken her place among the great singers of the post-war generation.

Spanish singers generally mature very early, and often make their débuts in their teens. De los Angeles was no exception, for her first public appearance was made in a performance of Monteverdi's *Orfeo* when she was only eighteen. True, she was still studying at the Barcelona Conservatory, but even at that early age she displayed a vocal quality and emotional power rare in one so young.

She was born in Barcelona. Her father was an employee of the University, and she lived with her family in a house attached to it. When still a child, she discovered that she could sing, and used to accompany herself on a guitar. University lectures were interrupted by the young de los Angeles, who would break into a class-room in order to try out its acoustics! Her formal education was carried out at a school attached to the University. One day a professor who had heard her singing suggested that she should go to the Conservatory and study singing seriously. As in many cases of budding singers, her father forbade her even to think of a musical career, so she did what many other aspiring opera artists have done—studied secretly. When she was accepted by the head of the Conservatory she finally had to break the news to her father, and as her own mother had been similarly forbidden by her parents to take up a professional singing career, mother and daughter soon overcame the male opposition in the family.

The singing course at the Conservatory normally took six years; de los Angeles completed it in three, obtaining every prize. On one occasion when her professor was unable to take a class because of illness, he gave the young singer the task, saying: 'You know much more about it than I do'.

After her early appearance in Monteverdi's *Orfeo*, two more years of musical study followed. Then in May, 1944, she gave her first public concert—a lieder recital in Barcelona. A few days later she was heard in Mozart's *Coronation Mass*, and then in a series of concerts and lieder recitals in other cities. Her professional operatic début took place at the Teatro Liceo in Barcelona as the Countess in *Figaro* in January, 1945. Then followed appearances in Portugal and a return once more to Barcelona, where during the next two opera seasons she sang Manon and Marguerite in French, Mimi in Italian, and Elisabeth in *Tannhäuser* in German. In 1947 she participated in the International Festival at Geneva, and out of a hundred competitors she gained the first prize. A year or two elapsed, however, before her fame spread outside Spain and Portugal. It was in 1948 that the B.B.C. invited her to come to London to sing in a broadcast of Falla's *La Vida Breve*. Such was her success that even Ernest Newman was moved to write an enthusiastic notice about her in *The Sunday Times*.

She returned to London the following year to give a Wigmore Hall recital, and then in February, 1950, made her Covent Garden début as Mimi. This was one of those occasions not easily forgotten. A packed house, including nearly every singer in London, active or retired, was on hand to applaud the new soprano. Her success was never for a moment in doubt. In 1951 she returned to sing Mimi, Manon, Elsa and Cio-Cio-San. London had to wait another six years before it heard her again in opera. That was in April, 1957, when she sang a series of *Butterfly* performances, that were among the most moving ever heard at Covent Garden. The following summer she sang Salud in Falla's *La Vida Breve* at Edinburgh. In 1960 London again heard her Mimi and Manon and in the summer of 1961 she sang Santuzza and Nedda on one evening in a gala performance of *Cavalleria Rusticana* and *Pagliacci* in aid of the Opera Houses benevolent fund.

Since 1950, most of de los Angeles's operatic appearances have been at the Metropolitan in New York, with occasional visits to Milan, Stuttgart and Buenos Aires, and the inevitable sessions in the recording studios. Her roles at La Scala are most interesting, for they are not parts in which New York and London know her—Ariadne, Donna Anna, Agathe, and Laodice in Scarlatti's *Mitradate*

Eupatore. In New York too she has sung parts that London has not yet heard her in—Mélisande, Violetta, Micaela, the Figaro Countess and Rosina (in the original key).

There has been much discussion among musicians whether in fact de los Angeles is really a soprano, or merely a very high mezzo-soprano. It should be remembered however that although today mezzo-sopranos generally sing roles like Carmen and Azucena, last century they could be heard as Anna Bolena or Norma; and even today we have sopranos and mezzo-sopranos sharing certain roles—Santuzza, Eboli, Octavian, Venus, Ortrud and Kundry.

But whatever role she sings, she lavishes on it a highly developed musical style, and one of the most beautiful voices of the day.

GIUSEPPE DI STEFANO

LA SCALA's leading tenor during the late 1950's has been Giuseppe Di Stefano, who, in the absence abroad of Mario Del Monaco, was asked to assume dramatic as well as lyric roles, in which he was so outstanding earlier in his career.

Di Stefano was born in Catania, Sicily, on July 24, 1921. His father was a professional soldier, and his mother, Angelina Gentile, came from a well-known Sicilian family. He went to school at a Jesuit Seminary, where he was considered a brilliant pupil. One of his closest friends at the Seminary was a law student who was also an opera enthusiast. He heard Di Stefano singing a popular song, and was so excited by the natural beauty of his voice, that he suggested to him that he take up singing as his career.

His family made many sacrifices so that they could give their son a musical education, and came to Milan, where Di Stefano studied for five years with the baritone, Luigi Montesanto, making his début in April, 1946, at the Teatro Municipale, Reggio Emilia, as Des Grieux in Massenet's *Manon*, with Umberto Berrettoni conducting. His initial success was phenomenal, the natural beauty of the voice was such that he was immediately engaged for a series of concerts in Switzerland. On his return he appeared at Bologna, Piacenza, La Spezia, Faenza and Lucca, singing Alfredo (*Traviata*), Elvino (*Sonnambula*), Fritz (*L'Amico Fritz*) and repeating his successful Des Grieux, in which role he made his début at the Scala, Milan, in March, 1947, with Mafalda Favero as Manon. During the 1946-7 season he also appeared at the Rome Opera, the San Carlo, Trieste and Venice, singing Nadir in *The Pearl Fishers*, the Duke in *Rigoletto*, and Wilhelm Meister in *Mignon*. He also made his first operatic appearances outside Italy singing at the Teatro Liceo, Barcelona.

The complete list of artists for the 1947-8 season at the Metropolitan, New York, did not originally include Di Stefano among the tenors; but he was engaged a little after mid-season by Edward Johnson, and arrived in New York with his teacher, Montesanto, towards the end of February. His début took place on February 25th as the Duke in *Rigoletto*. His fame had preceded him, and as one New York paper said, 'The walls bulged and the ceilings resounded when Giuseppe Di Stefano, 26-year-old tenor from Milan, made his début as the Duke in the fourth *Rigoletto*. Rejoicing behind the rails was a fever heat, and though it was not exactly prejudicial to the success of the newcomer, it was still enough of an irritant to disturb many. In other words what seemed to be a claque was a real nuisance, and, in the view of the majority, who liked the tenor, an unnecessary one. The outbursts which greeted his tender beginning grew wilder and wilder, until there were "bravos" even in the midst of arias, and one shout "Boy, you're a natural", which nearly upset the lad, already in an agony of nervousness. His recovery was swift, however, and his assurance grew as the evening waned . . . . Soberer customers had reasons to approve him as well. Mr. Di Stefano's voice is clear, manly and fluent. It has some sweetness in the middle range, and in moderate or soft passages; and if he does not yield to an inclination to force on attacking higher notes, his top voice should open up and really ring. He is free from too much portamento, and turns a phrase neatly, so that there is hope for musicality, although he was tempted into holding final high notes too long. His rhythmic sense improved after some false starts and stumblings in "Questa o quella", from which Pietro Cimara saved him by some adroit conducting. His best singing came in the third act, when "Parmi veder le lagrime" was movingly and ringingly delivered. He also showed a feeling for florid style in "La donna è mobile" and was secure in the Quartet.

Almost painful shyness made for stiff and decidedly amateurish acting, but a feeling for the stage is obviously present, and it is to be hoped that he can learn. With any sort of artistic humility, so that he is not spoiled by too much adulation and not led astray by the antics of the claque, the youth should be a fine lyric tenor-actor, and a distinct addition to the American stage'.

This critique has been reproduced almost in full, because it gives a good idea of Di Stefano's potentialities in 1948, and of the hopes that were nurtured by many lovers of bel-canto for his future. Indeed, Cecil Smith, at that time editor of *Musical America*, wrote of his Des Grieux a month later, that 'his tone was unfailingly beautiful and unusually expressive, and had the rich velvety sound we have seldom heard since the days of Gigli and Lauri-Volpi'. He also mentioned the 'exquisite pianissimos in The Dream'.

Following the Metropolitan success, Di Stefano was engaged for Rio de Janeiro and Mexico in the summer of 1948; at the latter city he added the part of Alfredo to his quickly growing repertory. The next two years he spent entirely in America. At the Metropolitan during the 1948-9 and 1949-50 seasons he was heard as Wilhelm Meister, the Duke, Alfredo, Nemorino (*L'Elisir d'Amore*), Rinuccio (*Gianni Schicchi*), Fenton (*Falstaff,*) Rodolfo (*Bohème*), The Singer (*Rosenkavalier*) and Faust. In Mexico in the summer of 1949 he added Werther and Ferrando to his repertory, and in San Francisco in the autumn of 1950, Edgardo (*Lucia*) and Almaviva (*Il Barbiere*). In addition to this large number of new parts, Di Stefano was singing too frequently, especially in New York, and his beautiful voice tired and became heavy. This was a great pity, for even today he has not quite recovered that 'velvety' quality that was noticed in those early years.

In the summer of 1950 Di Stefano returned to Italy, singing Nadir in *The Pearl Fishers* at the Verona Arena. A critic writing in *Opera* about that performance remarked that the tenor was in thrilling voice but that his performance was marred by a tendency on two occasions to sing flat. The tenor's Italian appearances, however, were confined to autumn and spring, and it was not until the 1952-3 season that he decided to leave New York and to pursue his career in Italy.

His return to the Scala was as Rodolfo in the third *La Bohème* of the 1952-3 season, with Carteri as Mimi. It was noticed that his voice was not as perfect as it had been three years previously, but that he sang his part with rich warm tones. He followed this, with some very successful appearances as Enzo in *La Gioconda* with Callas and Stignani.

In the 1953-4 season he began to sing heavier roles; his style became less elegant and the voice larger and less beautiful. By the end of the 1957-8 season his repertory had expanded to include such parts as Don Josè, Canio, Turiddu, Radames, Alvaro, Osaka in *Iris*, Manrico and Calaf. Thus when he was heard at the 1957 Edinburgh Festival, his Nemorino had less of the vocal charm than many people had hoped for. Yet there were moments which were reminiscent of his early days ten years previously, when his voice possessed a rich velvety tone, unfailingly beautiful and capable of exquisite pianissimo. These attributes were noticeable to a great extent when he made a long-delayed Covent Garden début in the spring of 1961 as Cavaradossi.

MATTIWILDA DOBBS

ONE of the most pleasing aspects of post-war operatic activity has been the number of American coloured singers who have made careers for themselves, not only in their own country, but in Europe. One of the most successful and charming of these is the soprano Mattiwilda Dobbs.

She was born in Atlanta on July 11, 1925. Her vocal studies were at Spelman College, Atlanta, and then in New York with Lotte Leonard. In 1947 she won a Marian Anderson scholarship; and then other awards and finally in 1950 a $3,000 scholarship which brought her to Europe where she studied in Paris with Pierre Bernac.

In October, 1951, she won first prize in the Geneva International contest, which led to appearances with orchestras in France, Holland, Sweden and other European cities. In June, 1952, she sang the title role in Stravinsky's *Le Rossignol* at the Holland Festival. 'I shall not quickly forget those floating lyrical tones as they caught and caressed the most exacting of coloratura phrases. This was easy, accurate coloratura, such as one virtually never hears nowadays, and it fell very gratefully and consolingly on the listener's ear. We need talent in opera today, as perhaps never before, and when it is allied, to such beauty of voice, such expressive and exact musicianship, the combination should take its possessor to the top of the singing tree'. So wrote Lord Harewood in *Opera* of her performance in the Stravinsky opera.

It was not long before she was heard in Italy—Elvira in *L'Italiana in Algeri* at La Scala, and Queen of Night at the San Carlo, Naples. In the summer of 1953 she sang Zerbinetta at Glyndebourne. Covent Garden heard her soon after as the Woodbird in *Siegfried*, as a most attractive Queen of Shemakahn in *The Golden Cockerel*, and as Gilda, a role in which, according to Andrew Porter, she 'displayed a ravishing quality of sound, and consistently sensitive musical phrasing'.

She has returned to Covent Garden on a number of occasions since then, where she has added The Queen of Night and Olympia in *Les Contes d'Hoffmann* to her repertory. While she was at Glyndebourne again in the summer of 1954 she was released by the management to participate in a Gala performance of *The Golden Cockerel* at Covent Garden before the British Royal family and the King and Queen of Sweden. After the performance King Gustav decorated her with the Order of the North Star.

Mattiwilda Dobbs made her New York début in a concert performance of *Ariadne* during the 1953-4 season. She was engaged for the Metropolitan, New York, for the 1956-7, making her début there as Gilda. Ronald Eyer writing in *Musical America* commented on the soprano's 'fine, beautifully schooled voice of considerable size, and innate musicianship of the highest order'. During her second New York season she sang Lucia with great success. 'Her tone was unfailingly lovely', wrote one critic, 'the tones squarely on pitch and effortlessly produced, the high climatic notes sustained and secure, the fioriture deftly and accurately negotiated. Accompanying all the technical display required by Lucia's music was a disarming simplicity in style that gave Miss Dobbs' performance a basically lyric quality, and it was appropriately matched by her gentle, wistful and sweet portrait of the unhappy heroine'.

In 1961 Mattiwilda Dobbs sang a series of guest performances at Hamburg, and so successful were they, that she was invited to join the company for the following season. She has now sung Sophie in *Rosenkavalier*, Gilda in Felsenstein's production of *Rigoletto*, Rosina, Olympia and Constanze in Hamburg. It is good that this singer should have found a place for herself in a firmly-established German company, as this will give her the opportunity of developing her art and tackling new roles which she might have little chance to do elsewhere.

OTTO EDELMANN

AMONGST the post-war interpreters of Hans Sachs and Wotan Vienna's Otto Edelmann holds a high place. He was born in Vienna in 1916 and his first career was very far removed from music—he was a professional boxer. He was persuaded to study singing and went to the Vienna Conservatory where his teachers were Professor Lierhammer and Gunnar Graarud.

Edelmann's first engagement was in the small company at Thüringen, where he made his début as Figaro (Mozart) in 1938, following it with Kecal. The following year he was engaged for Nuremberg, but soon was called up for military service, and spent the next seven and a half years first in the army and then in a Russian prison camp. When he was released in 1947 and returned to his native Vienna he was quite unknown, but after an audition he was engaged by the State Opera where he made his début as the Hermit in *Freischütz* under Knappertsbusch.

At the Vienna Opera he soon became a leading singer, and although he was heard in serious roles, such as the Speaker in *Zauberflöte* and King Philip in *Don Carlos*, he found that he was in great demand as Falstaff, Dulcamara, Plunkett and Leporello.

In 1948 Edelmann was first heard at Salzburg, and he has been a regular visitor there ever since, where he has sung in *Fidelio*, *La Clemenza di Tito*, *Don Giovanni* and *Der Freischütz*. In 1951 he was chosen to sing Hans Sachs at the first Bayreuth Festival, a role he repeated the following year and in which he made his début at the Metropolitan, New York, in November, 1954. He has

MARIO DEL MONACO

as *Andrea Chénier*

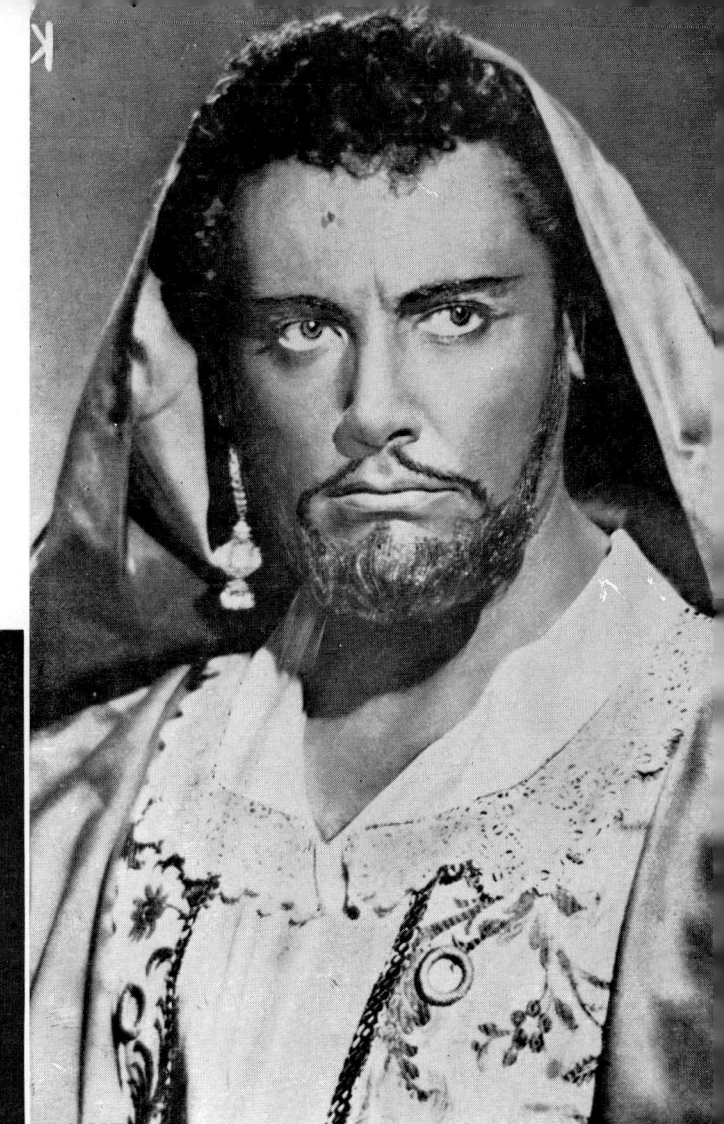

as *Otello*

VICTORIA DE LOS ANGELES — as *Manon* in 'Massenet's Opera'

VICTORIA DE LOS ANGELES

as herself

as *Madama Butterfly*

GIUSEPPE DI STEFANO

as *Nemorino* in 'L'Elisir d'Amore'

as *Riccardo* in 'Un Ballo in Maschera'

MATTIWILDA DOBBS
as *the Queen of Shemakhan* in 'The Golden Cockerel'
with Howell Glynne as *King Doran*

OTTO EDELMANN
as *Baron Ochs* in 'Der Rosenkavalier'

GERAINT EVANS

as *Beckmesser* in 'Die Meistersinger'

as *Falstaff* as *Figaro* in 'Mozart's Opera'

SYLVIA FISHER

as *Sieglinde* in 'Die Walküre'

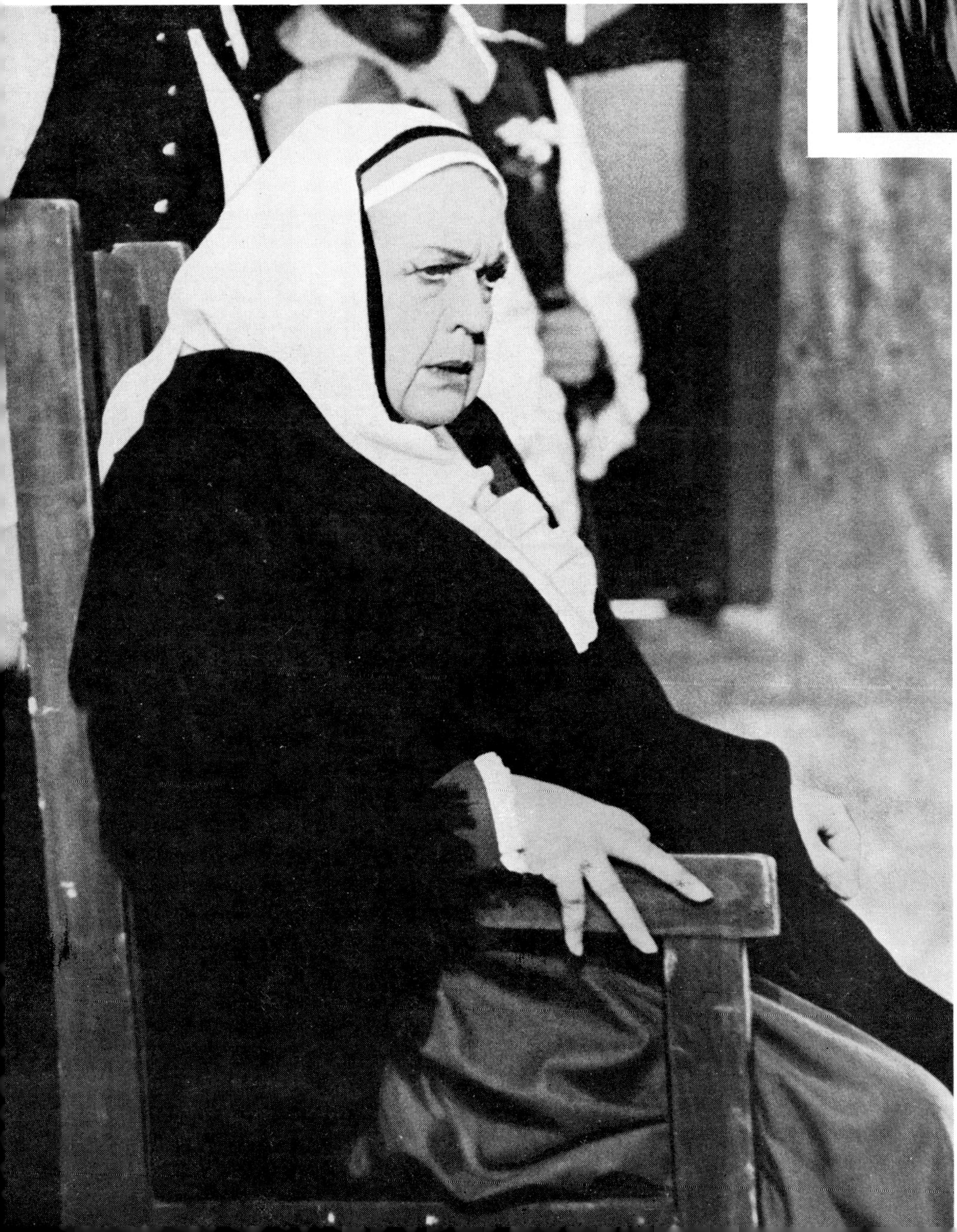

as the *Kostelnicka* in 'Jenufa'

as *Wozzeck* and *Falstaff*

DIETRICH FISCHER-DIESKAU

as *Amfortas* in 'Parsifal'   as *Wolfram* in 'Tannhäuser'

remained a member of the Metropolitan since, adding Heinrich in *Lohengrin* to his repertory in November, 1955—'a distinguished performance' according to *Musical America*; Ochs the following February—'sly, lecherous, bumptious, and for just a moment at the end, movingly wistful'; Gurnemanz a month later, to which part, according to one critic, 'he brought a searching spiritual perception'; Wotan in 1957 and King Marke in 1958. His Wagnerian repertory also includes the Dutchman which he has sung in Europe, but not so far in America.

One of the highlights of Edelmann's career was being chosen to sing Wotan in the Act 3 recording of the *Die Walküre* opposite Flagstad. He had always admired her since her Salzburg *Fidelio*, but never dreamed that the soprano herself would choose him for the recording.

GERAINT EVANS

ONE of the handful of British artists to have achieved true international status in the post-war operatic world is the Welsh baritone Geraint Evans, whose appearances at Covent Garden and Glyndebourne have marked him out as one of the finest baritones in opera today.

Geraint Evans was born in Pontypridd in 1923, and after leaving school embarked on a business career. When he was seventeen he began to take singing lessons, and then participated in a number of local amateur performances. The outbreak of the war found him in the Royal Air Force, and at the end of the war, he was in Hamburg helping Trevor Harvey to organize programmes for the British Forces Network and sometimes singing in them himself. He was heard in one such programme by the famous bass Theo Hermann, who took him on as a pupil.

On his return to England Evans went to the Guildhall School of Music, where he studied with Walter Hyde; and he has also had periods of study with Fernando Carpi in Geneva.

Geraint Evans joined the Covent Garden Company in 1948, making his début in the small role of the Night-watchman in *The Mastersingers*. He followed this by appearances as the Marquis in *La Traviata*, and a Police Officer in *Boris Godunov*. During his second season he began to consolidate his position at Covent Garden. First there was the Count Ceprano in *Rigoletto*, then Schaunard in *La Bohème*, and in January, 1949, his first big chance as Figaro in the new production of the Mozart opera.

At first, Evans's Figaro was merely very full of promise, then gradually as he got into the skin of the part, it became one of the best interpretations of the role to be seen or heard. His Figaro was certainly a person with whom the Count had to reckon, and at the same time he was a warm-hearted and lovable character. Evans's warmth and spontaneous charm were also much in evidence in his interpretation of another Mozart role, Papageno. Both these roles he also sang at Glyndebourne in their original language. Evans's first Glyndebourne appearance had been in 1950 when he sang Guglielmo in *Così fan tutte*, a role he has repeated there on several occasions. This was followed by Masetto, The Music Master (*Ariadne auf Naxos*), Abbate Cospicuo (*Arlecchino*), Leporello, the Papageno and Figaro already mentioned, and perhaps his greatest triumph, Falstaff.

Evans's Falstaff was received with critical and public acclaim. 'Mr. Evans has crowned with this interpretation a reputation that has been steadily growing for versatility in characterization, for incisive delivery of the words of several languages, and for the sheer tonal resources of an excellent voice' wrote *The Times*. And in 1958 when he opened the Glyndebourne season in the same role, Desmond Shawe-Taylor commented 'His utterance both musical and verbal has acquired a fine wit and distinction, and his ripe impersonation is worthy to be remembered in the historic sequence of famous Falstaffs'. Covent Garden endorsed this opinion when it asked him to sing the role in Zeffirelli's production of Verdi's Opera in 1961.

Almost as successful had been his impersonation of Beckmesser in the Covent Garden production of *The Mastersingers* in January, 1957. Such is Geraint Evans's seriousness of approach when tackling a new role, that he specially visited the Bayreuth and Munich Festival performances of the same opera the previous summer, in order to study at close quarters two other famous Beckmessers, Karl Schmitt-Walter and Benno Kusche. That is not to say that Evans's Beckmesser had nothing original about it—far from it. He refrained from turning the role into the caricature it often becomes, and offered a complete musical and dramatic portrait of a small-minded, mean and petty townclerk.

Other roles in which Covent Garden has heard this fine baritone include Escamillo, Sharpless, Lescaut, Spalanzani, Mr. Flint in *Billy Budd*, Mountjoy in *Gloriana*, Balstrode and Ned Keene in *Peter Grimes*, Antenor in *Troilus and Cressida*, Enrico in *Lucia di Lammermoor*, Wozzeck, and Falstaff. In a word he is a leading baritone of which any major opera house might well be proud, and as such has been invited to sing in San Francisco, Vienna, at La Scala, Milan, the Salzburg Festival, and at the Metropolitan, New York.

DIETRICH FISCHER-DIESKAU

It might come as a surprise to English and American readers of this book that Fischer-Dieskau is admired as much as an opera singer in Germany and Austria as he is as a lieder singer in England and America. Indeed, like most foreign singers, it was in the opera house that his career began.

He was born in Berlin on May 28, 1928, and studied at the Hochschule für Musik of that city. His family was a musical one, and in Bach's day there was a Kammerherr von Dieskau, for whom Bach wrote his 'Peasant Cantata' in 1742. His father and mother were both musicians, and he himself originally intended to become a conductor.

After his training in Berlin, he was conscripted into the army, and was a prisoner of war in Italy. Soon after his return to Germany in 1947, he was called on to replace a sick colleague in a performance of the Brahms *Requiem* at Mulheim. In 1948 he was engaged by Tietjen for the Städtische Opera, Berlin, where he still sings regularly.

His roles in Berlin for the first five years of his career included Valentine, Wolfram, Posa, Jokanaan, Don Giovanni, Don Fernando and Dr. Faustus (Busoni). Then in 1954 he went to Bayreuth where he sang Wolfram and the Herald in *Lohengrin*. Andrew Porter writing in *Opera* about his Wolfram commented, 'The intensity of his declamation and his phrasing, and the wonderful quality of his voice made his Wolfram unforgettable'.

The following year he added Amfortas to his Wagnerian repertory, and was also heard in the small but significant role of Kothner in the Wieland Wagner production of *Meistersinger*. His Kothner was pompous, knowing, smug and self-important, and vocally impeccably sung.

At Salzburg too, Fischer-Dieskau has become a regular visitor, where his 'charming and dangerous' Count Almaviva and romantic Mandryka have been greatly admired.

His regular operatic appearances are now divided between Berlin, Munich and Vienna, and he has added several more roles to his repertory, including Renato in *Un Ballo in Maschera*, Falstaff (Verdi), which took Berlin by storm, Gregor Mittenhofer in Henze's controversial *Elegy for Young Lovers*, and the title role in Einem's *Dantons Tod*.

On records he has also been heard as Pizarro in *Fidelio*, Olivier in *Capriccio*, and the Dutchman; and by the time these words appear in print, he may well have sung them on the opera stage. It is remarkable that an artist who spends so much time touring the world as a lieder singer can find time to add to his operatic repertory in the way Fischer-Dieskau does. And it is not often that one finds in an opera singer the art of the lieder singer used to such advantage. That, added to his beautiful voice, sensitivity and musical feeling, all add up to make Fischer-Dieskau one of the most distinguished baritones to have come out of Germany this century.

SYLVIA FISHER

It has been said, with some truth, but for the supply of singers from Australia, post-war British opera might have been in a very bad way. One has only to think of the soprano voice alone to see the truth of this statement. Joan Hammond, Elsie Morison, Joan Sutherland, Elizabeth Fretwell, Marie Collier, Una Hale, Patricia Howard, June Bronhill are names that we all know—and of course the finest Sieglinde and Marschallin of the post-war period at Covent Garden, Sylvia Fisher.

She was born in Melbourne and studied piano and singing while still at school. She then entered the Melbourne Conservatory and while still a student took part in a performance of Lully's *Cadmus and Hermione* at the Comedy Theatre in 1932. This was her only operatic appearance until she came to England after the war, but it lead to oratorio and concert appearances; and she did sing in radio performances of a number of operas and was heard as Donna Anna, Ortrud and Aida.

Sylvia Fisher's teacher at the Conservatory was Mary Campbell, but after she had taken her diploma she studied with Adolf Spivakovsky, brother of the famous violinist, with whom she remained for twelve years. About the immense amount she learned from him, Fisher is in no doubt; and she has written: 'My teacher, Adolf Spivakovsky, was very exacting about matters of style, which are so important in creating character, and about the differences between one composer and another. For many years my study comprised learning the differences between Wagner and Mozart, between Brahms and Schubert. And this holds good even in different roles by the same composer. The voice will always obey the stimulated imagination. There are few singers that concern themselves enough with these matters, too many that are content to be just themselves'.

In December, 1947, she decided to come to England and pursue a career as a lieder singer or on the operatic stage. Her first year in London was a lonely one, and during that time she gave no less than five Covent Garden auditions! Finally she was engaged as a solo artist, and asked to prepare the role of Leonore in *Fidelio*, which was receiving its first post-war production at Covent Garden under Karl Rankl. The producer was Friedrich Schramm; his advice to her, when he heard that she had never been on the stage before, was 'Good. All you need do is to leave your hands at your sides and sing. Let the music speak for itself'. To this day Sylvia Fisher follows that advice, and with great effect.

It was exactly one year after her arrival in England that she made her operatic début. The *Fidelio* was followed by appearances as the Countess in *Figaro*, and in the summer of 1949 she sang her first Wagnerian role—the Third Norn in *Götterdämmerung*.

During the 1949-50 season Elsa, Sieglinde and the Marschallin followed; then Senta, Elsa and Gutrune the year after. The touching, human quality of her Sieglinde was in evidence from the very beginning. Eric Blom, writing in *The Observer* commented, 'One has never regretted more that Sieglinde was not spared to greet her god-sent daughter at her awakening'.

It was during the 1950-51 season that Erich Kleiber came to Covent Garden, and his faith in many of the British artists of the company, and in Sylvia Fisher in particular, had a beneficial effect on the singers—that plus Kleiber's genius as an operatic conductor. Kleiber's influence and work at Covent Garden made a great impression on Sylvia Fisher, and in an article she contributed to *Opera* in May, 1957, she had some most illuminating things to say about working with him: 'Erich Kleiber used to say that the repertory was the singer's worst enemy; the endless repetition of the same operas, night after night, season after season, was likely to become mechanical, and so the role would suffer, would become deadened instead of brought to life ever more fully. He said he always guarded against this—and I think it is good advice for everybody—in that in every performance he concentrated his full powers on one passage, perhaps one page of the score, and tried to do it on that occasion better than ever before. When the moment comes, he said, use your whole being in the effort to get just that one bit perfect for just once. Of course you may fail! But next time you may succeed, and then each time you will go on improving. This is a wonderful remedy against the effect of routine performances.

'Kleiber knew the great value of the pause in opera. No-one does anything without thinking, after all, and there must be time for thought and decision before making a movement. I wish more producers would think the same! For instance, if someone enters the room on stage, you must at least have time to see who it is before singing to him or about his arrival. At one particular place near the end of Act I of *Der Rosenkavalier* Kleiber always gave me time to sigh. I complained to him that I couldn't sigh in a convincing natural manner as quickly as the music wanted me to. He said, "You just sigh and I'll be there." And he was. How well he understood the importance of things like this.'

Desmond Shawe-Taylor writing about Fisher's Marschallin under Kleiber pointed out that no-one had benefited more from the flexibility and new lightness of the orchestral playing than she—'Her performance is now both vocally and dramatically distinguished'.

Kleiber then took her to Rome to sing Sieglinde in his *Ring* performances there; and when she sang the same role in the new Covent Garden *Ring* of 1954, Ernest Newman singled out her performance as 'outstanding' and 'beautifully sung'.

The season before she had faced perhaps the greatest challenge of her career. She was asked to sing Isolde at Covent Garden. Not only did she have to contend with the memory of her immediate predecessor, Kirsten Flagstad, but also with the great amount of head-shaking that went on, and mutterings that this role would surely ruin her voice. She overcame both these obstacles successfully; for first she went to Berlin to study the role with another great pre-war Isolde, Frida Leider, and then proceeded to confound all the critics by singing one of the most womanly and moving Isoldes heard at Covent Garden. The top notes held no terror for her, and the great moments of the score which called for power and vehemence were encompassed with skill and ease.

In the 1955-6 season she sang the *Walküre* Brünnhilde on tour with the Covent Garden company, and then in the autumn of 1957 was heard in London in the same role in an extra performance of the opera after the *Ring* cycles. Helped by the magnificent Wotan of Hotter, she offered one of the most moving interpretations of Brünnhilde seen or heard at Covent Garden. Other roles in which this artist has appeared at Covent Garden include Ellen Orford in *Peter Grimes*, Agathe in *Freischütz*, and Elisabeth in *Tannhäuser*.

Another of Sylvia Fisher's triumphs was as the Kostelnicka in Janácek's *Jenufa* in December, 1956. According to *The Times* she 'revealed characterization and dramatic power of a high order'. While Shawe-Taylor, a Janácek expert if ever there was one, wrote, 'Hers was in every way a beautifully complete and rounded portrait, alike in gesture, gait, make-up, and vocal inflection.

Later the same season she sang her first Turandot. That she triumphed in this role cannot be denied. But the music Puccini wrote for this opera is a voice-killer, and Sylvia Fisher's voice certainly suffered from having to sing this role. Indeed during the 1957-8 season she was not in good vocal health, and her Isolde in the summer of 1958 showed vocal strain. Other artists have gone through similar crises—Mödl, Varnay, to mention but two; and one can only hope that Sylvia Fisher will after a period spent repairing her voice, emerge again as the glorious singer we have long admired.

GOTTLOB FRICK

ONE of the few real 'black' basses in German opera today, is the Munich and Vienna singer, Gottlob Frick. He was born in Olbronn in Württemberg on July 28, 1906, and studied at Stuttgart. His début was made in 1927 at the Stuttgart Landestheater; seasons followed in Coburg, Freiburg and Königsberg; and then in 1941 he joined the Dresden State Opera, remaining a member of that organization for ten years.

While Frick was a member of the Dresden ensemble he sang Favar in the Dresden première of Kienzl's *Der Kuhreigen*, Caliban in the world première of Sutermeister's *Die Zauberinsel*, Tischlermister in the first performance of Haas's *Die Hochzeit des Jobs*, as well as such roles as Rocco, Pogner, Gremin (*Eugene Onegin*), Falstaff (*Lustige Weiber*), Tommaso (*Tiefland*) and the more popular bass parts in the German and Italian repertory.

In 1947 Frick went to Berlin where he sang Daland, Marke, Gurnemanz and Osmin at the State Opera, and the Landgrave, Fafner and Ramphis at the Städtische Oper. He then became a member of the latter company and from 1950 began to appear in other European cities.

During the 1950-51 season he sang in the German season at the Liceo, Barcelona, at the Scala, Milan, and at Covent Garden (Fafner, Hunding and Hagen). In 1952 he went to the Edinburgh Festival as a guest artist with the Hamburg State Opera as Caspar, Sarastro and Rocco. Lord Harewood writing in *Opera* of his Edinburgh performances, commented on 'his brilliantly incisive singing of Caspar, notably the drinking song, which was as near perfection as it is easy to imagine'.

Frick's connection with Munich began in 1951 and with Vienna the following year; and today he divides his time between both houses, singing both in Wagner and Verdi —his King Philip and Padre Guardiano are especially admired—as well as in other roles in his repertory.

In the autumn of 1957, Covent Garden gave two extra

performances of *Götterdämmerung* after the two annual *Ring* cycles, and Frick, returning to London for the first time since 1951, sang Hagen with great success. 'He dominated the opera for most of the time', wrote *The Times*. He returned the next year to sing Fafner, and he repeated his excellent Hagen. In May 1959 he sang Gurnemanz in Covent Garden's new production of *Parsifal*, and with the exception of Ludwig Weber, one can think of no other bass of our time who has sung the role so movingly and with so consistently musical and beautiful a tone.

In 1960 Frick was heard at Bayreuth for the first time, and now he is at the very peak of his career. His is perhaps the only German bass voice, like those possessed by Helgers, List, Andresen, which possesses that dark, sonorous quality, which Wagner specially required in his bass roles.

NICOLAI GEDDA

ONE of the most versatile and gifted of contemporary tenors is the Swedish Nicolai Gedda. He was born in Stockholm of a Russian father and Swedish mother in 1925. His father, a member of the original Don Cossack Choir, whose name was Ustinov, was the choir-master of the Russian church in Leipzig, and it was there that Gedda (he took his mother's surname for the stage) first began to sing.

He began his professional training in Stockholm in 1948, when he studied with Carl Martin Oehmann, a famous tenor who sang in German at the Metropolitan and Covent Garden in the 1920's and 1930's. Gedda's début took place at Stockholm in 1952 in Adam's *Le Postillon de Longjumeau*. He was heard by the conductor Issay Dobrowen and Walter Legge of E.M.I. Records, who were both so impressed that he was engaged to sing Dimitri in the complete recording of *Boris Godunov* in Paris with Christoff in 1953.

In the same year he was engaged for La Scala, Milan to sing Don Ottavio under Karajan, and in Orff's *Trionfi*. In 1954 he was heard as Huon in Maurice Lehmann's magnificent production of *Oberon* at the Paris Opéra. Not long afterwards he made his Covent Garden début as the Duke in *Rigoletto*, and then he sang Faust and Tamino in Paris, and Vincent (*Mireille*) and Belmonte at the Aix-en-Provence Festival. At Aix also he sang the tenor version of Gluck's *Orfeo* in 1955. This most difficult role contains high B flats, C's and even a high D, all of which the tenor was able to take easily.

Much of 1956 and 1957 was spent making gramophone records for Gedda is in great demand in the recording studio and his six languages (French, German, Italian, Swedish, Russian and English) make him into one of the most versatile singers of the day. Musically too he is equally at home in Johann Strauss's sparkling *Fledermaus*, Lehar's *Merry Widow* or Bach's B Minor Mass.

In November 1957 Gedda made his Metropolitan début as Faust, when his refined style and ability to sing *piano* were favourably commented upon. Later that season he was heard as Ottavio and the Tenor in *Rosenkavalier* and he created the role of Anatol in Samuel Barber's *Vanessa* when his superb diction stood out from among a cast of English-speaking singers. At Salzburg in the summer of 1958 he repeated this role,—he had previously been heard there the previous summer in Liebermann's *School for Wives*.

Gedda began his second Metropolitan season singing the title role in Offenbach's *Contes d'Hoffmann*, following it with Tamino, Lensky in *Eugene Onegin*, and the Duke in *Rigoletto*. Of his Tamino, *Musical America* wrote, 'Nicolai Gedda sang with refinement and authority, and once again his English diction was a model for our native-born artists'; and as Lensky, the same paper wrote, 'It is perhaps the finest thing he has done here, and it was as notable for finished and inspired acting as for hauntingly beautiful singing'.

During the 1960-61 season Gedda sang Tamino in a concert performance in London of *Die Zauberflöte* under Klemperer, and displayed a new assurance and a voice that seemed to have assumed more heroic proportions. This was confirmed a few months later in Holland, when the tenor sang the title role of Berlioz's *Benvenuto Cellini* in the 1961 Holland Festival—indeed Gedda's singing was the one entirely pleasing aspect of the performance. If there is to be a Meyerbeer revival in our time, here surely is the ideal tenor for Raoul in *Les Huguenots* and John of Leyden in *Le Prophète*.

HOWELL GLYNNE

ONE of the most popular figures in post-war British opera has been the Welsh bass, Howell Glynne. He was born in Swansea in 1907 and studied singing with the great Ben Davies, and then with Reinhold von Warlick.

He joined the Carl Rosa Company for their 1931-2 season, and after singing small roles, became the company's leading bass by the outbreak of the second world war. Returning to England in 1945 he spent a season with the Carl Rosa, singing Méphistophélès, Sparafucile and other parts, and then in 1946 was engaged for Sadler's Wells where he made his début as Bartolo in *The Barber of Seville*, following it with Kecal, Ford in *Sir John in Love*, and Mr. Crusty in the first production in England of Wolf-Ferrari's *School for Fathers* (*I Quatro Rusteghi*).

Glynne's success in this role, as well as in other buffo parts, led to his being engaged to sing as a guest artist at Covent Garden as Varlaam in *Boris Godunov* in the 1947-8 season and Bartolo the year after. But it was not only in comic roles that he was heard for he was chosen to sing Fiesco in the first English performance of *Simon Boccanegra* at Sadler's Wells in October 1948. His sonorous bass voice, and sympathetic study of the role made a deep impression. Completely in contrast was his assumption of the role of the Devil in Weinberger's *Schwanda the Bagpiper* later that season.

In the autumn of 1949 Glynne joined the Covent Garden Company and opened his first season there as Lavatte in the world première of Bliss's *The Olympians*. Later he sang his first Baron Ochs, which with the help he received from Kleiber and the bass Fritz Krenn became one of his best sung interpretations. Rocco in *Fidelio* was another role which Glynne sang with considerable success at Covent Garden.

In 1951 as part of the Festival of Britain celebrations, Covent Garden combined with Sir Thomas Beecham to put on a revival of Balfe's *The Bohemian Girl*, and Glynne was chosen to sing Devilshoof in this production. But perhaps his greatest triumph at Covent Garden was as King Dodon in Rimsky-Korsakov's *The Golden Cockerel* in 1954.

At the end of the 1955-6 season Glynne left Covent Garden and once again became a member of the Sadler's Wells Company. He began his new engagement there as Plunkett in *Martha*; then he took over the title-role of *Don Pasquale*, and was heard as Sarastro. He was given leave from the company during the season to return to Covent Garden to sing an excellent King Fisher in the revival of Tippett's *The Midsummer Marriage*.

During the 1957-8 and 1958-9 seasons, he was heard in three more new roles, Baron Mirko Zeta in *The Merry Widow*, Falstaff in Verdi's opera of that name, and the Waterman in Dvorak's *Russalka*, when it had its first English stage performance. And when the Sadler's Wells Company began its operetta season at the London Coliseum in April 1959 with *Die Fledermaus*, Glynne was of course there in another of those comic roles which he has made so much his own, Frosch, the drunken jailer.

TITO GOBBI

WHEN the history of post-war Italian opera comes to be written, the name of Tito Gobbi will undoubtedly occupy an honoured place in it; for there is little doubt that this one artist nobly carries on the art of such legendary figure as Ronconi, Maurel and Battistini, and in our time Mariano Stabile.

Gobbi was born at Bassana del Grappa near Venice on October 24, 1915. He studied law at Padua University, and began to take vocal lessons. His vocal possibilities were seen by a friend of the family who persuaded Gobbi's father to allow him to study professionally; and accordingly he studied for five years (1933-8) with the tenor Giulio Crimi. In 1937 he won a scholarship to the Scala School, and was also one of the first prize winners in the Vienna International Competition.

Gobbi's name appeared on the 'cartellone' for the 1937-8 season at the Teatro Reale dell'Opera in Rome; but it was not until the summer of 1938 that he was heard in an important role, the Herald in *Lohengrin*. During the following season he was heard as Jokanaan in *Salome*, and in roles in Montemezzi's *La Nave*, Pizzetti's *Fra Gherardo* and *Boris Godunov*. From then onwards Gobbi has never missed a season at Rome. Besides appearing there in the great Verdi and Puccini roles, he has sung such parts as

Tepurlov in the world première of Rocca's *Monte Ivnor*, the Story-Teller in the first performance of Napoli's *Il Tesoro*, Rambaldo in Puccini's rarely-performed *La Rondine*, and perhaps most important of all, the title-role in *Wozzeck*. This opera by Berg was most courageously given its Italian première during the German occupation of Rome in 1942 in a season of modern opera organized by Tullio Serafin.

Gobbi repeated his Wozzeck at Naples in 1949 and at the Scala in 1952. Such is his versatility that he could sing this role one night, and the next appear as the gay Figaro, the rascally Schicchi or the scheming, sadistic Scarpia.

Gobbi's Scala début took place in 1942 when he sang Belcore in Donizetti's *L'Elisir d'Amore*; and he opened the 1952-3 season there as Ford in *Falstaff* under De Sabata. It was in both these roles that he made his first London appearances in the short but memorable Scala season in 1950 at Covent Garden.

Two years later he returned to London and sang Figaro and Scarpia with a scratch Italian company at the Stoll theatre. In the Rossini part he was apt to play to the gallery, but as Scarpia he showed his true metal in London for the first time, giving a performance that was both authoritative and finely sung. Then there was an interval of another two years before he returned to the London opera stage, this time as a substitute for an indisposed baritone at Covent Garden, where he was called in to sing at very short notice, two performances of *Un Ballo in Maschera*. As Andrew Porter wrote in *Opera* 'This sudden impact of a performance in the finest Scala tradition, with bearing and gesture geared to the grand scale, and big confident, stylish singing, was startling'.

From that time Gobbi has been a welcome visitor at Covent Garden and his appearances have been eagerly awaited by all lovers of good singing and acting. The critics too have accepted him for what he is, a singing-actor in the great Italian tradition. In 1955 Covent Garden heard his Scarpia with Milanov and Tagliavini; the following year Rigoletto, and in 1958 his greatest London impersonation, Posa in *Don Carlos*. That most demanding of critics, when it comes to voice, Desmond Shawe-Taylor, wrote in the *New Statesman*, 'The finest performance of all —impeccable in bearing, in declamation and in solidity and purity of musical line—came from Tito Gobbi.'

While the usually sober *Times* was moved to exclaim 'Mr. Gobbi is a joy to see and hear, for dramatic singing seems to be a natural function with him, so does art conceal art'. Since then London has been able to enjoy this singer in the title roles of Verdi's *Macbeth* and *Falstaff*, *Iago*, *Count Almaviva* and *Don Giovanni*.

In *Don Carlos* Gobbi was partnered by his brother-in-law, Boris Christoff, and fortunately they have recorded their performances in this opera for H.M.V. Verdi's *Simon Boccanegra* is Gobbi's favourite role, and he chose this part to celebrate his twentieth anniversary as a singer, when that event was celebrated at the San Carlo in Naples, on December 28, 1958. His Boccanegra too has been recorded, again with Christoff (as Fiesco), and Gobbi's portrayal of the Doge, one of Verdi's finest creations, confirms his position as one of the greatest singing-actors of this generation.

America first heard Gobbi in 1948, when he sang at San Francisco. He now appears regularly with the Chicago Opera, but has made only a few appearances at the Metropolitan in New York. In Vienna he is heard in the yearly Italian performances at the State Opera, and there his Falstaff, Scarpia, and Iago under Karajan have earned for him the highest praise.

Gobbi's repertory is immense; besides the roles already mentioned he sings Michele (*Tabarro*), Jack Rance, Germont, Amonasro, Nabucco, Macbeth, Don Giovanni, Tonio, and other parts totalling some ninety roles in all.

How does this great artist study a role? He begins by making a coloured plastic model of the character. 'First of all', he says, 'I must see the chap physically before me, if I want to understand what he feels and thinks'. He then compiles a dossier on the character, psychological and physiological, having read all he can about him if he is an historical character. If only other artists would take half as much time and care preparing a role! But neither study, nor voice, nor natural acting ability can make a person into a great artist. He must be born with that rare thing, the 'star quality' in him. Perhaps some people would call it genius, for that is after all what it really is. But Gobbi would not agree to that. He is just a singer who loves opera and takes pleasure making the public enjoy itself.

CHRISTEL GOLTZ

Germany has always taken its opera far more seriously than any other country, and so it is not surprising that there has been a tradition of great operatic actresses on the German stage, starting with Schröder-Devrient—one of the most famous of Leonores—who made such an impression on the youthful Wagner. Nearer our own day one has only to think of Frida Leider and Martha Fuchs to realize how strong that tradition is. Christel Goltz is another of the outstanding singing actresses of German opera.

She was born in Dortmund in 1912 of a theatrical family. It comes as a surprise to learn that her parents were successful circus acrobats who toured with the famous Barnum and Bailey circus troupe, and were billed, with another member of their family, as the Goltz Trio! The youngest of eight children, Christel Goltz was left an orphan when she was ten. She began her musical studies at the Ornelli-Leeb School in Munich, working at handcraft, tapestry and needlework to pay for her lessons. She originally intended to become a dancer, and indeed her first engagement was in that capacity in Munich. Then she went to Fürth, the little town near Nuremberg from which the maidens in *Die Meistersinger* came to dance with the apprentices. She was a member of the chorus there in 1935, but she got her chance of singing a solo role, and an important one at that—Agathe in *Der Freischütz*. This was a production for young people by the Intendant, and Goltz's success in it led to her engagement at Plauen the following year. There she graduated to such roles as Santuzza, Octavian and Eva. In the 1936-7 season she was engaged by Karl Böhm for the Dresden State Opera as a solo singer. Her Dresden début was as Reiza in *Oberon*, and she remained a member of the Dresden ensemble until the end of the 1949-50 season.

During her fourteen seasons at Dresden she built up an enormous repertory—today it totals more than one hundred parts—including Leonore in *Fidelio*, Fiordiligi, Elisabeth in *Tannhäuser*, Desdemona, Tosca, Aida, Ariadne and Salome. Her success in the Richard Strauss operas was such that Karl Böhm, who had been the Generalmusikdirektor at Dresden, subsequently invited her to sing all the major soprano parts in the 1943-4 Strauss Festival in Vienna. While in Dresden she married Theodor Schenk, who was a pupil of Hindemith and a horn-player in the Dresden Staatskapelle. He now acts as her coach and accompanist, and has never missed a single one of his wife's performances.

Between 1947 and 1950 Goltz divided her time between Dresden and Berlin, singing at both the Staatsoper and Städtische Oper in the latter city. It was in Berlin that she scored a great personal success as Jenufa and as Amelia in *Un Ballo in Maschera*.

Before 1950 the name of Christel Goltz meant little or nothing outside eastern Germany although a few enthusiasts were beginning to talk about the reports they had received of a wonderful new Salome in Dresden. In the summer of 1950 Goltz sang that role at the Munich Festival, and it was not long after that Covent Garden engaged her to sing the same part. Besides Salome, her London appearances have included Leonore in *Fidelio* and Marie in *Wozzeck* in the first stage performance of the opera in England, under Kleiber. The provinces however had been a little luckier, for during the 1953 tour of the Covent Garden company she sang Musetta in *La Bohème*—an interpretation which those who heard it still say is one of the best they have witnessed of this part. When she made her début during the 1954-5 season at the Metropolitan Opera, her Salome was greeted with the same success as elsewhere.

Another Strauss role in which Goltz is widely acclaimed is Elektra, which she sings regularly in Vienna, Munich and elsewhere in Europe, as well as in Buenos Aires. She made her South American début at the Colon in Buenos Aires in 1951, and returned there in 1952 and 1953 singing Jenufa, Elektra, Elsa, Senta, Salome, Marie (*Wozzeck*), Leonore, and Octavian.

As can be seen Goltz's repertory is large and varied. In Vienna, Munich and Berlin she is to be heard in the Italian repertory, Aida, Elisabeth de Valois, Tosca; in Mozart as Donna Anna and the Countess; and recently she has added Isolde to her Wagner repertory which also includes Elisabeth, Sieglinde and Kundry.

It is surprising that with so large a repertory Goltz has so far only created one part. That was the title role in Liebermann's *Penelope* at Salzburg in 1954, for which she earned the unanimous praise of the critics, Austrian and

HOWELL GLYNNE

as *Lavatte* in 'The Olympians'

GOTTLOB FRICK

as *Hagen* in 'Götterdämmerung'

GOTTLOB FRICK

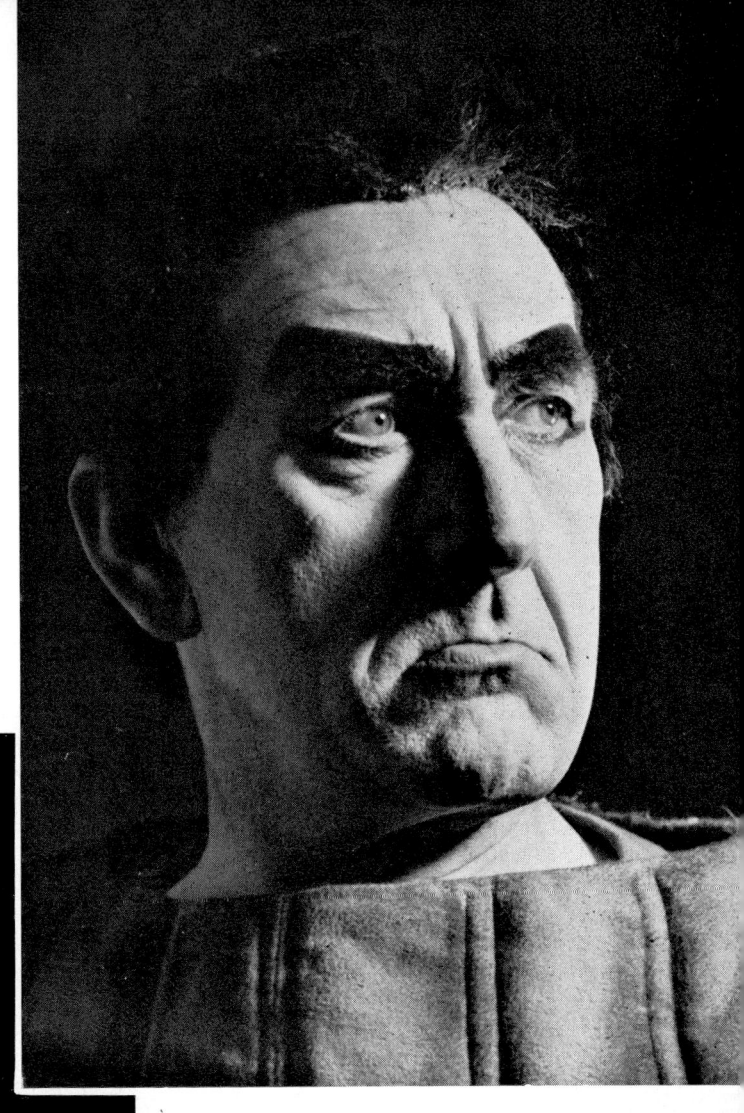

as *Hunding* in 'Die Walküre'

as *King Philip* in 'Don Carlos'

NICOLAI GEDDA

as *Anatol* in 'Vanessa'

as *Lensky* in 'Eugene Onegin'

as herself   as *Dalila*

RITA GORR
as *Fricka* in 'Die Walküre' with HANS HOTTER as *Wotan*

TITO GOBBI

as *Iago* in 'Otello'

as *Gianni Schicchi*

as *Falstaff*

CHRISTEL GOLTZ

as *Elektra*

as *Antigonae*
in Carl Orff's opera

ELISABETH GRÜMMER

as *Eva* in 'Die Meistersinger'

as *Donna Anna* in 'Don Giovanni'

HILDE GUEDEN

as *Anne Trulove* in 'The Rake's Progress'

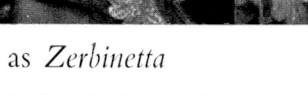

as *Zerbinetta* in 'Ariadne auf Naxos'

foreign. Another modern opera for which she has a special liking is Carl Orff's *Antigonae*, in which she sings the title role, and she has said she would very much like to perform this opera in London.

Goltz's voice is not of the quality one generally associates with heavy dramatic parts—and she hopes one day to sing Brünnhilde—it is clear and brilliant, three octaves in range, but not inherently beautiful. Like many of her German colleagues her acting is intense, and she prepares her roles with enormous care, studying the background both of the opera and its characters. Her career is already some twenty years old, but there is no reason at all why it should not continue for just as many more for Christel Goltz seems to thrive on hard work, and obviously enjoys singing in opera as much as her audiences enjoy hearing her.

RITA GORR

ONE of the characteristics of post-war Bayreuth has been the appearances, on what was once an almost exclusively German stage, of singers from other countries—America, Canada, Holland, France and Belgium. In this later category is the mezzo-soprano Rita Gorr.

She was born in Ghent in 1926, where she began her musical studies. She then went to Brussels and in 1948 she won the first prize in an international competition at Verviers. In 1949 she was called to Strasbourg to replace an indisposed artist as Brangaene—and this was her début. She sang for three seasons at Strasbourg, where she was heard as Amneris, Orfeo, Venus, Delilah, Herodiade, Margaret (*Le Roi d'Ys*), and Ursula in Hindemith's *Mathis der Maler*.

In 1952, Rita Gorr entered for the Lucerne International Contest and was awarded first prize. This led to her being engaged at the Paris Opera, where she made her début as Magdalena in *Meistersinger*, and where she has sung ever since. Her roles in Paris have included Venus, Fricka, Marguerite in *La Damnation de Faust*, Delilah, Marina in *Boris Godunov*, Amneris, Octavian, Herodias in *Salome*, and Mère Marie in *Dialogues des Carmelites*.

In the opera houses of Belgium this singer is also heard regularly. Besides the roles already mentioned, she sang Jocaste in Enesco's *Oedipus* at the first performance in Belgium at La Monnaie in Brussels in March 1956, and the Princess de Bouillon in the first performance in Belgium for more than fifty years of *Adriana Lecouvreur* at Ghent in 1957. Leo Riemens, Holland's most knowledgeable opera critic, who heard her in this last role and as Delilah, commented 'Here at long last is a real French contralto in the tradition of Delna or Gervile-Réache'.

The Belgian-born conductor André Cluytens, who had conducted a number of Gorr's performances in Paris, suggested that she should audition for Bayreuth, which she did and was accordingly engaged for the 1958 Festival to sing Fricka. According to Andrew Porter, she was a 'bright voiced, subtle and triumphant Fricka'; and it was no surprise that she was re-engaged for 1959. Meanwhile she had sung Kundry at the Rome Opera with great success in the spring of 1958 and this in its turn led to engagements for the 1958-9 season elsewhere in Italy and in Lisbon.

Rita Gorr's London début was as Amneris in May, 1959, when her beautiful, full mezzo voice, even throughout its register and used with the utmost musicality and intelligence, clearly demonstrated that here was the kind of French mezzo-soprano voice one used to hear. Reviewing this performance I said that one could foresee many possibilities for her at Covent Garden, and suggested five roles in which she might well be heard. These included Orfeo, Fricka and Eboli.

Although she has not sung Orfeo in London, she has been heard in a Gluck role—the title part in his *Iphigénie en Tauride*, which opened Covent Garden's first visit to the Edinburgh Festival. Her Fricka a few weeks later under Georg Solti, in a new production of *Die Walküre* by Hans Hotter, was generally considered the greatest interpretation of the role heard in London since the days before the last war, when Maria Olczewska, Sigrid Onegin and Kerstin Thorborg were all heard in this role. Gorr's Fricka was a virtuoso performance, vocally and histrionically. Not only Wotan but the audience cowered beneath her lashing tongue and imperious glance.

Her Eboli in *Don Carlos* which she sang for the first time at Covent Garden in 1962, was a veritable *tour-de-force*, 'a Princess Eboli in the grand old-style heroic manner' wrote Andrew Porter; 'The most beautiful mezzo-soprano of

France and Navarre' wrote a leading French critic, an opinion which is now confirmed by audiences the world over.

JOSEF GREINDL

ONE of post-war Bayreuth's most familiar artists is the bass Josef Greindl, who is regularly to be heard there as Fafner, Hunding and Hagen and has also sung there as Pogner, Titurel, Gurnemanz, and Herman.

He was born in Munich on December 23, 1912. When he was fifteen he attended a performance of *Der Freischütz* in Munich in which the role of Caspar was sung by the celebrated bass, Paul Bender. The performance so impressed Greindl, that when a few years later he decided to forsake the violin and study singing, it was to Bender that he went for lessons. At the Munich Academy where he studied he also benefited from coaching with Anna Bahr-Mildenburg.

Greindl's début was made in peculiar circumstances. The father of a young conductor hired a Munich theatre so that his son might have a chance to conduct. The opera chosen was *Don Carlos* and Greindl was given the role of Philip. The first two performances of the opera, mostly performed by students, proved so successful that the Intendant of the Munich Opera forbade any more!

Greindl's professional début followed the next year at Krefeld as Hunding. From Krefeld he went to Düsseldorf, and thence to the Berlin State Opera in 1942, where Tietjen was then Intendant. Tietjen took him to Bayreuth in 1943 and 1944 to sing Pogner, and engaged him for the West Berlin Städtische Oper in 1949, of which ensemble he still is a member.

In Berlin he has sung all the Wagner bass roles, Sarastro, Rocco, Osmin, Ochs, Méphistophélès, Padre Guardiano, King Philip, and Boris Godunov. In 1949 he was first heard at Salzburg as Sarastro and Rocco, and has appeared there at subsequent festivals. The singer's international career began about the same time. In the summer of 1950 he went to Buenos Aires, then followed the first of many appearances in Italy, at La Scala, Rome, Naples and elsewhere. In the 1952-3 season he went to the Metropolitan in New York where he was heard as Heinrich and Pogner. His belated London début was as Hans Sachs at Covent Garden in 1963; a wonderfully rounded and moving performance.

ELISABETH GRÜMMER

ONE German soprano perhaps, more than any other had a special place in the affections of the operagoers of the 1930's, Tiana Lemnitz. She was a beautifully schooled singer, whose exquisite *piano* singing was in a class on its own; in Mozart and as Octavian and Eva she had few equals. In the post-war operatic scene, Elisabeth Grümmer occupies a similar position.

She was born in Niedergentz in Alsace-Lorraine on March 31, 1911, and shortly after the first world-war, moved with her parents to Thuringia. She studied for the stage at Meiningen, and appeared as a professional actress for three years at Aachen; there she married the leader of the orchestra. Until then she had no idea of becoming a singer, although she possessed a very beautiful natural voice. She was then persuaded to study singing, and after six years made her début at Aachen as one of the Flower-maidens in *Parsifal*; this was followed by a successful Octavian. She next was engaged as first lyric soprano at Duisburg, and then went to Prague. When the German theatres were all closed in 1944, she worked for a time as a post-office sorter, while her husband went into a factory.

When the war ended in 1946 she went to Berlin where she was engaged by the Städtische Oper, of which company she is still a permanent member. Between 1946 and 1950 she was heard in a variety of roles in Berlin, including Agathe, Desdemona, Eva, Pamina, Marenka, and Ellen Orford in the first Berlin performance of *Peter Grimes*.

Her Eva was so successful that she was asked to repeat it in East Berlin and Dresden. It was in this role too that she made her London début in the summer of 1951 at Covent Garden under Beecham.

In the summer of 1952 she sang a most elegant and beautiful Octavian at the Munich Festival, and a few weeks later delighted many people in the same role at Edinburgh, where she appeared as a guest artist with the Hamburg State Opera; she was also heard as Agathe, Pamina, and Eva.

In 1953 she began to appear regularly in Vienna and Salzburg; and today she divides her time equally between Berlin, Hamburg and Vienna. Her Salzburg roles have included Agathe in the 1954 *Freischütz* under Furtwängler, and Donna Anna. It was as Anna that she returned to London in 1954 with the Vienna Opera. Eric Blom in *The Observer* wrote about her 'ravishing tone and phrasing', while Desmond Shawe-Taylor, besides commenting on her impeccable musicianship, remarked that 'she is the only Donna Anna of recent years who has sounded not only comfortable, but beautiful, in "Non mi dir".'

In 1956 Grümmer was first heard at Glyndebourne as Ilia in *Idomeneo* and the Countess in *Figaro*; and the following year she paid her second visit to Edinburgh with the Hamburg Company and offered one of the most touching and exquisite performances of Pamina possible.

The 1957-8 season was one of the most successful in this singer's career. In Berlin she was heard as the Countess in Strauss's *Capriccio*—'with such a beautiful voice as hers one would not complain if the final monologue went on for another quarter of an hour. She radiates such human warmth and womanly charm, and she is so lovely to look at, that I for one prefer her to any other singer who has so far tackled the role, and I have heard them all'—so wrote a leading Berlin critic. Then came Elisabeth in *Tannhäuser*, and in the summer her first Bayreuth Eva.

Early in the 1958-9 season Grümmer was cast as Elsa in the Wieland Wagner-Heinz Tietjen *Lohengrin* production at Hamburg. 'The cast was dominated by Elisabeth Grümmer who sang her first Elsa in a way that can properly be described only as heartrending' wrote one of the Hamburg critics. At Bayreuth she has repeated her Eva and has also been heard as Freia and Gutrune.

So far Grümmer has not appeared in America, nor are her appearances in England as frequent as they ought to be, for seldom do we hear such beautiful singing allied to so aristocratic a style and innate musicianship.

HILDE GUEDEN

BORN in Vienna of an Austro-Italian father and Hungarian mother, brought up in Rome, a student at the Vienna Conservatory, an expert linguist and a mistress of German, Italian and French opera, briefly sums up Hilde Gueden.

She was born on September 15, 1917. When she was sixteen she entered the Vienna Conservatory to study dancing and the piano, but it was not long before vocal studies took first place, with Madame Wetzelsberger as her teacher. At seventeen she made her début in an operetta: called *Servus, Servus*, by Robert Stolz, and a year later became a member of the Zurich Opera, making her début, as Cherubino. In 1941 Clemens Krauss, who was then Generalmusikdirektor of the Munich Opera, engaged Gueden as first soubrette. Her performance of Despina in *Così fan tutte* was seen by Richard Strauss, who suggested that she sing the part of Sophie. This she learned not only in German, but in Italian for a performance in Rome, which led to a series of engagements in Italy at the Scala, Florence and other leading opera houses. After her first appearance as Sophie, Richard Strauss gave her a photograph of himself with the inscription 'to my Sophie Gueden'.

Although she sang frequently as a guest artist in Vienna from 1941, it was not until the 1946-7 season that she became a permanent member of the Vienna ensemble. Her Covent Garden début was made in September, 1947, with the Vienna company, as Zerlina, and during their London visit she also sang Cherubino. In 1950 she was given the title of Kammersängerin, one of the youngest singers ever to be accorded this title in Vienna.

Gueden's connection with the Salzburg Festival dates from 1946, and she has been heard there almost every summer since then. Besides singing the Mozart soubrette roles—Zerlina and Despina—she has been heard as Ilia in *Idomeneo*, Amor in *Orphée*, Sophie in *Der Rosenkavalier*, Julia in Boris Blacher's *Romeo und Julia*, Lucia in *The Rape of Lucretia*, Norina in *Don Pasquale*, and most surprising of all, as Zerbinetta in 1954, when she first displayed her newly acquired coloratura technique. Her performance in this role came as a revelation, and to her already fresh and charming voice and youthful personality, she added an agility and élan which gained for her a great personal triumph. Indeed there had been much opposition to her singing this role for the first time, and one of the Salzburg orchestra had bet her six bottles of Hungarian Tokay that she would not succeed. She did, and the orchestra stood in the pit and applauded! Five years later she assumed another difficult Strauss role for the first time, again at Salzburg, Aminta in *Die Schweigsame Frau*. This is a role which demands a lyric-dramatic-coloratura soprano—its range goes up to 'e' in altissimo!

New York first heard Gueden in 1950, when she made her début as Gilda. She has sung there nearly every season since, and has been heard as Rosalinda in *Fledermaus*, Anne Trulove in *The Rake's Progress*, and Zdenka in *Arabella*, all of which she sings in English, Musetta, Susanna, Micaela, Mimi, Sophie, Zerlina, Euridice, Norina and Marguerite.

Gueden's versatility is such that she has been much sought-after to appear in modern works. She has sung in Weill's *Mahagonny* in Venice and in the Britten, Blacher and Stravinsky works already mentioned.

If there is any reservation about Gueden's singing, which is technically secure and always beautiful to hear, it is that she is inclined to be too reserved and some of her interpretations are too cool. Yet her personal beauty and stage presence are such that a leading American critic was moved to write about her: 'Lovely to look at and lovelier to listen to'.

JOAN HAMMOND

To the British opera-goer the war years were a particularly lean period. With Covent Garden closed and later used as a 'palais de danse', with Sadler's Wells occupied by bombed-out families, opera was kept alive by the touring Carl Rosa and the homeless Sadler's Wells company. Among the brighter spots of the Carl Rosa's wartime seasons in London were the appearances of Joan Hammond. This artist, with her Italian-sounding voice, and on the stage a real prima donna personality, brought something of the atmosphere of grand opera to those performances.

She was born in Wellington, New Zealand, in 1912, but received both her formal and musical education in Sydney, Australia. In her early life her chief interests were golf and tennis; indeed it was as a golfer that she attained fame in Australia, before she had sung a note.

At the Sydney Conservatory she trained to be a violinist, and played with the Sydney Symphony Orchestra. She discovered quite by accident that she had a voice, and in order to train it had to find some money. This she earned by writing sports reports for local newspapers. Her actual début was made while she was still a student, in a concert, when she sang in Vaughan Williams's Pastoral Symphony. Shortly after this she joined an opera company singing in the chorus, dancing in the ballet and occasionally taking small roles like Siebel.

In 1936 Joan Hammond left Australia for Europe and continued to study in Vienna. She sang some small roles at the Volksoper, and was engaged for the opera company at Aussig, a small town on the Austro-Czech border. There she sang such roles as Constanze, Martha and Nedda. While visiting Salzburg she met Dino Borgioli with whom she studied for some time. In 1937 she paid her first visit to London and was heard in a recital at the Aeolian Hall, and then the following year at the Wigmore Hall. She sang in a *Messiah* under Beecham; and then was heard singing Violetta's 'Ah fors è lui' on the opening night of the 1939 Promenade Concert season. War broke out shortly after, and she remained in England.

During the early war years she was an ambulance driver, and then with the formation of both ENSA and CEMA offered her musical talents to entertain the forces. It was not until 1942 that she made her first stage appearance in Great Britain. This was as Violetta in *La Traviata*, a role she had sung most impressively in a radio performance of that opera for the BBC a year previously. From 1942-45 she appeared regularly with the Carl Rosa Company, and her roles at that time included Marguerite in *Faust*, Leonora in *Il Trovatore*, Tosca and Cio-Cio-San. Within a short time she had built up a tremendous following, and I can think of no artist who has such a devoted band of 'fans' as Joan Hammond. Her records, too, have had enormous sales, and an indication of the wide appeal that she has for non-operatic audiences is the frequency with which her recordings have been requested in programmes like "Housewives' Choice" and "Forces' Favourites". In this way she has made an important contribution to opera, by bringing it to audiences composed largely of people who generally fight shy of serious music.

In 1947 Joan Hammond was the first British artist to sing at the Vienna State Opera since before the war. There she was heard in four of her most famous roles: Mimi, Tosca, Cio-Cio-San and Violetta. Although the Covent Garden Opera Company was formed in 1946, it was not until the 1948-49 season that Joan Hammond sang there. Leonore in *Fidelio* and Aida were two parts which she added to her repertory at Covent Garden, and among the other parts she has sung there have been Cio-Cio-San and Tosca. Sadler's Wells engaged her to sing the part of Elisabeth de Valois in *Don Carlos* in the Verdi year, 1951. Joan Hammond has also appeared with the New York City Center Opera Company, and has sung a number of other roles for the BBC, including Tatiana in *Eugene Onegin*, and the title-roles in *Thais*, *Manon Lescaut* and *Turandot*. She has also sung Tatiana in Russian; on the first occasion at the Teatro Liceo, Barcelona, in 1955, where she sang the leading soprano role in Rimsky-Korsakov's *The Invisible City of Kitezh*, and then two years later at the Bolshoi, Moscow, where she also sang Aida in Italian.

It was not until 1957 that she was heard in opera in her native Australia, when she sang Tosca and Desdemona, the latter for the first time in her career. In 1959 she was again heard on the London opera stage, when she sang the title role in Dvorak's *Russalka* in its first English stage production at Sadler's Wells, and then she was heard as Butterfly.

William Mann writing in *Opera* prior to her return to the London operatic stage said: 'I shall be surprised if her return to Sadler's Wells does not lead to regular operatic appearances in London. The British do not give much honour to their great musicians (though the Queen recognized Joan Hammond's merits by decorating her with the O.B.E. in 1953), but here in our midst we have a Turandot and a Desdemona, who can rank with the greatest sopranos of today, and a Marschallin long overdue at Covent Garden.'

MARGARET HARSHAW

AMERICA has produced a number of outstanding Wagnerian sopranos in its time—Nordica, Fremstad, Varnay, Traubel and most recently Margaret Harshaw. Like Fremstad and a number of other famous Isoldes and Brünnhildes including Elisabeth Ohms, Martha Fuchs and Martha Mödl, Harshaw began life as a contralto.

Margaret Harshaw was born in Narbeth, Pennsylvania. She began her vocal studies in Philadelphia and in the 1930's won a scholarship to the Juilliard School of Music. After four years study there she appeared at the Lewisohn Stadium, New York, in a summer concert. Her first operatic engagement was at the Chautauqua Summer Opera in 1940.

In the spring of 1942 she won the famous Metropolitan Auditions of the Air Contest (other artists who have also been successful in this competition include Eleanor Steber, Arthur Carron and Leonard Warren), and she was engaged by the company for its 1942-3 season, making her début on November 25, 1942, as the Second Norn in *Götterdämmerung*. Miss Harshaw was at that time a contralto, and her other roles that year were the Third Lady in *The Magic Flute* and Flosshilde in *Walküre*. During her second season she sang a number of major roles, including Azucena, Amneris and Mistress Quickly in *Falstaff* under Beecham, with Tibbett and Steber in the cast. Of her Quickly, *Musical America* wrote, 'Margaret Harshaw was one of the chief vocal assets of the performance. Her Dame Quickly was a pretty and youthful—almost too youthful—minx, provided with an opulent voice of fresh quality which was a joy to hear.'

During the next four seasons she sang regularly at the Metropolitan and also at the San Francisco Opera; her roles at this time included Erda, Waltraute, Fricka, Ortrud, Brangaene, Herodias, Geneviève (*Pelléas*), La mère (*Louise*), Ulrica, La Cieca (*Gioconda*), Amelfa (*The Golden Cockerel*) and the Nurse (*Boris*). There were also appearances in Mexico and Rio, and in 1948 Harshaw came to Paris to sing Brangaene, Delilah and Amneris at the Opéra.

In 1950 her voice had changed, and during the 1950-51 season she sang her first dramatic soprano role, Senta, in *The Flying Dutchman*; she followed this with *Götterdämmerung* Brünnhilde in 1952, and then Isolde, first at Philadelphia, and then later in February, 1953 in New York, where she also sang Donna Anna during the course of the season. The Wagner performances in New York were conducted by Fritz Stiedry, who chose Harshaw for Brünnhilde in the new *Ring* production at Covent Garden in the summer of 1954. These appearances were preceded in the autumn of 1953 by performances of Brünnhilde in *Walküre* and *Siegfried*, both of which she was singing for the first time in her career. It was noted on this occasion that she revealed bright top notes and was able to trill on the F sharp of 'heiaha' in the Battle Cry. In the full cycle in the summer of 1954, it was generally agreed that her Brünnhilde promised much for the future, and by the time she had sung her third complete London *Ring* in 1956 the London *Times* was able to write: 'Miss Harshaw's Brünnhilde has consolidated into a finely controlled conception of the part, capable of asserting its authority majestically when she comes to the bier of Siegfried'. While in England in 1954, Harshaw also was heard as Donna Anna at Glyndebourne, one of the best sung performances of the role ever heard there.

At the Metropolitan Harshaw continued to sing each season. In recent years however she has confined herself to Wagnerian roles, with perhaps an occasional Donna Anna. Thus she has been heard as Brünnhilde, Isolde, Sieglinde, Elisabeth, Ortrud and Kundry. Of her Elisabeth Ronald Eyer wrote in *Musical America*: 'Miss Harshaw's performance placed her unmistakably among the finest Elisabeths it has been our privilege to hear at the Metropolitan in the last quarter of a century'; and her Ortrud likewise has been highly praised.

In these days of curtailed German repertory at the Metropolitan, Harshaw's operatic appearances are not as numerous as her admirers would like; but her voice is admirably suited to the Italian dramatic soprano roles. And should someone contemplate casting a soprano, as originally intended, instead of a mezzo for Adalgisa in *Norma*, she should fill the role admirably.

JEROME HINES

STILL in his forties Jerome Hines has an impressive list of operatic achievements to his credit. He was the first American to sing Gurnemanz in *Parsifal* at Bayreuth; he was chosen to sing the title role in Handel's *Hercules* at La Scala; and has a repertory of nearly forty roles, most of which he has sung at the Metropolitan, New York.

He was born in Hollywood on November 8, 1921. He began to display vocal promise while still in his teens, and in May, 1938, commenced his vocal studies with Gennaro Curci. He then went to the University of California where he studied chemistry and mathematics. While still at college he sang the role of Bill Bobstay in *H.M.S. Pinafore* with the Los Angeles Civic Light Opera. During the war he taught chemistry to army students— he had been rejected for military service because of his extreme height, he was six foot six!

In October, 1941, he was engaged for the San Francisco Opera, making his début with the company on tour, as Biterolf in *Tannhäuser* and Monterone in *Rigoletto*. In 1942 he sang with the San Carlo touring company as Ramphis; in 1943 he appeared as Méphistophélès with the Opera Company of the Golden West. The next year he repeated the role with the New Orleans Opera Association and also sang Osmin. Following his success in these last two parts, his teacher arranged an audition for him at the Metropolitan in March 1946, and he was awarded a contract for the 1946-7 season.

Hines's Metropolitan début was on November 21, 1946, in the small role of the Sergeant in *Boris Godunov*. Three weeks later he sang Méphistophélès. *Musical America* wrote: 'His "veau d'Or" music came as the true climax of a fine performance and placed Mr. Hines in the front rank of the Metropolitan's new generation'. From that time the singer has not looked back. In New York he built up for himself an impressive repertory. Among the more important roles he has sung there have been Ramfis, Don Basilio, Lothario in *Mignon*, Raimondo in *Lucia*, Dossifé in *Khovanshchina*, Gurnemanz, the Grand Inquisitor and King Philip, Sarastro, Il Padre Guardiano, Colline, Pimen and Boris, Arkel in *Pelléas*, Hermann, King Marke, and Don Giovanni.

Of his first assumption of King Philip in *Don Carlos* in December, 1950, *Musical America* wrote: 'The characterization was by considerable measure the best the young bass has given in his Metropolitan career so far.... He has seldom if ever before sung so well as in the "Ella giammai m'amo"; to a beautifully controlled legato line he added an introspective quality that bespoke a new maturity in his musicianship'.

In February, 1954, he sang the title role in *Boris* for the first time. For this event he made a careful preparation, making a psychiatric study of the mental derangement of Boris with the assistance of physicians. Thus his performance was 'an authentic portrait of manic depression, ending in death by cerebral haemorrhage', so wrote Ronald Eyer in *Musical America*. The critic continued, 'Having a set pattern of behaviour before him, Mr. Hines was never at a loss how to act and one never got the feeling that he was improvising gestures and pieces of business simply for the immediate theatrical effect.'

The previous summer Hines had been heard as Nick Shadow in *The Rake's Progress* with the Glyndebourne Company at the Edinburgh Festival, which until his appearances at Bayreuth and La Scala in 1958, was his only visit to Europe. Of his Gurnemanz at Bayreuth, Andrew Porter wrote 'Jerome Hines has a magnificent bass voice, grave and wise, and when he has sung the role more often he should become a Gurnemanz to succeed Ludwig Weber'.

Hines himself is a deeply religious man, which may go a long way to explain why he brings to roles like Gurnemanz, Sarastro, and Il Padre Guardiano such deep humanity and warmth. There is little doubt that he must count as one of the great bass singers of our day.

ELISABETH HOENGEN

One of the minor tragedies of the war years and the period immediately after when German artists had still not begun to sing in England, was that a handful of singers who reached their prime in the early 1940's, were not heard in their great roles by English audiences. One such artist was Elisabeth Hoengen.

She was born in Gevelsberg in Westphalia and from 1928-30 studied music at Berlin University; and then until 1933 at the Berlin Academy of Music. Until 1932 she had intended to specialise in church music, but she then discovered she had a fine voice and was in addition a natural actress. Her teacher was Ludwig Hörth, and she made her first public appearance when she was eighteen. From 1933-5 she was a member of the Wuppertal Company and from 1935 to 1940 she sang at Düsseldorf. At this time she was singing the usual mezzo-soprano repertory—Octavian, Amneris, Brangaene, etc., but even at this stage in her career she had already appeared in one of her greatest roles, Lady Macbeth in Verdi's *Macbeth*. In 1939 she made her first guest appearances in Munich where she was heard as the Nurse in Strauss's *Die Frau ohne Schatten*, and in Berlin where she sang Fricka, and Adriano in Wagner's seldom performed *Rienzi*.

From 1940-43 she was a member of the Dresden State Opera, and while there she sang Octavian under Strauss's own baton. She also took part in the first performance of Orff's version of Monteverdi's *Orfeo*, singing the role of the Messenger and in Sutermeister's *Die Zauberinsel*, singing the part of Ariel (the opera is based on Shakespeare's *The Tempest*). In 1943 Hoengen was engaged as dramatic mezzo-soprano at the Vienna Opera, of which company she still is a member, being made a Kämmersängerin in 1949.

In 1943 she scored one of the greatest successes of her career as Lady Macbeth in the Vienna revival of the Verdi opera. Other roles in which she was heard in Vienna during the next few years included Herodias, Eboli, Marina in *Boris*, Carmen, Clytemnestra, Amneris, Fricka, Dorabella, Octavian and the Countess in *The Queen of Spades*.

Hoengen's international career began in 1947 when she sang Dorabella with the Vienna Company in Paris and London, and Herodias in Geneva and London. While in England she took part in a broadcast performance of *Elektra* under Beecham, singing Clytemnestra, also recording excerpts from the opera. She then went to Barcelona and Buenos Aires; and in the summers of 1948 and 1949 sang Orfeo at Salzburg. The following summer she sang Clairon in *Capriccio* and Lucretia in Britten's *The Rape of Lucretia*. In the summer of 1951 she was the Bayreuth Fricka and Waltraute.

By this time she had sung in the *Ring* at La Scala, Milan under Furtwängler, and made appearances in other Italian opera houses. Then, in the 1951-2 season she made her American début at the Metropolitan as Herodias. Cecil Smith writing in *Musical America* found her 'a vital and assured actress, a handsome woman, and a vocalist of assured skill'. Later in the season she sang Clytemnestra.

The same critic wrote: 'Taken on its own terms Miss Hoengen's Clytemnestra was magnificent. Her appearance had the rottenness of self-indulgence. Her fear of Elektra left one unpitying, as it should; her jubilation upon receiving word of Orest's death was hellish'.

Hoengen's career was interrupted by a serious illness shortly after this, and it was quite a considerable time before she recovered her vocal powers. By the time the Vienna Opera re-opened its doors in November, 1955, Hoengen was singing again with her former authority, and was heard as the Nurse in *Die Frau ohne Schatten*, one of her greatest roles. Since then she has sung all her old roles with great success, and her Clytemnestra, Herodias, Fricka and Erda continue to be a feature of the Vienna performances. In the first Vienna performance of Poulenc's *Dialogues des Carmélites* she sang the role of the First Prioress, and in the summer of 1959 she created the part of the Nurse in the première of Erbse's *Giulietta* at Salzburg. Two further roles that gave this artist ample scope to display her gifts as a singing-actress of the first order.

GRACE HOFFMAN

The influx of American singers to the opera stages of Europe has been one of the phenomena of the post-war period. Helped by Fulbright and other financial grants, many promising young American artists have been able to study in Europe, and then pursue a career in the opera houses of Germany and Italy. Grace Hoffman is such an artist.

She was born in Cleveland, and studied at the Western Research University. Her vocal studies began with Friedrich Schorr. She then won a Fulbright and Blanche Thebom scholarship, and went to Europe where she studied in Milan with the baritone Mario Basiola. She then won further awards in vocal competitions in Vercelli and Lausanne. Her operatic début was at the Teatro Comunale, Florence, where she sang during the 1951-2 season as the Priestess in *Aida*, Enrichetta in *I Puritani*, and Ludmilla in *The Bartered Bride*. During the 1952-3 season Grace Hoffman sang the Princess de Bouillon in a series of performances of *Adrianna Lecouvreur* in Lyons and Marseilles, and made a trial guest appearance at the Zurich Opera as Azucena. Her success was great, and she was engaged as leading mezzo-soprano there for the next two seasons. Her roles at Zurich included Dorabella, Orfeo, Carmen, the Nurse in *Die Frau ohne Schatten*, Maddalena (*Rigoletto*), Fenena (*Nabucco*), Fricka, Kundry, and Ortrud.

Grace Hoffman made a number of guest appearances in Italy during this period, and was then engaged as leading dramatic mezzo-soprano by the Stuttgart State Opera for the 1955-6 season, a position she has held ever since. She made her London début with the Stuttgart Opera at its season at the Royal Festival Hall in September, 1955, as Brangaene, the Third Lady in *Die Zauberflöte,* and the Third Maid in *Elektra*. In Stuttgart she quickly established herself as one of the finest mezzos of recent years, equally at home in Verdi as in Wagner, and in such modern works as *Jenufa* and Orff's *Antigonae* as in Handel and Mozart. Her work at Stuttgart brought her into contact with Wieland Wagner, who engaged her for Bayreuth in 1957, where she has sung Brangaene, and other roles. In Stuttgart she has been heard as Fricka, Waltraute, Ortrud, Brangaene, and Kundry, and her Wagnerian repertory also includes Venus and the *Walküre* Brünnhilde.

In America Grace Hoffman's appearances have been limited to Brangaene at the Metropolitan and the San Francisco Opera in 1958, and Brangaene, and Marina in *Boris*, which she sang in Russian, with the Chicago Opera in the same year. She has also appeared in Lisbon, Bordeaux, and as a guest artist in many German opera houses.

In the summer of 1959 she made her Covent Garden début as Eboli in a revival of the Visconti production of *Don Carlos*, conducted by Giulini. Her Italian training, attractive stage presence, and beautiful warm voice ensured a success for her. She won further laurels for her Kundry the following year, which she also sang in Vienna, with the Stuttgart Opera in the autumn of 1959, and which lead to her being engaged for the 1960-61 Vienna season for twenty-five evenings. In 1963 she sang the title-role in the first performance in Germany for over a century of Donizetti's *Maria Stuarda*.

Grace Hoffman's voice has great warmth in the middle register, and is particularly bright at the top. She sings with great intelligence and displays a musical feeling in

JOSEF GREINDL

as *Hagen* in 'Götterdämmerung'

JOAN HAMMOND

as *Tosca*

ELISABETH HÖNGEN

as *Venus* in 'Tannhäuser'

MARGARET HARSHAW

as *Brünnhilde* in 'Götterdämmerung'

JEROME HINES

as *Don Giovanni*

as *Méphistophélès* in 'Faust'

as *Wotan* in 'Die Walküre'

HANS HOTTER

as himself

as *Wotan* in 'Die Walküre'

HANS HOTTER

as *Borromeo* in Pfitzner's 'Palestrina'

as *The Holländer*

SENA JURINAC

as *Desdemona* in 'Otello'

as *the Composer* in 'Ariadne auf Naxos'

as *Leonore* in 'Fidelio'

SENA JURINAC

as *Madama Butterfly*

JAMES JOHNSTON

as *Calaf* in 'Turandot'

GRACE HOFFMAN

as *Brangaene* in 'Tristan und Isolde'

all that she does. Her acting is perhaps a little subdued, but she is always an appealing figure on the stage.

HANS HOTTER

THE supreme Wotan of our day, and according to some people the greatest exponent of the role since the almost legendary Van Rooy, was born in Offenbach-am-Main on January 19, 1909. Hotter's early musical studies were directed towards his becoming a conductor, and at the Munich Academy he studied the organ, piano, counterpoint and theory. While still a student he became organist and choirmaster in one of the Munich churches, and it was not long before his bass-baritone voice was discovered by Matthaeus Roemer, a concert singer and former pupil of Jean de Reszke. Roemer persuaded Hotter to study singing with him, and so he had the benefit of studying the de Reszke method. In 1929 he made his first public appearance singing the bass part in Handel's *Messiah* at Passau; then he was engaged by the Troppau Opera for the 1929-30 season, making his début as the Speaker in *Die Zauberflöte*. In his first season he also sang Wolfram and Tonio.

Engagements soon followed in Breslau and Prague where he added Amfortas, Pizarro, Amonasro, Jokanaan and Kurwenal to his repertory. From 1934 to 1938 he was a member of the Hamburg Opera and then in 1938 he joined the Munich State Opera, of which organization he is still a member; since 1939 he has also sung regularly at the Vienna Opera.

Hotter's first important role at Munich was in the summer festival of 1938 when he created the part of The Commandant in Strauss's *Friedenstag* under the direction of Clemens Krauss. Later he sang Mandryka in *Arabella*, created the role of Olivier in Strauss's *Capriccio* (Munich 1942), and took the part of Jupiter in the public dress rehearsal of Strauss's *Die Liebe der Danae* at Salzburg in 1944—the official première did not take place because of Hitler's edict closing all German theatres. By the time the war had ended Hotter had a considerable reputation in Germany and Austria, and a large repertory, including roles in the Italian and Russian as well as the German repertory.

In the autumn of 1947 Hotter made his Covent Garden début with the Vienna Company as Don Giovanni and Count Almaviva. He was not at that time in the best of health, and did not make the impression he was later to make. However the Covent Garden Company engaged him for the 1947-8 season to sing Hans Sachs, Wotan and The Speaker in English, and Kurwenal in German. The following autumn he really came into his own when he repeated the Wotan, this time in German, and also sang the Wanderer, thus beginning a series of performances in the *Ring* (he has also sung Gunther in London on two occasions), which have continued for more than fifteen years. By the time of the great Kempe performances of the *Ring* in 1956 and 1957 Ernest Newman was able to write of Hotter's 'subtle, noble and sensitively sung Wotan'; while of his performance in *Siegfried* he wrote 'Hotter's Wanderer was a fine piece of work; he was equally impressive as the contemplative philosophic Wanderer of the first two acts and the vehement frustrated god of the third, making his last futile stand against fate'.

Much of Hotter's time is spent each summer at Bayreuth, where under Wieland Wagner he has sung year after year in the *Ring* and also been heard as Sachs, Pogner, Kurwenal and Amfortas. Between the Bayreuth *Ring* cycles Hotter generally manages to find time for a few appearances at the Munich Festival, generally as Jokanaan, or as Cardinal Borromeo in Pfitzner's *Palestrina*, one of his most telling and subtle impersonations.

Hotter's Metropolitan Opera début took place on the second night of the Bing régime in November, 1950, in the title role of *Der fliegende Holländer*. His personal magnetism was compared to Chaliapin, and he was highly praised for his singing and acting. Later in the season he made his Grand Inquisitor in *Don Carlos* 'a magnificent figure of towering rage'. He continued to appear in New York until the end of the 1953-4 season and he has also sung with the San Francisco Opera.

Hotter has been called an intellectual artist, by which term one means that his interpretations are thought out to the last detail and illuminated by a fine intelligence. None the less they appear as entirely spontaneous creations. Hotter himself however always stresses that an artist would be lost without 'tricks'—the many subtle devices that are acquired through years of experience. Yet

Hotter's 'tricks' are so much a part of his stage work, and are controlled so carefully by the brain behind the man, that it is impossible to spot them. And thus even when his voice is not in its best state, and he displays a little tiredness, which is understandable when one witnesses the immense amount of energy that he puts into his performances, the audience is completely under the spell of his magnetic stage presence, and the spell of one of the few truly great singers of the day.

In the autumn of 1961 Hotter fulfilled an ambition he had long nurtured, namely to produce an opera. This event took place appropriately enough at Covent Garden where he had established himself as a great favourite during the post-war Wagner seasons, and marked the beginning of Covent Garden's new Ring production under the musical direction of Georg Solti. The first opera chosen was *Die Walküre*, and Hotter as well as producing sang Wotan. His long experience of Wagner showed itself in many felicitous touches, especially in the human and moving way he drew the characters of Siegmund and Sieglinde. Undoubtedly when the time comes for this great artist to give up singing, he will begin a new career as an opera producer. And many a German opera house could do worse than invite him to become its Intendant.

JAMES JOHNSTON

ONE of the most popular tenors in British opera since the end of the war has been Belfast-born James Johnston. It was only by accident that he became an opera singer—for he was too polite to refuse an offer from the Dublin Opera Company to sing in 1940.

Before that James Johnston had sung in occasional performances of oratorio and indulged occasionally in Irish folk songs, but most of the time he spent running his three Belfast butcher shops. In 1940 he happened to be appearing in *Merrie England* when he was heard by Colonel O'Kelly, one of the directors of the Dublin Opera, and was invited to sing *Faust*, an opera that Johnston had never even seen, let alone studied. He wired back that he couldn't sing Faust but knew the tenor lead in *Rigoletto*. Johnston explained that *Rigoletto* was the only opera he had ever seen up to then, and he wanted to be polite to the Dublin Company, but hoped they would lose interest in him. But so eager were they to get him to sing in opera that they changed the opera from *Faust* to *Rigoletto*.

During the next five years he was heard in Dublin as Pinkerton, Alfredo, Don José, Cavaradossi, Turiddu and Canio. A leading Dublin critic, writing about his début said: 'Here is a singer who can sing Verdi as Verdi wrote the music: but his lovemaking and acting—oh, dear!'

In 1945 Tyrone Guthrie and Joan Cross, who were then responsible for the Sadler's Wells Company, went to Dublin to hear him sing, and rewarded him with a contract for the first season at Sadler's Wells after the end of the European war in the summer of 1945. He sang Jenik in *The Bartered Bride*, followed by the Duke in *Rigoletto*, Rodolfo, Turiddu, and Pinkerton.

During the 1946-7 season he took part in his first new production at the Wells, that of *Tosca*, in which his Cavaradossi was singled out for high praise. 'In James Johnston the company possesses a tenor whose natural gifts include special aptitude for lyrical expression', wrote the late Bonavia in the *Telegraph*. The following season he sang the title role in *Faust* in Dennis Arundell's controversial production of that opera. The *Times* wrote, 'Mr. James Johnston brings a real tenor voice to the music of Faust, and is now acting with more freedom and conviction'.

October 22, 1948, was a memorable night for Sadler's Wells and for Johnston. It was the occasion of the first performance in England of Verdi's *Simon Boccanegra* with Johnston as Gabriele Adorno. 'The singers rose splendidly to the occasion', wrote Desmond Shawe-Taylor, 'if James Johnston alone possessed the white-hot intensity demanded by the music, the other principals had their fine moments'; while Lord Harewood in *Opera* wrote, 'James Johnston sang Adorno with ringing tone and a truly dramatic style, and gave a stirring performance.'

Not long after the *Boccanegra* performances, Johnston scored yet another success as Don José in a new production of *Carmen* by Tyrone Guthrie; and during the same season he was hastily summoned to Covent Garden to sing Alfredo in *Traviata* opposite Schwarzkopf at twenty-four hours notice. It was a foregone conclusion that Johnston would, before very long, be invited to join the

Covent Garden Company, and this he did at the beginning of the 1949-50 season, remaining with them until the end of the 1957-8 season.

Johnston's first new role at Covent Garden was that of Hector in the world première of Bliss's *The Olympians*, which was followed by José, Alfredo, the Duke, Cavaradossi, and Manrico. He continued however to sing at Sadler's Wells, and during the next two seasons scored two further successes there, first in the title role of *Hugh the Drover*, one of his best parts, and then in the title-role of *Don Carlos* opposite Joan Hammond.

At Covent Garden, where he had become a firm favourite, Johnston added to his list of roles Calaf in *Turandot* and Radames in *Aida*. The former he sang on the opening night of the 1951-2 season, and the latter he added later that season. He was also invited to Glyndebourne in the summer of 1952 to sing Macduff in *Macbeth* under Gui. Max in *Freischütz*, Riccardo in *Ballo in Maschera*, and Hoffmann were other roles he sang at Covent Garden before deciding to return to Ireland. He still sings occasionally with the Dublin Opera. His contribution to Covent Garden however during his nine seasons with the company cannot be over-estimated.

SENA JURINAC

THOSE people who are lucky enough to have been operagoers in 1924 will remember that that was the year in which International Opera returned to Covent Garden after the First World War. In those days opera fans were not prepared in advance for new singers by having first heard them on the radio, while the volume of gramophone records was only a fraction of what it is to-day. So in that 1924 season the arrival of a whole new generation of Central European singers who had grown up since 1914 came as a complete surprise. Frida Leider, Lotte Lehmann, Delia Reinhardt and Elisabeth Schumann were four names to conjure with.

Something of the same kind of thing happened in the autumn of 1947 when the Vienna Opera paid its first post-war visit to London. But unlike 1924 Londoners were rather better prepared by the radio and gramophone for some of the newcomers. Some people, however, were a trifle wary about forming opinions purely on the evidence of the gramophone, and so it was more than gratifying that a group of artists was introduced to them who could well be termed the successors of Leider, Lehmann, Reinhardt and Schumann—Ljuba Welitsch, Sena Jurinac, Elisabeth Schwarzkopf and Irmgard Seefried.

Srebrenka (Sena for short) Jurinac was born in Travnik in Jugoslavia on October 24, 1921. Her mother is Viennese and her father Croatian. She was educated in Zagreb and studied at the Musikakademie for two years. From 1939 she studied with Maria Kostrencic, the teacher of Zinka Milanov, the only teacher with whom she worked regularly for an appreciable time. In 1942 she made her début at the Zagreb Opera as Mimi. While a member of the Zagreb company she created the part of Isabella in Werner Egk's *Columbus* and the title-roles in two Jugoslavian operas—*Suncanica* (Papandopulo) and *Morana* (Gotovac). She also sang the Countess in *Figaro*, Marguerite, Freia and a Flower Maiden in *Parsifal*.

In 1944 she was engaged by the Vienna State Opera, making her début there on May 1, 1945, in the first performance of opera in Vienna after the liberation. This was as Cherubino in *Figaro*, under Josef Krips. By the time she came to London with the Vienna Company in the autumn of 1945, she had already been heard in Vienna in a variety of roles including Rosalinde, Cherubino, Mimi, Antonia, Octavian and the Composer in *Ariadne*. The only role she sang in London however on that occasion was Dorabella in two performances of *Così fan tutte*, a part she had previously sung at the 1947 Salzburg Festival. In 1948 at Salzburg she sang Amor in *Orfeo* and Cherubino.

In 1949 she began her long connection with Glyndebourne, singing Dorabella with the company at Edinburgh. In 1950 she graduated to Fiordiligi, a part she continued to sing there—never in Vienna—with success. 'The best Fiordiligi of our time. She has youth, beauty, fine taste and a beautifully solid, yet flexible tone', wrote Desmond Shawe-Taylor. The following summer she was heard as Ilia in *Idomeneo*, providing some 'meltingly beautiful singing'. In 1953 came her greatest Glyndebourne triumph, the Composer in *Ariadne auf Naxos*. Again she reaped a harvest of superlatives in the various critiques that appeared. 'Simply perfection, with lovely tone streaming out', wrote Eric Blom; 'her singing was a reassurance that the art is not yet dead in the world', wrote the *Times*.

Donna Elvira was Jurinac's next Glyndebourne role; but she only sang it for one season, 1954, deciding to graduate to the heavier roles of Donna Anna the next year. This was the year of decision for Jurinac, for although she still continued to sing Octavian and Cherubino, Mimi and Micaela, she had set her heart on assuming more dramatic roles. Donna Anna and the *Figaro* Countess at Glyndebourne were the beginning; and then came Leonora in *La Forza del Destino* at Edinburgh. The voice at that time did not seem quite ready for these roles, and lost some of its bloom; and indeed two not particularly happy seasons vocally followed, including Eva at Bayreuth and Marzelline in *Fidelio* at Bayreuth and Salzburg in 1957. Perhaps she was not in the best of health, for an illness developed which caused her to cancel her American appearances for the 1957-8 season—she was to have created the title role in Barber's *Vanessa* at the Metropolitan.

But there were consolations however, for in the 1957-8 season she sang her first Desdemona and Butterfly in Vienna. These in their turn led to her being chosen to sing Elisabeth de Valois in the Salzburg production of *Don Carlos* in the summer of 1958.

In January, 1959, came her début with the Covent Garden Company as Butterfly, and she treated her audience to an evening of exquisite vocalism and sensitive singing—though some people felt that she failed to capture the innocence of the character. In the autumn of 1959 she made her long delayed American début singing Butterfly, Eva and Donna Anna at San Francisco.

In December, 1959, London heard Jurinac's unsurpassed Octavian in the first 'German' *Rosenkavalier* at Covent Garden since 1938. The following season she sang her first Leonore in *Fidelio* on any stage at Covent Garden in the memorable Klemperer performances of the Beethoven opera. She offered an interpretation that was womanly, sincere, and moving, in fact a real-life person. Even if her voice was a trifle light for the great 'Abscheulicher', there was so much else she had to offer that one did not mind this. She returned to London during the 1961-2 season as Donna Elvira and a year later as Mimi. In Vienna she has added Tatiana in *Eugene Onegin* and Poppea in Monteverdi's *L'Incoronazione di Poppea* to her repertory.

Her enormous successes have not done anything to spoil her essential charm. She is still, as she was ten or so years ago, the same unspoiled, almost unsophisticated person. In fact she is the most un-prima donna-like prima donna one could hope to meet. That is her great charm, that and her delicious sense of humour both on and off the stage. That is why she is adored by everyone wherever she happens to be appearing, from her most senior colleague down to the newest arrival in the chorus; from the producer to the humblest scene shifter.

In her early forties with her voice in fine condition, and still growing, the future indeed looks exciting for her, with the prospect of more dramatic roles in both the Italian and German repertory. Already yesterday's Cherubino and Marzelline is today's Countess and Leonore. There is little doubt that in the not too distant future that the Composer will have become Ariadne, and Octavian the Marschallin.

PETER KLEIN

ONE of the finest character actors in opera, and certainly the greatest Mime of the day, was born in Zuendorf, a village just outside Cologne. Klein's father who owned an inn wanted his son to enter the hotel business, but the young man had other plans and began to take lessons in secret. When he had finished his training at the Cologne Academy, he appeared in some operetta performances at the Reichshallentheater with Richard Tauber.

Klein's early engagements included Düsseldorf, Kaiserslautern where he appeared in *Fra Diavolo*, *Die lustigen Weiber von Windsor*, *Der Waffenschmied* and other works, Zurich, where he was heard as Goro, and David in *Meistersinger*; and from 1937 to 1941 Hamburg. Klein's Hamburg engagement established him as a first rate character singer—Shuisky, Mime, the Podestà in *La Finta Giardiniera*, Eroschka in *Prince Igor*; then Vasek in *The Bartered Bride*, Bardolph, Pedrillo, Jacquino and Valzacchi. The latter role he had first sung as a guest in Vienna in

1934;—it was to Vienna that he went in 1942, and he has remained a member of the ensemble ever since.

Vienna and Salzburg see and hear him regularly; at the Salzburg Festivals he has sung Basilio, Valzacchi, Pedrillo, Monostatos, Monsieur Taupe in *Capriccio*, the Captain in *Wozzeck* and other roles. Of his Captain in *Wozzeck*, Lord Harewood writing in *Opera*, said: 'Peter Klein was the best member of the cast, perhaps because the only one who had taken the pains to memorize his music entirely accurately, and *from* it to produce a consistent characterization; his was a good musical performance'.

Klein first sang in London with the Vienna company in the autumn of 1947. In November, 1948, he sang his first Covent Garden Mime 'about the best I ever remember to have seen' remarked Desmond Shawe-Taylor; while Ernest Newman wrote: 'Klein's Mime was of the right kind one so rarely sees . . . . a thing wholly evil, differing from Alberich only in the degree of his capacity to achieve the evil his heart is set on. Klein *sings* the part too, instead of making it sound like the creaking of a rusty hinge; and that is all to the good'. Nine years later the same critic was still able to write that Klein was without a superior in the part.

Klein's New York début was made on the opening night of the 1949-50 season as Valzacchi, and during his first season he sang a number of small roles as well as David in *Meistersinger*. During his second season at the Metropolitan he added Mime and Jacquino to his New York roles. But Klein would seem to prefer the less rushed life of Vienna, for he has refused invitations to return to America, and indeed other than his many visits to London for the *Ring*, he spends most of his time at the Vienna State Opera singing two or three times a week, and giving his countless admirers much pleasure with his admirably studied characterizations. Toscanini's dictum that there are no small roles in opera is amply borne out when an artist of Klein's calibre is seen in one of the characters from his gallery of operatic personages.

OTAKAR KRAUS

BORN in Czechoslovakia, trained in Italy, creator of important roles in operas by Britten, Walton, Tippett and Stravinsky, and now a naturalized British citizen, sums up the highlights of Otakar Kraus's career.

He was born in Prague in 1909. He studied in his native city with Konrad Wallerstein and with Fernando Carpi in Milan where he heard all the great baritones of the 1930's —Stracciari, Galeffi, Franci. He made his début at Brno in 1935 as Amonasro, and from 1936 to 1939 was leading baritone at the Bratislava Opera. When Hitler occupied Czechoslovakia, Kraus came to London, where he has lived ever since.

During the war years he was heard in the production of *The Fair at Sorotchins* at the Savoy and Adelphi Theatres. Then he joined the Carl Rosa Opera with whom he sang a variety of roles, including Valentine, Germont, Scarpia, Dapertutto and Dr. Miracle. In 1946 when the English Opera Group was formed, Kraus was invited to sing with them and he created the role of Tarquinius in Britten's *The Rape of Lucretia* at Glyndebourne. He also sang Lockit in *The Beggar's Opera* and the Vicar in *Albert Herring* with the Group.

For the 1950-51 season Kraus was engaged for the Netherlands Opera where he sang a number of roles including the title part in *Der fliegende Holländer*. In the summer of 1951 he was heard as Alberich in the *Ring* at Covent Garden, as a guest artist, and then joined the company for the 1951-2 season, and has remained a member of the company ever since. Of his first Covent Garden Alberich, Ernest Newman wrote, 'The outstanding thing has been the Alberich of Otakar Kraus. For the first time in my experience the part has been *sung*, and that splendidly; and the most casual listener must have been conscious that it is infinitely more meaningful when the notes that Wagner took such care over are really sung instead of being barked, or rasped, or screeched. This is certainly the finest, because the most Wagnerian, Alberich I have ever heard'. And year after year Kraus's Alberich, like Peter Klein's Mime, has become an outstanding feature of the London *Ring*. He has also sung this role in Rome under Kleiber, in Munich under Knappertsbusch, in Vienna under Karajan, and at Bayreuth under Kempe.

Other roles Kraus has made particularly his own at Covent Garden have been Scarpia, Klingsor, Orest, Jokanaan and Kurwenal. He also sang a sinister Doctor in *Wozzeck* under Kleiber, and created the roles of Diomede in Walton's *Troilus and Cressida*, and King Fisher in Tippett's *The Midsummer Marriage*. In addition to Scarpia, other roles in the Italian repertory that Kraus has sung include Renato, Amonasro, Rigoletto and Iago. This latter part he sang in the *Otello* production that ushered in Kubelik's three-year tenure as Covent Garden's Musical Director. Kraus replaced Gobbi in this role, who arrived too late for rehearsals. To quote Newman again, 'Otakar Kraus was the perfect foil to his [Vinay's] commanding Otello; his fine voice seemed capable of an infinity of psychological nuances, so that it was always the forceful yet subtle villain of Shakespeare and Boito that we saw before us'.

Another important role that Kraus created was Nick Shadow in Stravinsky's *The Rake's Progress* at the Venice Festival of 1951, repeating the part at the Scala during the 1951-2 season and at Glyndebourne in 1958. In Rio in 1952 he sang Pizarro, the Dutchman and other roles in his repertory; and he is always a welcome guest in Amsterdam and the Hague with the Netherlands Opera.

Kraus is a first rate singing-actor. He is a master of make-up and a vital and striking figure on the stage. He never lets a performance down, and often lifts it from the mere routine and gives it that extra something, which suddenly brings it to life.

ERICH KUNZ

To visitors to Salzburg since the war there has been but one Figaro, Leporello and Papageno, the baritone Erich Kunz. He was born in Vienna on May 20, 1909, and studied with Lierhammer, the teacher of Welitsch, in Vienna. His first engagement was at Troppau in the 1935-6 season, where he made his début as Osmin. Also at this time, he came to Glyndebourne as an understudy and sang in the chorus—a fact that is not generally known. Engagements at Plauen, and Breslau followed, and then in 1940 he was engaged by the Vienna Opera, where he has sung ever since. One of his early roles in Vienna was Beckmesser, which he sang at Bayreuth in 1942 and 1943, and again after the war in 1951. He was at Salzburg in 1942 and has sung there most summers since 1946.

When the war ended and the Vienna Company began to pay visits abroad, Kunz was one of the most admired Mozart artists. London first heard him in 1947 with this company as Leporello, Figaro and Guglielmo. He then sang Guglielmo with the Glyndebourne Company in 1948 and 1950. He sang Leporello, Beckmesser and Faninal at the Metropolitan during the 1952-3 season, adding Figaro the following year.

Kunz has been heard widely in the leading Italian opera houses, and has also sung in Paris, Zurich, Munich, Brussels. He has a much larger repertory than the roles for which he is internationally famous. In Vienna he has sung some fifty parts including Malatesta in *Don Pasquale*, Gianni Schicchi, Spalanzani in *Hoffmann*, Harlequin in *Ariadne* and countless roles in the operettas of Strauss, Millöcker and other Viennese composers.

Kunz's sense of humour is legendary, and on the stage his colleagues never know what to expect. An example of this was reported in a performance of *Così fan tutte* in the summer of 1957, when Kunz who was singing Guglielmo 'took it into his head to insert a little impromptu business, so that while lying "unconscious", he began one of those back-bends, which female acrobats usually do in the *Folies Bergères*. This time Don Alfonso in company with other members of the cast were convulsed with laughter. The purists will be glad to know that Mozart did not suffer and the whole incident was extremely funny'. Should Kunz decide to give up opera, he would be certain to make an equally successful career in cabaret or musical comedy!

BENNO KUSCHE

ANOTHER Leporello, Papageno and Beckmesser, who has made himself extremely popular in the years since the war is Benno Kusche. He was born in Freiburg in 1916, his mother was a concert singer and his father a scenic designer. When he was nineteen he went to Karlsruhe where he studied to become an actor, but fortunately he changed his mind and decided to pursue a musical career.

In the 1938-9 season he made his début at Coblenz singing mostly in operetta. His first engagement as a buffo bass was at Augsburg in 1942. His career was then interrupted by the war, and he was first in an arms factory and then on the land. In 1946 he joined the Munich State Opera, and quickly made a name for himself in such roles as Melitone, Schicchi, Don Alfonso, Alberich, Leporello, Rangoni and Beckmesser. It was in this last part that he made his Covent Garden début in the 1951 revival of *Meistersinger* conducted by Beecham.

Kusche's 'truly remarkable Beckmesser', to quote Ernest Newman, was a great success with the public and he was invited back to London to repeat the part in 1953. In the autumn of that year, the Munich Opera came to Covent Garden and Kusche appeared on the opening night of the season as Count Waldner in *Arabella*. The first London performance of Strauss's *Capriccio* had to be postponed because Kusche fell a victim of bronchitis, and although still ill, he sang in the postponed performance, taking the part of La Roche, the theatre director.

In 1954 Kusche appeared at Glyndebourne as Leporello. The *Times* wrote: 'The most interesting individual performance was the Leporello of Benno Kusche .... He is a singer in whom the music is shot through with a natural wit—a small example of his insight into character was his imitation of Don Giovanni's voice when he was impersonating him at the beginning of Act II'. In 1954 he was also chosen to sing Papageno in the now-famous Felsenstein production of *Die Zauberflöte* at the East Berlin Komische Oper.

When the Deutsche Opera am Rhein was established at Dusseldorf and Duisburg in 1956, Kusche joined the company. His most recent successes have been as Falstaff, Titus Feuerfuchs (Sutermeister), Arnolphe in Liebermann's *Die schule der Frauen*, and the Devil in *Schwanda*.

GERDA LAMMERS

One of the most exciting things that can happen in an opera house is when an entirely unknown singer makes an unheralded appearance, scores a success and receives an ovation of the proportions generally reserved for a Callas. Such an event was the occasion of Gerda Lammers's Covent Garden début in November, 1957, in the highly taxing role of Elektra.

Gerda Lammers was born in Berlin in 1917. She studied there at the famous Hochschule under Lula Mysz-Gmeiner, and later with Margaret Schwedler-Lohmann. The first fifteen years of her career were spent on the concert platform and she had, by the 1950s, established herself as a fine lieder singer, and a Bach-Handel artist.

In the summer of 1955 she was engaged for Bayreuth to sing Ortlinde. In the autumn of the same year she began her engagement at the Cassel Opera, where her first role was the highly difficult part of Marie in *Wozzeck*, which she followed with the title role in *Elektra*. During the next two seasons at Cassel she sang Senta, Penthesilea in Schoeck's opera of that name, Alceste, the Sängerin in *Cardillac*, and Santuzza.

In November, 1957, Lammers was in London to sing in a private concert. At the same time Strauss's *Elektra* with Christel Goltz in the title role was scheduled for Covent Garden. Goltz fell suddenly ill with an appendicitis, and it looked as if *Elektra* would have to be cancelled. But there were a few people in London who had read reports of Lammers's success in Cassel, and she was rushed to the opera house for an audition. Rudolf Kempe, the conductor, agreed to accept her in the place of Goltz, and so on November 16, 1957, she made her début before one of the most critical opera audiences in the world. Her success was phenomenal, and the ovation that greeted her at the fall of the curtain was one of the greatest in the theatre's history.

Ernest Newman writing in *The Sunday Times* remarked 'Her voice proved itself one of commanding power, dramatically the right thing for Elektra, yet always gratifyingly musical and always dead in tune, while towards the end of the exacting work, after all the strain of the opening and middle portions of the drama, her voice was extraordinarily appealing by the tender beauty of its timbre in the more relaxed portions of the great "recognition" scene'. While Desmond Shawe-Taylor wrote about 'an impact of genius' and a performance that was 'all music, all drama, all intensity, all passion. It could be all these things at once' he continued, 'because it was all of a whole, all one'. And a very famous actor who was present at the performance, compared Lammers's acting with that of the legendary Rachel.

It was not surprising that she was re-engaged to repeat

the role at Covent Garden's centenary celebrations, in the summer of 1958. A few weeks later she was heard as Dido in Purcell's *Dido and Aeneas* at Ingestre Hall.

During the 1958-9 season in Germany she was invited to sing Elektra at Hamburg and elsewhere, and at Cassel she added another famous classical role to her repertory, that of Medea in Cherubini's opera of that name. A British critic who was present at the performance wrote that she seemed almost like a 'soprano Fischer-Dieskau', and that her performance was as shattering in its impact as had been her Elektra in London. Later in the season she was to sing the title role in Handel's *Rodelinda*, Cassel's contribution to the Handel bi-centenary celebrations. Before that however London heard her once again; this time as Kundry in Covent Garden's new production of *Parsifal*.

In Cassel she has added Isolde, Brünnhilde, and the Dyer's Wife (*Die Frau ohne Schatten*) to her repertory, and has sung as a guest artist in Vienna. In 1962 she made her New York début as Elektra. Still in her early forties, there is no reason why Lammers should not continue to sing for many more years—her years as a lieder singer and her perfect technique stand her in good stead for that.

ADÈLE LEIGH

ONE of the most versatile of present-day opera singers is the soprano Adèle Leigh. Not only has she made a name for herself on the opera stage, but she has become known to a much wider public through her many appearances on Television, and in taking part in 'Large as Life', a popular variety entertainment, that ran for nearly a year at the London Palladium.

She was born in London in 1928, and after studying at the Royal Academy of Dramatic Art she went to America, where she began to take music lessons at the Juillard School in New York. Her voice teachers were first Julius Gutman and then Maggie Teyte. Returning to England, she joined the Covent Garden Opera Company when not quite twenty, making her début in the small role of Xenia in *Boris Godunov* during the 1947-48 season. Rather like any young opera singer in a German opera house, she only sang small roles during her first few seasons such as the Page and the Countess Ceprano in *Rigoletto*, Barbarina in *Figaro* and Kate Pinkerton in *Madama Butterfly*; and just as the young German artist with promise is then given a larger role, so Adèle Leigh was asked to sing Cherubino in *Figaro*. And what a delightful Cherubino she was!— one of the best post-war English interpreters of this part Covent Garden has heard. In 1949-50 season she succeeded Shirley Russell as Madeleine in Bliss's *The Olympians*.

By the 1951-52 season she had made great strides, and her first real test came in the exacting role of Pamina in *The Magic Flute*. This she sang with a sweetness of tone that came as a surprise to most people. She soon followed this role with Susanna in *Figaro*, and Sophie in *Der Rosenkavalier*. This latter part, with its high *tessitura* and soft top notes, was just right for her vocal equipment. She was, however, apt to be somewhat arch and a little self-conscious, and it took three or four years before she was able to overcome these weaknesses on the dramatic side of her performances.

Oscar in *Un Ballo in Maschera*, Marzelline in *Fidelio* and Micaela in *Carmen* were added to her repertory, and as Anne in *Der Freischütz* she had another role that suited her voice and temperament. In February, 1955, she created the part of Bella in Tippett's *The Midsummer Marriage*. This is not the place to discuss the musical merits of this work, but in the role of the hard-boiled typist for which Adèle Leigh was dressed in a creation worthy of Dior, she scored another personal success. A few weeks later she was asked at very short notice to sing the title role of Manon in Massenet's opera, and once again she showed what a hard worker she is, and how natural is her sense of stage. She sang three other new roles during the 1954-55 season—Esmeralda in *The Bartered Bride*, in which she displayed amazing comic talent, the Wood Bird in *Siegfried*, in which she was heard but not seen, and Liù in *Turandot*.

During Kubelik's first Covent Garden season, in addition to repeating a number of her more popular roles, she was heard as Musetta in *La Bohème*, a part she had always wanted to play since her student days. *The Times* thought she gave the role a delightful charm and elegance. She sang the same role in her American operatic début at Boston in 1959, when according to one American critic

ERICH KUNZ

as *Figaro* in 'Mozart's Opera'

PETER KLEIN

as *Mime* in 'Der Ring des Nibelungen'

as *Alberich* in 'Der Ring des Nibelungen'

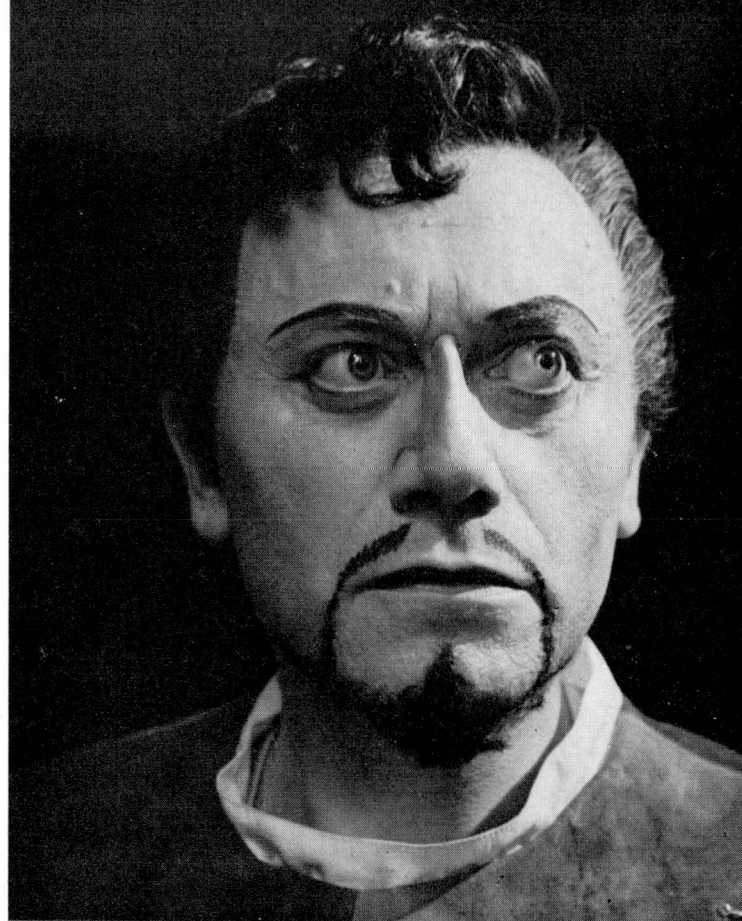

as *Iago* in 'Otello'

as *Orestes* in 'Elektra'

OTAKAR KRAUS

BENNO KUSCHE

as *Beckmesser* in 'Die Meistersinger'

as *La Roche* in 'Capriccio'

as *Elektra*

GERDA LAMMERS

as *Dido* in 'Dido and Aeneas'

RICHARD LEWIS

as *Troilus* in 'Troilus and Cressida'

as *Don Ottavio* in 'Don Giovanni'

as *the Captain* in 'Wozzeck'

ADÈLE LEIGH

as *Manon* in 'Mozart's Opera'

JAMES PEASE

as *Harapha* in Handel's 'Samson'

WILMA LIPP

as *Martha* in 'Flotow's Opera'

as *Constanze*
in 'Die Entführung aus den Serail'

GEORGE LONDON

as *Amfortas*

as *Don Giovanni*

she 'sang and acted with style, and dominated the second act'.

By this time Adèle Leigh had become the wife of the American bass-baritone, James Pease, whom she had met in Dublin in December, 1957, when she was singing Susanna to her future husband's Figaro. In the spring of 1959 she sang her first Octavian to her husband's Baron Ochs, with the Covent Garden company on tour.

Abroad, in addition to her appearances as Musetta in Boston, Adèle Leigh has sung at the Vienna Volksoper as Rosalinde in *Fledermaus*, at Nice as Susanna, as Pamina in Holland, Despina in a series of concert performances of *Così fan tutte* in America (this time with her husband as Don Alfonso), and the soprano role in Chabrier's *L'Etoile* recorded for the Italian Radio.

RICHARD LEWIS

It must be a rare achievement for a tenor to be chosen to create the leading roles in two operatic world premières in the same opera house, within a period of less than two months. Rare indeed in Germany or Italy, unique in England; yet to Richard Lewis fell the task of being the first Troilus in Walton's *Troilus and Cressida*, and the first Mark in Tippett's *The Midsummer Marriage* at Covent Garden during the 1954-5 season.

The day after the first performance of the Tippett opera, Lewis was flying off to Amsterdam to sing in two performances of Mahler's *Das Lied von der Erde* with the Concertgebouw Orchestra under Ormandy; and a week later, after two more performances of *The Midsummer Marriage*, he was off to Rome to sing for the Italian radio's Third Programme in Handel's *Judas Maccabeus* conducted by Vittorio Gui, with Maria Stader, Oralia Dominguez, Petre Munteanu and Boris Christoff as his distinguished colleagues.

Richard Lewis was born in Manchester of Welsh parents on May 10, 1914. When he was twelve years of age he was heard singing by one of his school teachers who encouraged him to enter for various musical competitions as a boy soprano; he did so, and between the ages of twelve and sixteen, he won a number of gold medals and other prizes. In 1930 he competed at fourteen festivals, winning thirteen first prizes and one second; as a result of this he was invited to record for Parlophone, but unfortunately his voice began to break before he was able to begin making records.

When he was sixteen, Lewis left school, and began work in the office of a cotton manufacturer; he spent all his spare time studying harmony, counterpoint and the piano. He continued his vocal training with T. W. Evans of Manchester. In 1939 he won a scholarship to the Royal Manchester College of Music, where he began his serious vocal studies under Norman Allin. He was only able to complete four terms at the College, before the outbreak of war; he joined Ensa, with whom he toured for a year.

In 1941 he was asked to sing with the Carl Rosa Company, and for two months he appeared with the company in the Northern provinces as Pinkerton and Almaviva. Then came his call-up, and for four-and-a-half years he served with the Royal Corps of Signals. While he was still in the army, he sang with the Brussels and Oslo Philharmonic Societies, made appearances with the Danish Radio Orchestra, broadcast from Hamburg, and gave recitals in Antwerp and Liège. When Lewis was demobilized, he thus had quite a number of foreign engagements to his credit, but at home, he still had to establish himself.

In January, 1947, he and his wife (he had married in 1943 Mary Lingard, daughter of Joseph Lingard, professor of the flute at the Manchester College of Music, and one of the oldest members of the Hallé Orchestra) decided to move to London. In the same month came his first concert engagement, the Britten *Serenade*, with the Southern Philharmonic Orchestra at Brighton under Herbert Menges. Meanwhile Lewis continued his vocal studies with Norman Allin, who was now a professor at the Royal Academy in London. In the summer of 1947 came Lewis's first important operatic engagement, the Male Chorus in *The Rape of Lucretia* at Glyndebourne. 'Of the new singers, Mr. Richard Lewis may be commended for his delivery of the elaborate declamation assigned to the Male Chorus' wrote *The Times* critic.

In November of the same year, Lewis sang the title role of *Peter Grimes* at Covent Garden. Scott Goddard writing in the *News Chronicle* said 'Richard Lewis gave a very moving performance in the name part. His voice is clear, his diction unforced, he has an excellent dramatic sense, and is altogether a great gain to the cast of the opera'. Appearances as the Simpleton in *Boris*, Tamino, and Alfredo in *Traviata*, at the Royal Opera House, and as Ferrando in *Così fan tutte* at Sadler's Wells, followed during the next few seasons.

It is perhaps with Glyndebourne that Richard Lewis's name has been most closely associated, and it is certainly Glyndebourne that gave him his greatest opportunities between 1948 and 1953. Like many other artists he is ungrudging in the gratitude he expressed to the late Fritz Busch and to Carl Ebert.

In 1948, he appeared for the first time with the Glyndebourne company at Edinburgh, singing Don Ottavio in *Don Giovanni*. 'Richard Lewis contrived to make Don Ottavio into a sympathetic personality, and sing the music with a superior sense of phrasing, and what is rare in the role, consistently on pitch.' So wrote Lord Harewood in *Ballet and Opera*, in October, 1948.

In 1950, Lewis sang Ferrando in *Così* at Glyndebourne, a role he has repeated on many occasions since. In 1951, '52 and '53 he sang the title role in *Idomeneo*, in 1953 and '54 the part of Admète in *Alceste*, Tom Rakewell in *The Rake's Progress*, and Bacchus in *Ariadne auf Naxos*; this last role he took over and learned at virtually the eleventh hour, when the tenor originally engaged was unable to sing the part; and in it, incidentally, he has scored one of his greatest successes.

Between 1955 and 1958 at Glyndebourne Lewis repeated roles that he had already sung there; but in 1959 he broke new ground, as did Glyndebourne, by singing Florestan in the first performance there of *Fidelio*, opposite Gré Brouwenstijn.

In 1955 Lewis made his American operatic début. This was at San Francisco, where he was heard as Troilus, in the America première of Walton's *Troilus and Cressida*, and Don José in Carmen. According to Alfred Frankenstein, one of America's leading opera critics, Lewis's José was 'one of the greatest interpretations of the part I have yet heard'. In 1956 he sang Ferrando, Pinkerton and Dmitri there; in 1957 Ferrando and Bacchus; in 1958 Jason in *Medée*, Jenik, and Des Grieux; in 1959 Don Ottavio; in 1960 the Drum Major in *Wozzeck;* and in 1962 Tom Rakewell.

Other operatic appearances have included Gwyn in the first performance of Arwell Hughes's *Menna* in November, 1953, Paolino in *The Secret Marriage* for the London Opera Club in 1949, and many B.B.C. opera performances, including *L'Elisir d'Amore*, *Castor et Pollux* and *Iphigénie en Tauride*. Abroad Richard Lewis has sung with the Zagreb Opera in *The Rape of Lucretia* and in Stravinsky's *Persephone* in Paris under the composer's own direction; and in September, 1961, he sang Amphytryon in the première of Klebe's *Alkmene* at the new Deutsche Oper in West Berlin.

Lewis made a welcome return to Covent Garden during the 1961-2 Season, when he was heard as Tamino, Don Ottavio, Hermann in *The Queen of Spades*, and Achilles in Tippett's *King Priam;* in this latter role he gave what many people considered to be the finest performance of his career.

Those are the facts behind this singer's career; what about the man himself? The first thing that strikes one is that he is completely unspoiled; he still retains the wonderful sense of humour that must have helped him through many a difficult crisis, operatic and otherwise. He is a very quick learner, and that together with his natural musicianship and his interest in modern music, has made him much sought after as an interpreter of contemporary works. He admits that he prefers to specialize in this kind of music, and therefore he is more inclined to participate in the specially prepared operatic performance, in festivals, in works like the Tippett and the Walton. That does not mean that he would not sing in repertory performances, but he quite naturally feels, that his special gifts should be utilized in a special way.

Although Richard Lewis finds it easier to sing in Italian than in English, his diction when singing in his native tongue is always clear, as those who heard him as Troilus and Mark will testify. It is his diction, his completely professional and sincere approach to all that he undertakes, that makes Lewis's contribution to an operatic performance so satisfying.

WILMA LIPP

ONE of the fine group of Mozart singers in post-war Vienna, the charming soprano Wilma Lipp, was born in

Vienna on April 20, 1925. She originally was intended for a business career, and went to a commercial school in Vienna. She herself however had decided on becoming a singer, and studied voice with Friedl Sundl and dramatic art with Anna Bahr-Mildenburg and Alfred Jerger.

When she was seventeen she sang in a concert conducted by the composer, Josef Marx, and the following year made her operatic début as Rosina in *Il Barbiere di Siviglia* in a cast that included Anton Dermota, Alfred Poell and her teacher, Alfred Jerger.

Lipp became a member of the Vienna Opera in 1945, and was made a Kämmersängerin ten years later. In Vienna she has sung German, French and Italian roles, including Queen of Night, Blöndchen, Constanze, Zerbinetta, Sophie, the Italian singer in Strauss's *Capriccio* (which she sang in the opera's first performance at Salzburg in 1950), Lady Harriet in *Martha*, Adele, Violetta and Gilda.

In 1950 she made her Covent Garden début as Gilda; 'a fluent lovely-voiced Gilda' wrote Lord Harewood in *Opera*. She subsequently sang Queen of Night, Olympia in *Hoffmann*, and in 1955, Violetta. At Glyndebourne in 1957 she sang Constanze; and she has, of course, sung at most of the European Festivals—Salzburg, Florence, Holland, Wiesbaden, Bregenz, and even Bayreuth where she has been heard as the Voice of the Woodbird.

During the 1957-8 season Lipp began to extend her repertory from coloratura to lyric roles, and was heard as Pamina and Mimi in Vienna and Marenka at the Bregenz Festival. She has also been heard more recently in Vienna as Ursula in *Mathis der Maler*, Wellgunde and Nedda in a new production of *Pagliacci*. Of her interpretation of this last role, Joseph Wechsberg wrote, 'Lipp was magnificent as Nedda. Her beautiful voice, always lovely at the top, has expanded greatly in the middle range, and there was an exciting voluptuous quality in it. Her phrasing and style were impeccable, and she gave a sharply drawn portrait of the unfaithful wife'. In 1960 she sang her first Eva in *Meistersingers* and then Donna Elvira in *Don Giovanni*.

As Lipp is still in her thirties, and her vocal technique is secure, there is every reason to hope that she will, during the course of the next few years, build up an entirely new repertory. If she can, at the same time, retain her coloratura technique, and there seems to be no reason why she should not, there are a number of roles, especially in the Italian repertory, in works by Donizetti, Bellini and Verdi, in which she should make a great success.

GEORGE LONDON

BORN in Canada of Russian-Jewish parents, brought up in America, and leading baritone of the Metropolitan and Vienna State Operas. Those are the brief facts about George London, one of the outstanding bass-baritones of the day.

London was born in Montreal on May 30, 1920. The son of Russian emigrée parents, his real name is Burnstein, he moved to Los Angeles in 1935. There he took lessons with Richard Lert, and under the name of George Burnson, made his début in a small role in Albert Coates's *Gainsborough* at the Hollywood Bowl in 1941. The following year he appeared as the doctor in *Traviata*. But other than these small parts he spent most of his time until 1949 in operetta and musical comedy, singing leading roles in *The Vagabond King*, *The Desert Song*, and other works.

In 1947, after a period of study in New York with Paola Novikova, he toured the United States as a member of the 'Bel Canto Trio' (its other members were Frances Yeend and Mario Lanza). After two seasons of touring, London decided to go to Europe for some operatic experience. In June, 1949 he auditioned for Karl Böhm in Brussels, where the Vienna State Opera Company happened to be appearing. He was immediately engaged for the autumn, and made his début in Vienna in September 1949, as Amonasro, without any rehearsal, despite the fact he had never sung the role before—though the State Opera Direction did not know that. His success was immediate and he followed it up with appearances as Escamillo and Galitzky, which he sang in German; then came the four 'villains' in *Hoffmann* in French, Boris in Russian, and Mephistophélès, again in French.

In the summer of 1950 he sang with the Glyndebourne Company in Edinburgh as Figaro; and in the summer of 1951, he sang his first Amfortas at Bayreuth, a role he has sung there frequently since. In later seasons London sang the Holländer at Bayreuth.

This singer's Metropolitan Opera début was not long delayed, and he was first heard there on the opening night of the 1951-2 season as Amonasro. Of this event, the late Cecil Smith wrote in *Musical America:* 'Mr. London's début was, for me, the most significant event of the evening . . . the young Canadian bass-baritone gave a performance of such complete musical and tonal beauty, and such penetrating understanding of every facet of the part that I am willing to say I have never encountered a better Amonasro. A really important artist has suddenly risen above the horizon'.

During his second New York season, audiences saw and heard his Don Giovanni, Escamillo, Scarpia, Amfortas and Boris. His handsome and virile Don has been heard in Vienna and London; and Scarpia is one of his finest roles. Of his Boris, one leading New York critic wrote, 'He has the figure, mien, vocal equipment and technique, and, above all, intelligence to be one of the greatest Borises of our time'. And indeed it is just these qualities that mark London out as one of the finest operatic artist of our day.

Two other roles in which London has scored particular successes in New York have been Mandryka in *Arabella* and the title role in *Eugene Onegin*. But it is probably as a Wagnerian that George London's future lies. He has already recorded with success Hans Sachs's arias, and sung Wotan in the complete recordings of *Rheingold* and *Die Walküre*. The young, burnished bass-baritone voice, scales the heights with ease, and it will not be very long, one surmises, before he sings a complete *Ring* cycle in the theatre.

JEAN MADEIRA

ONE of the most glamorous and colourful personalities in present-day opera is the American mezzo-soprano Jean Madeira. She was born in Centralia, Illinois on November 14, 1924 and grew up almost on the bank of the Mississippi River, opposite St. Louis. Her father was superintendent of a coal mine and her mother a piano teacher. At first she pursued her musical studies with the idea of becoming a pianist, and at fifteen she played Beethoven's C minor Concerto with Vladimir Golschmann and the St. Louis Symphony Orchestra. Generous St. Louisans helped finance a trip to New York, where she auditioned for a scholarship at the Juilliard School of Music. The celebrated American pianist, Olga Samaroff, was struck by the girl's rich voice, and steered her into the vocal instead of the piano department.

Not wishing to strain the generosity of her St. Louis patrons, she found professional work (under her maiden name of Jean Browning) as soon as she was ready. With the summer opera company at the Chautauqua Institution, and then for two years with Fortune Gallo's touring San Carlo Opera Company, she gained experience as Ulrica, Frédéric (*Mignon*), Nicklausse, Delilah, Amneris, Azucena, Carmen, Maddalena (*Rigoletto*) and Lola. In the summer of 1948 she came to London and Paris as understudy to Marie Powers in *The Medium*.

In 1947 she married Francis Madeira, future conductor of the Rhode Island Philharmonic Orchestra, and it was as Jean Browning Madeira that she made her Metropolitan début as the First Norn in *Götterdämmerung* in the autumn of 1948. Her second part was Frédéric. In the succeeding years she has undertaken roles of increasing size and importance at the Metropolitan, and has appeared in many other American cities than New York. Her first important Wagnerian role came in 1951, when without rehearsal she replaced the indisposed Karin Branzell as Erda in *Das Rheingold*. By this time she had dropped the middle name, and was known simply as Jean Madeira.

During the next three years she sang more important roles in New York—Amneris, Azucena, Magdalene in *Meistersinger*, La Cieca, Preziosilla, Mother Goose, Baba the Turk and Ulrica.

Of her La Cieca in *La Gioconda* in December 1952, Ronald Eyer wrote: 'Among the most distinguished characterizations of the evening, was the blind mother of Miss Madeira, a rapidly maturing young artist'. A few weeks later, Madeira was called on at the last minute to sing two roles in a performance of *The Rake's Progress*, Baba the Turk and Mother Goose—she sang the latter owing to the sudden indisposition of a colleague.

In the summer of 1954 the mezzo-soprano was engaged

to sing Carmen in Puerto Rico and in the autumn of the same year Delilah at the Royal Opera, Stockholm—this was the beginning of her international career. Appearances followed in Munich as Carmen, and London and Bayreuth as Erda. She sang Orfeo under Monteux in Brussels, Carmen in Vienna and Amneris during the re-opening celebrations of the Vienna State Opera.

When she returned to the Metropolitan as Amneris in February 1956 after her Vienna success in the same role, *Musical America* wrote: 'Appearing as Amneris Miss Madeira revealed how seriously and effectively she had devoted herself to becoming an actress. In the Judgement scene her portrayal of the Princess maddened by unconquerable jealousy and grief made one forget indeed that she was acting. Amneris lived, a woman doomed to endure destruction of her own making, a woman crushed in the conflict of elemental passions, a woman to be pitied. Over the years Miss Madeira's singing has gained immeasurably in evenness and control'.

Later during the same season her Carmen was especially praised, and she sang this role in the summer of 1957 at the Aix-en-Provence Festival, and a highly individual and controversial interpretation it was. In the same summer she sang Clytemnestra at Salzburg, repeating the role there in 1958. Bayreuth has also heard her regularly as Erda, Waltraute and one of the Norns.

Madeira's voice is an excellent one, rich and dark in timbre. This coupled with a fine stage presence and dramatic intelligence make her a compelling figure on the stage.

ROBERT MERRILL

AMERICA has been rich in baritones these last thirty years—Lawrence Tibbett, Leonard Warren and Robert Merrill are three of the outstanding baritone voices of this generation.

Merrill was born in Brooklyn on June 4, 1917. He studied with his mother Lillian Miller Merrill, and began his career as a popular singer in Radio City Music Hall. His actual operatic début was as Amonasro with the Trenton Opera in New Jersey, and after appearances at Dayton and Detroit, he was entered for the auditions of the air at the Metropolitan and was rewarded with a contract for the 1945-6 season.

Merrill's first role at the Metropolitan was Germont. *Musical America* noted the young singer's 'Rich rotund voice which makes one forget that the Metropolitan is really much too large to allow singers to be heard at their best', and then went on to record 'Vocally he brought down the house.... his best singing was in the duets with Violetta, in which he displayed admirable refinement and control. Mr. Merrill is obviously an extremely valuable acquisition'.

During his first season he sang two more roles in New York, Enrico in *Lucia*, and Escamillo. Of the latter one critic wrote 'It was a treat to hear such flexible vocalism and beautiful tone in the Toreador song'. From then onwards Merrill continued to consolidate his position in New York, adding to his repertory during the next few years, Valentine, Amonasro, Figaro and Di Luna.

When Bing came to the Metropolitan in 1950 and launched his régime there with a new production of *Don Carlos* it was Merrill who was chosen to sing Posa. Cecil Smith wrote of his performance: 'Mr Merrill manifested a stylistic suavity that is new in his work. He bestowed flattering attention on many details of phraseology and he recognised—for the first time in my experience of hearing him—that the half voice may be a pertinent expressive medium'. Towards the end of this season differences arose between the young baritone and the management. Merrill was engaged to make a film in Hollywood and broke his contract to sing eleven performances with the company while on tour. Bing immediately dismissed him. Fortunately the quarrel was made up towards the end of the following season, and Merrill made a few appearances in the spring of 1952.

During the opening week of the 1952-3 season Merrill was heard for the first time in New York as Rigoletto; he had sung the part during the summer of 1952 at the Cincinnati Opera. Other than singing his first Marcello in November 1952, Merrill did not add any more new roles to his repertory until February 1955 when he was heard as Renato in *Un Ballo in Maschera*, a role in which 'he was unstinting in his vocal resources'. During the last few seasons Merrill has sung regularly in all his roles, which now also include Malatesta in *Don Pasquale*, Barnaba, Tonio, Gérard and Iago.

Although Merrill has sung widely in America, and has recorded a number of operas with some of his Metropolitan colleagues in Italy, he has not yet sung in any European opera house. More is the pity. But perhaps before very long he will be heard in opera in the flesh on this side of the Atlantic.

NAN MERRIMAN

ANOTHER outstanding American artist is the mezzo-soprano Nan Merriman. She was born in Pennsylvania in 1920 and came from a musical family. When she was fifteen she moved with her parents to Los Angeles, where she started her studies with Alexia Vassian. She spent twelve months singing background music for M.G.M. pictures, and in 1940 she toured the United States with Laurence Olivier and Vivien Leigh in their production of *Romeo and Juliet*. She did not act in this, but sang airs by Palestrina and Purcell as entracte music. During the same year she appeared in a concert in the Hollywood Bowl, and then decided to have a further period of study.

In the summer of 1942 Merriman was engaged for the Cincinatti Summer Opera season where she was heard as La Cieca in *La Gioconda*, Magdalena in *Rigoletto*, and Frédéric in *Mignon*.

It was in 1943 that her real chance came however. She went to New York and entered for a singing competition, which she won. Part of the prize was a quarter of an hour's broadcast; this was heard by Toscanini who immediately sent for her and gave her an audition which resulted in her being engaged for a Verdi programme he was going to broadcast. This was so successful that during the next few years she sang under his direction on many occasions as Orfeo, Meg in *Falstaff*, Magdalena in Act 3 of *Rigoletto*, and Emilia in *Otello*, all of which performances were recorded.

In 1953 Merriman was engaged for the Aix-en-Provence Festival where she sang Dorabella in *Così fan tutte*, a role with which she has become closely identified, singing it also at the Piccola Scala and Glyndebourne (1956) and with the San Francisco Opera (1957). She returned to Aix to sing the part in 1955 and 1959; while at the Piccola Scala she has also been heard as Laura in Darghmizhsky's rarely performed opera, *The Stone Guest*.

Of her Dorabella at Glyndebourne in 1956, William Weaver wrote in *Opera*: 'Nan Merriman's hilarious, pouting, eye-popping Dorabella was a splendid foil, and her rich warm voice also blended beautifully with Miss Jurinac's pure silver in all their scenes together'.

Nan Merriman is much in demand as a recitalist and concert singer, and it is a great pity that she cannot find more time, or even decide to give more time to opera. For there is no doubt that her voice, personality and dramatic ability are really fitted to this medium, and it would be a great pity if she were not to sing Carmen, Mignon and other roles in the mezzo-soprano repertory on the operatic stage.

ZINKA MILANOV

I DO NOT suppose that there can have been many sopranos in the history of opera who have been offered a contract for an engagement at a leading opera house which included two clauses, one stipulating that within three months she was to learn three roles in Italian, and the other that she lose at least twenty-five pounds of weight. That is what happened in the case of Zinka Milanov in 1937, when, virtually an unknown singer, she was offered an engagement in New York.

Zinka Kunc was born in Zagreb on May 7, 1906, and it was under that name that she was known until the time of her American début. Her brother was a talented child pianist, and composed some two dozen songs for his sister's early recitals. At the age of four she began to study singing, and when she was eight sang Carmen at a home performance of that opera. At twelve her voice began to change from contralto to soprano, and two years later she became a student at the Royal Music Academy in Zagreb. The following year she made her first concert appearance, and among those listening to her was Milka Ternina, one of the great Wagnerian singers of the early years of this century, and the first London and New York Tosca. She was enormously impressed by the young artist, and offered to coach her.

Three years of study with Ternina followed, and in October, 1927, she was ready for her début as Leonora (*Il Trovatore*) at the Ljubljana Opera. From 1928 to 1935 she was leading soprano at the Zagreb National Theatre and made guest appearances in Germany, Italy and Czechoslovakia. The turning point in this artist's career came in 1937, when she was invited by Toscanini to sing under his baton in the Verdi *Requiem* at Salzburg. In the same year she married the Jugoslav actor Predrag Milanov, and from then onwards she sang under her married name. Her Salzburg appearances were followed by the contract from the Metropolitan Opera already mentioned, and on December 17, 1937, she made her début there, again as Leonora in *Il Trovatore*.

Although most of the critics commented on a certain undependability as to pitch and on her imperfections as a vocalist, they all made allowances for the fact that she was singing her first role in Italian, and for the nervousness attendant on a Metropolitan début; at the same time they were able to remark on the translucent beauty of the voice, its power and the singer's inherent dramatic instinct. Milanov was able to overcome most of her vocal weaknesses in the course of the next ten years, during which time she studied in New York with Jacques Stueckgold; but even at the peak of her career she was not the perfect vocalist, and an impeccable performance on one evening could be followed by an erratic one on the next.

Except for a break covering the 1948 and 1949 seasons, Milanov has been the leading dramatic soprano at the Metropolitan over twenty-five years. There she has sung a wide variety of roles, ranging from Donna Anna (*Don Giovanni*) to Santuzza (*Cavalleria Rusticana*), and from the title-role in *Norma* to that of *La Gioconda*, but it is perhaps as a Verdi soprano that she has been supreme. While Tebaldi and Callas are both fine interpreters of such parts as Leonora and Aida, neither of these artists is a true *spinto* soprano. Milanov is, however, and when she sings Verdi's soaring phrases in *Un Ballo in Maschera*, *La Forza del Destino* and *Aida*, they sound as they must have done in the days of singers like Destinn and Muzio.

Milanov sang for three seasons at the Teatro Colon in Buenos Aires where she was heard in a number of roles she has not sung elsewhere, Reiza in *Oberon* and Maria in *Simon Boccanegra*. Two other roles she sang there, Desdemona and Madeleine de Coigney, she sang in New York in the late 1950s. She has only made rare appearances in the great operatic centres of Europe, Vienna, Milan and London.

Milanov's London début had actually been in 1938 when she sang in the Verdi *Requiem* under Toscanini, but it was not until July 1956 that London heard her in opera, when she made her Covent Garden début as *Tosca*, and scored an enormous success. It was a memorable evening.

Every opera-goer has his own personal treasury of memorable moments in the opera house; those rare occasions when he suddenly feels that he is in the presence of greatness, and those even rarer occasions when the whole audience also realises the same thing, and one can almost hear the silence. Such an atmosphere was created by Tiana Lemnitz when she sang 'Ach, ich fühl's' in 1938, by Callas and Stignani in 1952 when they embarked on the cabaletta of the great Norma-Adalgisa duet, and by Hotter and Kempe during the Wotan monologue in the second act of *Die Walküre*; and again during the second act of Milanov's Tosca, when she created an atmosphere that can only be described as sheer magic. She sang 'Visi d'arte' with a beauty of tone and a display of *legato* that we had thought no longer possible. Not that the rest of her performance was not also on a very high level, it was; but those few minutes in the second act were something to treasure for all time.

The following summer she returned to Covent Garden to repeat Tosca and to sing her regal and classic Leonora in *Trovatore* in which the ethereal beauty of her piano singing, and the way she tackled the soaring cantilena of Verdi's melodies will long remain in the memories of those who heard her. By the standard of the 1950's Milanov's acting was old-fashioned; but as Milanov is a 'diva' of the old school, that hardly seemed to matter.

MARTHA MÖDL

RICHARD WAGNER built Bayreuth so that he could have his operas sung and produced as he wanted them, and the tradition of Wagnerian acting there up to 1939 had changed very little since the beginning of the century.

One had become accustomed to stout Brünnhildes and Isoldes and to seeing a series of semaphore signalling movements which purported to be acting. It was left to Wagner's grandsons, Wieland and Wolfgang, to bring about a revolution in Wagnerian acting in post-war Bayreuth, and one of the artists who has worked with the Wagners there since 1951 is Martha Mödl. Her whole approach to the roles she interprets typifies the new ideas of operatic acting that are current in post-war Germany. These can be summed up briefly as the importance of acting before singing and an intensity in portraying the emotions that is rare on the operatic stage.

Martha Mödl was born in Nürnberg on March 22, 1912. She did not start her musical career until she was in her thirties, having spent most of her adult life as a secretary in a business house. She wished to take up an operatic career, and so while continuing to work during the day she studied at the local conservatory in her spare time. Her début was made as Azucena at Remscheid, a small town near Düsseldorf, in 1944. The following year she was engaged by the Düsseldorf opera as a mezzo-soprano, and made her début there as Dorabella in Così fan tutte. She remained a member of the Düsseldorf company until 1949, scoring notable successes as the Composer in *Ariadne*, Octavian, Clytemnestra in *Elektra*, Eboli in *Don Carlos*, Marie in *Wozzeck*, and Carmen. It was as Carmen that she made her Covent Garden début during the 1949-50 season. During the same year she appeared in Berlin as Kundry and her success in this role probably led to her first Bayreuth engagement.

During the 1950-51 Berlin season she sang the part of Lady Macbeth. This role had a great tradition behind it in Berlin, where Sigrid Onegin's interpretation had set a standard which no-one had equalled until Mödl. It is a role that either a high mezzo-soprano or a dramatic soprano can sing, and it was a sort of stepping-stone, so far as Mödl was concerned, to the dramatic soprano repertory. In 1952 she sang her first Isolde at Bayreuth.

Mödl's Isolde was one of the finest operatic creations of the day. It was almost impossible to describe it or analyse it. Her interpretation grew from within; she was Isolde. Vocally her voice, more mezzo than soprano, expressed the whole gamut of Isolde's emotions with colour and warmth. Rarely has there been an Isolde with so rich and vibrant a lower register. With Vinay as her Tristan, the emotional impact of their scenes together was unforgettable.

After Isolde the next step was Brünnhilde, and during the 1952 season she sang the role with a Bayreuth ensemble at the San Carlo in Naples. Then in the summer she sang it at Bayreuth itself. Many Germans regarded her the logical successor of Martha Fuchs, who like Mödl had started her operatic career as a mezzo-soprano. It has been as Kundry, which mezzo-sopranos as well as sopranos can sing, that Mödl has perhaps been most successful.

Mödl returned to Great Britain in 1952, when she sang Leonore in *Fidelio* and Octavian at the Edinburgh Festival as a guest artist with the Hamburg company, and in 1955, when she was heard as Isolde with the Stuttgart company in London. Perhaps the greatest honour that has yet been accorded her was to be chosen to sing Leonore in *Fidelio* at the re-opening of the Vienna State Opera in November 1955. It is at the Vienna Opera that she now spends most of each season; but also manages guest appearances in Hamburg and Stuttgart, and at the Metropolitan, New York, where she made her début in January, 1957 as Brünnhilde.

Mödl's intense and dramatic approach to the roles she sings have, it is true, an invigorating effect on the audience, but brings danger to the singer. After a series of performances such as those at Bayreuth, the voice is apt to tire quickly, and a period of vocal uncertainty results. Yet her voice, with its warm and beautiful lower register, an inheritance from her mezzo-soprano days, is always at the service of this highly individual and intelligent artist.

GEORGINE VON MILINKOVIC

YUGOSLAVIA has produced many fine opera singers since the first war. One has only to look at the list of artists who have sung at the Vienna Opera during the last quarter of a century—Bugarinovic, Dermota, Gostic, Jurinac, Neralic, Martinis, to mention but six; and of course the great Milanov, whose biography appears above, is also Jugoslav by birth.

Georgine von Milinkovic, leading mezzo-soprano of

JEAN MADEIRA

as *Carmen*

NAN MERRIMAN

as *Dorabella* in 'Così fan tutte'

GEORGINE VON MILINKOVIC

as *Fricka* in 'Der Ring des Nibelungen'

ROBERT MERRILL

as *Tonio* in 'Pagliacci'

as *Aïda*

as *Leonora* in 'La Forza del Destino'

ZINKA MILANOV
as *Madeleine* in 'Andrea Chénier'

as *Isolde*

MARTHA MÖDL

as *Leonore* in 'Fidelio'

ELSIE MORRISON

as *Marcellina* in 'Fidelio'

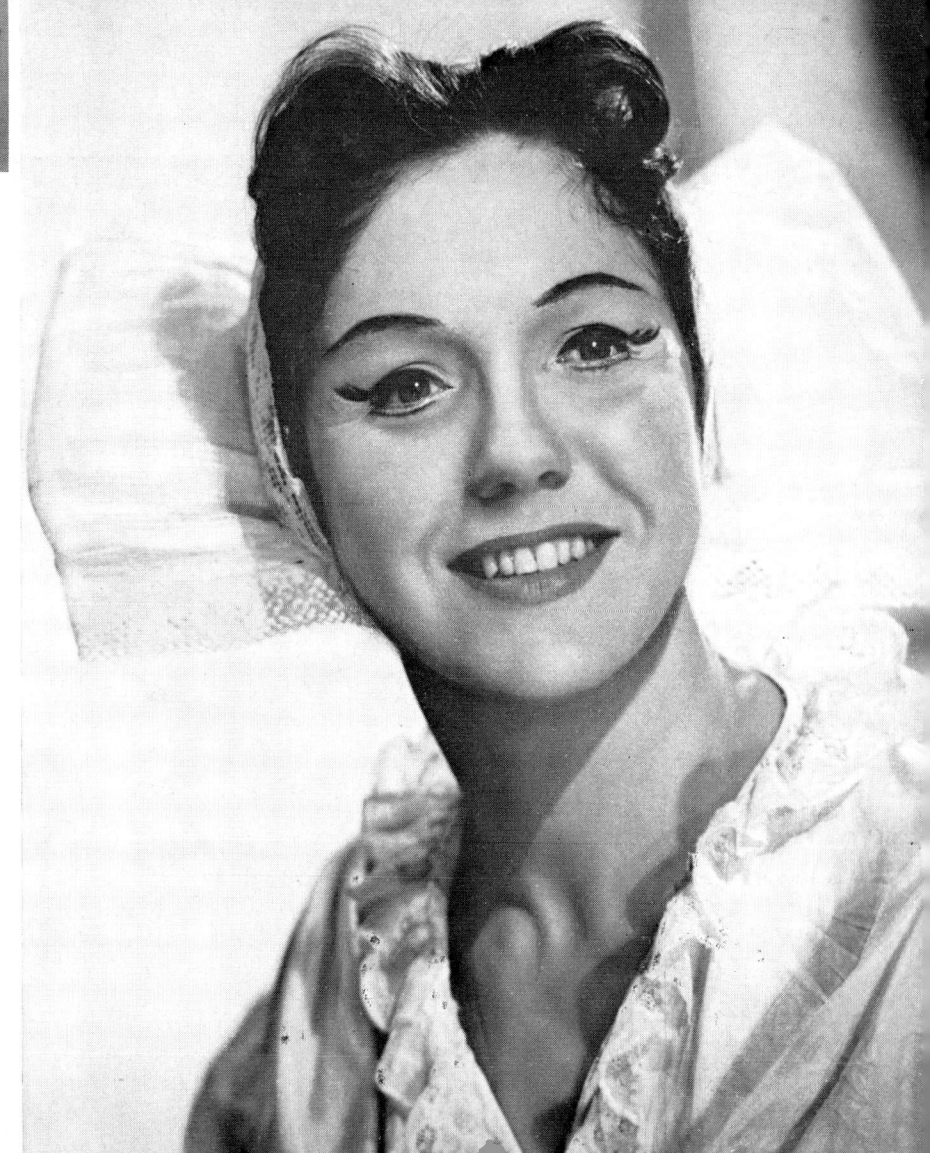

as *Marenka* in 'The Bartered Bride'

BIRGIT NILSSON

as *Isolde*

as *Turandot*

BIRGIT NILSSON
as *Brünnhilde*

PETER PEARS

as *Peter Grimes*

as *Vasek* in 'The Bartered Bride'

the Vienna Opera is another Yugoslav singer. She was born in Prague in 1913 of Croatian parents, but she studied singing in Zagreb, and later in Vienna. Her career began at the Zurich Stadttheater where she made her début in 1937, and she continued to sing there until 1940. During her engagement in Zurich she was heard in the usual mezzo-soprano roles, and scored special successes as Brangaene, as Countess Helfenstein in the world première of Hindemith's *Mathis der Maler* in 1938, and as Lady Macbeth in a production of Verdi's *Macbeth*. This production, the first in the German language of the revised 1865 Paris version, without any cuts, was a triumph for the young mezzo-soprano, and she was invited by Clemens Krauss to join the Munich Opera for the 1940-1 season, and there she remained until the end of the war.

While in Munich she sang in the first local performance of Strauss's *Daphne*, and was also heard as Octavian, Carmen, Amneris and Venus; and she took the part of Dorabella in *Così fan tutte* in one of the last performances at the Residenz Theater before it was destroyed.

Milinkovic's first appearance in Vienna was as a guest in 1944, when she was heard as Octavian, and five years later she joined the company of which she is still a member. In 1952 she was at Salzburg singing Alcmene in the first performance of *Die Liebe der Danae*, and two years later she was at Bayreuth singing Fricka in the *Ring*, in 1956 Magdalene in *Meistersinger*, and in 1957 the Alto Voice in *Parsifal*.

In the autumn of 1957 Milinkovic came to Covent Garden to sing Fricka in the *Ring*, following it a little later with Clytemnestra in the remarkable *Elektra* revival which introduced Gerda Lammers to London. Writing of this performance in *Opera*, William Mann said: 'But for Mme. Lammers, the Clytemnestra of Georgine von Milinkovic would have seemed superb; in the event one could merely be grateful that the central column of the opera's structure was so firmly supported, and that two greatly gifted artists were inspiring one another to drag more and more nourishing marrow from the bones of the action'. While Desmond Shawe-Taylor remarked that she 'made a splendidly corrupt Clytemnestra obtaining her effects entirely by singing, and not by that vulgar *sprechgesang* to which inferior exponents of that part revert'. What few people realised however was that this was the first time that Milinkovic was singing the part!

Another Strauss role in which she excels is Herodias in *Salome*, which she sings regularly in Vienna, but in which she has not yet been heard in London. There is little doubt that Milinkovic is one of the outstanding singing-actresses in present-day opera.

ELSIE MORISON

IN Great Britain before the war, despite the fact that Sadler's Wells and the Carl Rosa opera companies were permanent institutions, few singers were able to pursue operatic careers, and so they turned to oratorio for their livelihood. In recent years, with the establishment of Covent Garden as a permanent opera house, a young singer can hope to make a stage career; but tradition dies hard, and quite often young artists find themselves even now torn between the world of opera and that of oratorio. Too often a promising voice is lost to the opera house when its possessor decides to make a concert career, and this was very nearly what happened in the case of Elsie Morison.

She was born in Ballarat, a town in Victoria, Australia, in 1924. Until she was seventeen her musical studies were directed towards the piano, but at the same time her mother, who was herself a singer, was training her voice. In 1943 she won the Melba Scholarship which took her to the Melbourne Conservatory for three years. There she studied with Clive Carey, with whom she was able to continue in England, where he was appointed professor at the Royal College of Music in 1946. Her first important public appearance was at the Melbourne Town Hall in 1944, where she sang in the *Messiah*, and during the next two years she was heard mostly in recitals, oratorios and broadcasts. In 1946 she came to England and studied for five terms at the Royal College.

She made her first public appearance in England at the Albert Hall in February, 1948, in Handel's *Acis and Galatea*, and in the autumn of the same year she was invited to join the Sadler's Wells Opera Company. Her roles during the first season at the Wells included the Dew Fairy in *Hansel and Gretel*, Mercedes in *Carmen*, Lauretta in *Gianni*

Schicchi, Fiordiligi in *Così fan tutte* and the title-role in Rimsky-Korsakov's *The Snow Maiden*. Even for a young beginner of Elsie Morison's attainments, it was something of an undertaking to sing such a taxing role as that of Fiordiligi in one's initial opera season. To-day she says that if she had known then as much about singing and opera as she does now, she would never have dared to sing that role when she did.

Her second year at Sadler's Wells brought repetitions of her first season's roles, and the addition to her repertory of Nannetta in Verdi's *Falstaff*. In nearly a quarter of a century of opera-going I cannot recall a more charming interpreter of that part, and her ravishingly beautiful singing in the fairy music of the last act was an experience to treasure.

After two seasons at Sadler's Wells Elsie Morison began to sing more and more in oratorio throughout the country, and although she made a few appearances as Susanna it looked as if she was deciding to give up opera entirely. In the summer of 1953 she was invited to sing the part of Anne Trulove with the Glyndebourne Opera in the British stage première of *The Rake's Progress* at the Edinburgh Festival, and shortly afterwards to create the title role in Arwel Hughes's *Menna* with the Welsh National Opera Company in Cardiff. She also made one or two broadcasts in operatic programmes, but she was still undecided in which direction her future lay. Then, persuaded by several friends and admirers, she decided to accept an invitation to sing Mimi and Micaela as a guest artist with the Covent Garden company, first in London and then on tour. From the very outset her Mimi was a touching creation, and the simplicity and sincerity she brought to that role have been repeated in all her operatic interpretations. In the summer of 1954 she sang Marzelline in *Fidelio* under Clemens Krauss, and there the value of her training in Handel and Mozart combined with her unaffected stage presence to make that generally pale character into a real, living personage. The following year she was invited to become a permanent member of the Covent Garden ensemble, and to Mimi and Micaela she added the role of Antonia in *The Tales of Hoffmann* and Marenka in *The Bartered Bride*.

This last role she sang in May, 1955, in the new production of that opera which served to introduce Rafael Kubelik to Covent Garden audiences. Her gifts as a singer and her musicianship appealed to Kubelik, and she was his choice for Pamina in the Mozart bi-centenary production of *The Magic Flute* in January, 1956. Glyndebourne then invited her to sing Zerlina in *Don Giovanni* the same summer—the first British artist to sing the role there since Audrey Mildmay. She has re-appeared there as Anne Trulove and in the summer of 1959 sang Marzelline in *Fidelio*, when it received its first Glyndebourne production.

In 1957 Elsie Morison paid her first professional visit to her native country, and sang more than thirty performances as a guest artist with the Elizabethan Opera Trust. On her return to London in January, 1958, she scored one of the greatest successes of her career as Blanche in the first performance at Covent Garden of Poulenc's *The Carmelites*.

Elsie Morison has during the last few years achieved artistic maturity. Her voice, always sweet and well-placed, has taken on a new bloom, and has increased in size, so that from being just a good British singer, she has emerged as an artist of international stature. This was especially noticeable in her Marzelline in the Klemperer *Fidelio* at Covent Garden in 1961, and also as the Composer in *Ariadne auf Naxos* later the same year at Sadler's Wells. Since 1963 when she married Kubelik and settled with him in Munich, where he is conductor of the Bavarian Radio Orchestra, she has not sung in public; but one hopes that before very long she will return to the operatic stage.

BIRGIT NILSSON

SCANDINAVIA has produced some of the greatest Wagnerians of our time—Flagstad, Larsen-Todsen, Ljungberg, Branzell, Thorborg among the women, Melchior, Andrèsen, Svanholm, Berglund among the men. Since the war a new generation of Wagnerians has now emerged, including Nordmo-Loevberg, Kerstin Meyer, and Birgit Nilsson.

Nilsson was born in Karup in southern Sweden on May 17, 1918, the daughter of a farmer. When she was seventeen she met a singing teacher who advised her to study. Her parents however did not wish her to take up a singing career, and she was sent to a domestic science college. She was so eager however to sing, that her parents allowed her to audition for the Stockholm Royal Academy of Music. There were forty-seven applicants for two vacancies, and she won first place; that was in 1941, and she entered the opera class studying with Joseph Hislop and Arne Sunnegard. After five years' study, and one or two concert appearances, she made her début in 1947 as Agathe in *Freischütz*, following it up during the 1947-8 season as Lady Macbeth in a production of Verdi's *Macbeth* under Fritz Busch.

Between 1947 and 1951, Nilsson slowly built up her repertory at the Stockholm Opera singing the Marschallin, Sieglinde, Donna Anna, Venus, Senta, Aida, Tosca, and Lisa in *The Queen of Spades*. Her first important foreign engagement was at Glyndebourne in 1951 when she was heard as Electra in *Idomeneo*. On that occasion however she only made a slight impression, and it was to be another four years before her international reputation was really established. During these four years she added Elisabeth, Isolde, Elsa and the *Götterdämmerung* Brünnhilde to her repertory; and in 1954 sang Elsa at Bayreuth, her first appearance there. In 1955 she sang Brünnhilde in a complete *Ring* cycle in Munich, and has appeared there regularly since in a number of roles, of which her Salome is especially notable.

Nilsson's American début was at San Francisco in 1956 as Brünnhilde in *Walküre*, and the following year she sang the same role in Chicago, returning there in 1958 as Isolde and Turandot, and in 1959 as Senta and Turandot. 'Birgit Nilsson turned out to be the nearest thing we have heard to Flagstad since Flagstad herself,' wrote a leading American critic of her San Francisco début.

1957 was a great year for this singer, for not only did she come fully into her own at Bayreuth with her Isolde in the new *Tristan* production under Sawallisch, but she made her Covent Garden début as Brünnhilde in the *Ring* under Kempe. London hailed her as the finest Wagnerian since Flagstad, and the veteran Ernest Newman singled her out for special praise, writing that he considered himself fortunate to have lived long enough to have heard so promising a young Brünnhilde. In the summer of 1958 she fully confirmed this verdict when she returned to London to sing two Isoldes, producing a stream of beautiful tone reminiscent of the Flagstad of the 1930's.

Italy too has hailed this artist in no uncertain manner— she has been heard as Donna Anna in Naples, Brünnhilde and Isolde at Florence, and Brünnhilde, Senta and Turandot at La Scala. Indeed she opened the 1958-9 Scala season in this latter role, during the Puccini centenary celebrations, a great honour for a non-Italian.

Meanwhile Nilsson has joined the company of the Vienna Opera, where she is heard for long periods in between her engagements elsewhere in Europe and America. In Vienna she has sung, in addition to the German roles for which she is famous, Amelia in *Un Ballo in Maschera*, Tosca, and Aida. She joined the Metropolitan, New York for the 1959-60 season, and sang there among other roles Isolde in a new production of *Tristan*, and also Leonore in *Fidelio*. Bayreuth heard her as Brünnhilde in Wolfgang Wagner's new *Ring* production of 1960, and she has sung regularly in London since 1961.

This soprano seems to thrive on hard work, the voice never tires, and she possesses endless energy. Her voice is even throughout its range, pure in sound and perfect in intonation with a free ringing top; each successive performance shows artistic growth and development. Vocally she is already the supreme Wagnerian soprano of the day, and there is no reason why she should not also become supreme from the interpretative and dramatic points of view.

PETER PEARS

TENORS as a race are not on the whole blessed with great intelligence and musicality. Of course there are honourable exceptions to this generality, and towering high above the normal run of tenors is Peter Pears.

Born at Farnham, Sussex on June 22, 1910; educated at an English public school (Lancing); an organ scholar Oxford (1928-9); a schoolmaster (1929-33); spent a year at the London Royal College of Music (1934); was a member of the B.B.C. Chorus and then B.B.C. Singers (1934-8); toured the United States with the New English Singers (1936-8); a member of the Glyndebourne Chorus with a walking-on part in *Macbeth* (1938); went to America again, this time with Britten (1939-42) and while there studied in New York with Therese Schnabel and Clytie

Hine Mudie. Those are the facts behind the formative years of Pears's career.

In 1942 Pears was back in London, and he took the part of Hoffmann in a war-time production of *The Tales of Hoffmann* under Walter Susskind, sharing the title role with Henry Wendon. This was not actually Pears's operatic début, for he had sung in a performance of *Die Entführung aus dem Serail* at the College in 1934.

In 1943 came the real beginning of Pears's career as an opera singer; he was engaged by Joan Cross and Tyrone Guthrie for the war-time Sadler's Wells Company. Alfredo, the Duke of Mantua, Almaviva, Tamino were his first roles; then, in November, 1943, came Vasek in the new production of *The Bartered Bride*. 'A notable acquisition to the talented personnel is Peter Pears, whose study of the stuttering half-wit Vasek showed that he was as good an actor as singer', wrote the *Musical Opinion*.

In the autumn of 1944 came the memorable production by the company of *Così fan tutte* with Joan Cross as Fiordiligi, Owen Brannigan as Alfonso, Rose Hill as Despina and Pears as Ferrando. In June, 1945, occurred an event that changed the whole future of English opera, the première of Britten's *Peter Grimes* with Pears in the title role. 'Mr. Peter Pears commanded all the vocal resources required for a great and exacting part', wrote *The Times*; while Scott Goddard, writing in the *News Chronicle*, said 'Peter Pears as Grimes gave a profoundly sympathetic rendering of the part for which he will be remembered. Singing and acting were of one piece, and intensely moving'.

Since then Pears has sung the role abroad and at Covent Garden. He has also created a number of other parts in Britten operas—the Chorus in *The Rape of Lucretia* (Glyndebourne, 1946), the title role in *Albert Herring* (Glyndebourne, 1947), Captain Vere in *Billy Budd* (Covent Garden, 1951), Essex in Britten's Coronation opera, *Gloriana* (Covent Garden, 1953), Quint in *The Turn of the Screw* (Venice, 1954), and Flute in *A Midsummer Night's Dream* (Aldeburgh, 1960). As Thisby in the play-scene at the end of the opera, Pears's 'take-off' of a coloratura-soprano mad-scene was a *tour-de-force*: with the exception of *Budd* and *Gloriana* these Britten operas were produced by the English Opera Group of which Pears has been an invaluable member; he also sang Macheath in Britten's realisation of *The Beggar's Opera*, Aeneas in *Dido and Aeneas*, the Narrator in Monteverdi's *Il Combattimento di Tancredi e Clorinda*, Hawthorn in Bickerstaff's *Love in a Village*, Satyavan in Holst's *Savitri*, and Boaz in Berkeley's *Ruth*.

At Covent Garden Pears will be remembered, in addition to his performances in Britten operas, as a noble Tamino, as Vasek, as David in *Mastersingers*, and as Pandarus in Walton's *Troilus and Cressida*. He sings all his roles with an elegance and style rare among opera singers and with a natural feeling for the music and understanding of the text. His voice, not in itself a great instrument, is always at the service of the musician and, more important still, of the composer.

JAMES PEASE

THE list of the basses and baritones who originally trained for the learned professions before turning to the world of opera makes interesting reading; besides Christoff and Gobbi, already mentioned, it includes the American bass-baritone James Pease.

Pease was born in Indianapolis on January 9, 1916 and graduated in law at Indiana in 1939. At the same time he won a scholarship to the Philadelphia Academy of vocal art, and decided to renounce law for music. His début was made with the Philadelphia Opera Company in November, 1941, as Méphistophélès in *Faust*. Writing about his début the critic of *Musical America* said 'James Pease, a convincing Mephisto, brought an impressive stage-presence and sonorous tonal resources to his interpretation. Meriting special attention was his clear and well-defined articulation and phrasing'. Later in his début season he was heard as Ochs, Arkel in *Pelléas et Mélisande*, Schlemil in *Hoffmann* and Haramburu in the world première of Deems Taylor's *Ramuntcho*.

Shortly after this Pease had a successful audition for the Metropolitan, but having volunteered for the U.S. Air Force, he served for three years as a pilot with the U.S. Armed Forces Training Command.

After the war he joined the New York City Opera and from 1946-53 sang leading bass and baritone roles with the company—Sparafucile, Colline, Escamillo, Don Giovanni, Figaro, Ochs, Wozzeck, Kecal, Lunardo in *I Quatro Rusteghi*, Bluebeard in the Bartok opera, and roles in *The Love of Three Oranges*, *Ariadne auf Naxos*, and *Amelia Goes to the Ball*. The late Cecil Smith found his Figaro 'superb'; and his Sachs, for which he was coached by the great Friedrich Schorr, showed the promise of greater things to come.

Like many Americans, James Pease looked towards Europe; and after his seven years with the City Centre, he was engaged by the Hamburg Opera where he made his début in the autumn of 1953 as Orest in *Elektra*. Then during the next few seasons there followed Wotan, Falstaff, Tomksy in *The Queen of Spades*, the Count in *Figaro*, Briano in Verdi's *Aroldo*, Creon in *Oedipus Rex*, the Lawyer in *Der Prozess*, Sachs, and Boris. When the newly built Hamburg Opera opened its doors in November, 1955, Pease sang the Speaker in *The Magic Flute*, and then Socrates in the world première of Krenek's *Pallas Athene Weint*.

In 1954 Pease made his English début as Don Giovanni at Glyndebourne. The following spring he was heard as Wotan in the second *Ring* cycle that year at Covent Garden, since when he has sung regularly at Covent Garden, where his roles have included Hans Sachs, Ochs, Figaro, the Speaker, and Balstrode in Britten's *Peter Grimes* (he had sung in the American première of this opera at Tanglewood in 1946 and in the same composer's *Albert Herring* in 1949). His Sachs, while not as large in format as those of the very great German bass-baritones, was a beautifully conceived piece of work, young, warm and sympathetic; and his Ochs was one of the best in the post-war period. His diction, as was remarked at his début in 1941, has always been perfect.

In 1957 Pease appeared in Dublin as Figaro, his Susanna was Adèle Leigh, whom he married in the summer of 1958. Already they have sung together as Despina and Don Alfonso, Octavian and Ochs, Susanna and Figaro, and Zerlina and Don Giovanni.

JAN PEERCE

JAN PEERCE, often called 'Toscanini's own tenor', recently completed his twenty-first consecutive season as a leading tenor of the Metropolitan, New York. He began his musical life as a violinist and it was quite by accident that he became a singer.

Peerce was born in New York in 1904. In his teens he had thought of studying medicine, and indeed attended science classes during the day, and then played the violin, the instrument his father had decided he should learn, in the evenings in a restaurant. By 1932 he was a member of the house orchestra of the Astor Hotel, and one evening, when the little band was playing for a private banquet, Peerce sang a vocal number to help eke out the evening's entertainment. Among the people who heard him was Samuel L. Rothafel (Roxy) who invited him to sing 'four shows a day' at his Radio City Music Hall. There Peerce sang everything from popular ballads to Wagner.

In 1938 Samuel Chotzinoff, the Musical Director of the National Broadcasting Company, arranged for Peerce to audition for Toscanini who was seeking a tenor soloist for a performance of the Choral Symphony. Toscanini asked Peerce to sing 'Una furtiva lagrima'. He praised the tenor's *bel-canto* technique, his phrasing, and his Italian; and of course he engaged him for the performance of the Beethoven symphony. This was the first of many appearances with Toscanini, which continued until the conductor's final broadcast opera performance of *Un Ballo in Maschera* in January, 1954, and included the leading tenor roles in *La Bohème*, *La Traviata*, and *Fidelio*.

After the first Toscanini concert in 1938, Peerce was engaged to sing in Rachmaninoff's *The Bells* with the composer conducting. The following year he came under the management of the famous Sol Hurok; and in the summer of 1939 he made his stage début with the Cincinatti Summer Opera as the Duke in *Rigoletto*. In 1940 he sang the same role in Chicago, the following autumn at San Francisco, and then on November 29, 1941, he made his début at the Metropolitan as Alfredo in *La Traviata*. 'His voice is full and free and of quality, and he knows how to use it', wrote one critic; while another remarked on the 'ingratiating tone, vibrant high register, effortless emission, convincing passion, and pathos, and expert phrasing and diction'.

During the course of the next few years he was heard in

most of the Italian repertory at the Metropolitan—Edgardo, Cavaradossi, Riccardo, Rodolfo, and Pinkerton—and Don Ottavio. When he sang this last role in January, 1950, under Fritz Reiner in a cast that included Welitsch as Anna and Schoeffler as the Don, Olin Downes, the *New York Times* critic wrote: 'Jan Peerce sang his two great airs not only with beautiful tone quality and symmetry of line, but with sufficient masculinity to make these passages more than show-pieces for the tenor'.

The following summer Peerce made his first overseas appearances, in South America at Bogota, in Israel, where he sang in fourteen concerts, and in Europe. In 1955 he paid his first visit to Italy where he recorded Pinkerton in *Madama Butterfly* in Rome opposite Licia Albanese, and while in Rome he visited the Pope to whom he presented a rare collection of liturgical records of all religions—Peerce himself always includes some Jewish religious music in his concert programmes.

In the summer of 1956 at the invitation of the Soviet government Peerce made a month's concert tour of Russia, and while there he appeared in *Traviata* in Moscow, *Rigoletto* in Leningrad, and *Ballo in Maschera* in Kiev. He also officiated at a Sabbath morning service in a Moscow Synagogue.

Peerce did not sing opera in Europe until the summer of 1962, when his Alvaro in *La Forza del Destino* at the Holland Festival came as a revelation. He sang and phrased in the manner of a great artist, was scrupulous in his observance of Verdi's note-values and dynamic markings, and his whole performance had the stamp of sincerity. One regretted that he had delayed his European début so long and envied the American audiences who had been enjoying his artistry over the years.

ROBERTA PETERS

ROBERTA PETERS is one of the most popular and attractive young American sopranos now singing at the Metropolitan. Now in her early thirties, she has (summer 1962) twelve active New York seasons behind her.

She was born Roberta Peterman in New York on May 4, 1930, the daughter of a shoe salesman and a milliner, who recognised her musical gifts at an early age. When a young girl she used to attend performances at the Metropolitan as a 'standee'. When she was thirteen her grandfather, who knew Jan Peerce, asked him to listen to her sing. Peerce was so impressed that he sent her to William Hermann, who readily accepted her as his pupil. She studied with him for six years.

In November, 1949, she sang for Sol Hurok at her teacher's studio, and he was so impressed that he immediately gave her a contract. A few months later came a Metropolitan Opera audition for Max Rudolf, the theatre's Musical Secretary. He in his turn was so impressed that a second audition followed before Rudolf Bing, Fritz Reiner and Fritz Stiedry, for whom she sang (more than once) the Queen of Night's aria 'Der hölle Rache' from *Die Zauberflöte*. The result was a contract for the 1950-1 season.

The young soprano was scheduled to make her New York opera début as Queen of Night in January, 1951. Instead, at very short notice she was heard as Zerlina in *Don Giovanni* on November 17, 1950, replacing the indisposed Nadine Conner, with Fritz Reiner conducting. 'From her first entrance . . . . . . Miss Peters never faltered in what seemed an ideal embodiment of the peasant bride, and her gaiety and charm pervaded the scenes in which she appeared. Her voice was clear, accurate in pitch and focus, and lovely in quality'. So wrote the critic of *Musical America*. Later in the season she was heard as Queen of Night and Rosina. The late Cecil Smith writing about her in the latter role said, 'Without hunting out ancient recordings by Maria Galvany, it would be hard to call to mind scales of such swift rippling spontaneity or *staccato arpeggios* of such insouciance and brilliant accuracy'.

In the summer of 1951 she made her Covent Garden début as Arline in Sir Thomas Beecham's production of *The Bohemian Girl*, reminding this writer more than once of Lina Pagliughi with the ease and beauty of her florid singing, and invariably earning an encore for her singing of 'I dreamed that I dwelt in marble halls'.

Then as season succeeded season in New York and elsewhere in America, the young soprano added further roles to her repertory—Gilda, Lauretta, Lucia, Despina, Sophie, Adele, Susanna, Oscar, Lakmé, Norina, Olympia, as well as Amor in Gluck's *Orphée*, and Fiakermilli in Strauss's *Arabella*. A number of these roles she was specially asked to sing in the various new productions at the Metropolitan—Rosina in the 1953-4 season, and Norina in the 1955-6 *Don Pasquale*.

At the Cincinnati Summer Opera, Roberta Peters has been a favourite since her début there in 1951 as Gilda, when the critics agreed that her performance in this role was the best given there in all the years of the summer opera's life. When she sang Lucia there in 1954, she broke all records for attendance in the company's 33 years, and took 20 curtain calls, the greatest ovation ever accorded a singer there.

CLARA PETRELLA

'THE Duse of Singers' has been the appellation given by the Italians to Clara Petrella, one of the finest singing-actresses in post-war Italian opera, and a pupil of the famous Giannina Russ. She was born in Milan and made her début at Alessandria as Liù in 1941 opposite the famous Gina Cigna. After appearing in the Italian provinces she was engaged for La Scala, Milan, in 1947, where she made her début as Giorgetta in *Il Tabarro*. The following year she was heard there as Desdemona, and Fiora in Montemezzi's *L'Amore dei tre re*, and at the Scala she has created leading roles in Pizzetti's *Cagliostro* (1952) and *La Figlia di Jorio* (1954), as well as appearing in the same composer's *Debora e Jaele*.

Petrella's great acting abilities and the intensity she brings to such roles as Manon Lescaut and Nedda, have resulted in her being chosen for other contemporary works, besides those of Pizzetti. Thus she sang Magda Sorel in Menotti's *The Consul* and Katya in Rocca's *L'Uragano* at La Scala in 1952, and *Madame Bovary* in Pannain's opera of that name at Naples in 1956. Such is the soprano's versatility however that she has also sung the title-roles in Monteverdi's *L'Incoronazione di Poppea* and Cavalli's *Didone*.

In 1953 Petrella was chosen to sing the role of Manon Lescaut at the Rome Opera in a series of special performances to mark the twenty-fifth anniversary of the opening of the theatre as the Teatro Reale dell' Opera. In the 1953-4 season on the same stage, she sang the part of Maliella in the first stage performance in Italy of Wolf-Ferrari's *I Giojelli della Madonna*, a role that suited her perfectly.

Three other roles in which this singer excels are Charlotte in *Werther*, Nedda—her own favourite part and one which she thinks is ideally suited to her particular dramatic intuition—and Adrianna Lecouvreur in Cilea's opera of that name. This last role she has sung not only at La Scala and elsewhere in Italy, but also in Mexico and Portugal. She is also eager to sing Minnie in Puccini's *La Fanciulla del West*.

Giorgetta, the role of her Scala début in 1947, is another which suits her well, and she was chosen to sing it both in Rome and Milan during the Puccini celebrations of the 1958-9 season, and in both cities she received unanimous praise from the critics for the manner in which both voice and acting were one. That indeed is the great secret of Petrella's art. One is never conscious that she is a singer acting or an actress singing. She is that rare thing, the completely convincing singing actress.

ANNA POLLAK

THERE are one or two singers in the world of opera who never give a bad performance—they sometimes may be less good than usual, but they are so conscientious in all they do, and such complete artists that even their second-best is better than many other singers' best. Such a performer is the mezzo-soprano Anna Pollak, who was a member of the Sadler's Wells Company, 1945-61, and whom many people have come to take almost too much for granted.

She was born in Manchester in 1915 of Austrian parents. As a child she lived in Holland, and returned to England to complete her education. When she left school she became a member of Henry Bayton's Shakespearean company, then she acted in repertory, appeared in musical comedy, operetta, revue and pantomime all of which helped her to become one of the most assured and natural of operatic actresses of the present day. During the war she worked in A.R.P. and then appeared in concerts under the auspices of E.N.S.A. Her only orthodox singing training was with Joan Cross, who after an audition invited her to join the Sadler's Wells Company, with which she made her début in June, 1945 as Dorabella in *Così fan tutte*.

During her first two seasons she was heard in a number of small roles—Ludmilla in *The Bartered Bride*, Kate Pinkerton, and the Sandman in *Hansel and Gretel*; then she sang Mrs. Ford in Vaughan Williams's *Sir John in Love* and was invited to create the part of Bianca in the première of Britten's *The Rape of Lucretia* at Glyndebourne in 1946. It was in the 1946-7 season that she sang her first *travesti* role, Cherubino in *The Marriage of Figaro*, a part in which she has had few equals in recent years. *The Times* critic wrote 'The Cherubino of Anna Pollak is so convincing that one hardly notices the anomaly of a soprano voice in that of a young man, and she uses the voice well'. In this role she has had many successes, and was asked to sing it under Dobrowen at Covent Garden in 1952. Cherubino was followed the next season by Siebel in *Faust*, Hansel, and Orlofsky in *Fledermaus*, this latter to become one of her most brilliant portrayals.

In February, 1949, came perhaps the greatest challenge in her career, the title role in *Carmen*, in Tyrone Guthrie's controversial production of this opera. Desmond Shawe-Taylor wrote in the New Statesman, 'Anna Pollak's Carmen has been much under-praised; at any rate it gave me continuous pleasure, which is more than I remember to have felt in the presence of any other English Carmen'. The following year came another 'trouser-role', that of Lehl in *The Snow Maiden* and another Meg Page, this time in Verdi's *Falstaff*. In the summer of 1950 Anna Pollak was invited back to the country where she spent her childhood, Holland, to sing Fatima in Weber's *Oberon* at the Holland Festival. Glyndebourne heard her as Dorabella in 1952 and 1953 opposite the Fiordiligi of Sena Jurinac.

As season has succeeded season, so has this singer added still more roles to her repertory—the Sorceress in *Dido and Aeneas*, Mme. Larina in *Eugène Onegin*, Lady Capulet in the English première of Sutermeister's *Romeo and Juliet*, Lady Nelson in Berkeley's *Nelson*, the Secretary in *The Consul*—a most brilliant and sympathetic reading of the part—Nancy in *Martha*, Mrs. Strickland in *The Moon and Sixpence*, and Maurya in *Riders to the Sea*. All these were at Sadler's Wells. For the English Opera Group she created the title role in Berkeley's *Ruth* in October, 1956.

In 1958 when Sadler's Wells was faced with a serious financial and artistic crisis, Anna Pollak played a very important part in the formation of the 'Action Committee' which was largely instrumental in making the Arts Council and the Board of Directors of the theatre think again about the course of action that had been decided upon. In a short piece she wrote for *Opera* about Sadler's Wells, she explained why it is that she has become the artist she is: 'The resulting sense of security and achievement (at Sadler's Wells), which underlies one's work from day to day can hardly be assessed. It is what a theatrical career should be'.

REGINA RESNIK

THERE are quite a number of dramatic sopranos in the history of opera who began their careers as mezzos, but it is something of a rarity to find a singer who, after more than a decade as a successful dramatic soprano, decided to become a mezzo. Such however is the case of Regina Resnik, who is equally well known and appreciated on both sides of the Atlantic.

She was born in New York in August, 1922, of Ukranian parents. She studied at Hunter College where she sang many of the male roles in the productions of Gilbert and Sullivan operas. She then went to Rosalie Miller to study singing, and was introduced by her teacher to Fritz Busch, who engaged her to sing Lady Macbeth with the New Opera Company in New York on December 5, 1942, when only twenty! 'Miss Resnik won the audience immediately' wrote the *New York Times*. 'She has poise, and temperament. She is handsome and bears herself gracefully on the stage, and her voice is sure, steady, easily produced, and of lovely quality. What is more it is under perfect control, and she has the ability to colour it with emotion.'

In 1943 she entered for the Metropolitan Auditions of the Air and reached the finals, but she was unable to take part in them, for her success as Lady Macbeth had led to her being offered a contract to sing Senta and Leonore in

PETER PEARS
as *Pandarus* in 'Troilus and Cressida'

JAN PEERCE

as *Riccardo* in 'Un Ballo in Maschera'

as *Don Ottavio* in 'Don Giovanni'

ROBERTA PETERS

as *Norina* in 'Don Pasquale'

as *Zerlina* in 'Don Giovanni'

CLARA PETRELLA

as *Marguerite* in 'Faust'

with the composer Pizzetti after a performance of 'Debora e Jaele' in which she sang *Debora*

ANNA POLLAK

as *Carmen*

as *Lehl* in 'The Snow Maiden'

as *Carmen*

as *Princess Eboli* in 'Don Carlos' (top left)

REGINA RESNIK

as *Marina* in 'Boris Godunov'

ELENA RIZZIERI

as *Lesbina* in 'Il Filosolo di Campagna'

as *Mimi* in 'La Bohème'

NICOLA ROSSI-LEMENI

as *Henry VIII* in 'Anna Bolena'

as *Boris Godunov*

as *Becket* in Pizzetti's 'Assassinio nella Cattedrale'

Fidelio in Mexico under Kleiber. Then in the spring of 1944 she again sang in New York, this time with the New York City Opera Company, with whom she was heard as Santuzza and Micaela. At about the same time she again reached the finals of the Metropolitan Auditions, and was the only woman finalist that year. She was awarded a Metropolitan contract for the 1944-5 season and made her début there on December 6, 1944, as Leonora in *Trovatore*, taking over the part at twenty-four hours notice from Milanov. Three days later she was heard as Santuzza; and then on December 15 at a student performance she sang Aida.

As if this were not enough, she was chosen to sing Leonore in *Fidelio* in the revival of Beethoven's opera under Bruno Walter the following March. 'Regina Resnik, who had done well in other parts, showed that she had the voice, the high intelligence, and the dramatic sincerity required for Leonore's great role' wrote Olin Downes in the *New York Times*.

During the next two seasons, Resnik quietly consolidated her position at the Metropolitan adding Tosca, Butterfly, Delilah in the world première of Rogers's *The Warrior*, the First Lady in *The Magic Flute*, and Helmwige in *Die Walküre* to her repertory. She also appeared again in Mexico (Donna Elvira and Sieglinde), with the San Francisco Opera, in Montreal, where she sang her first Carmen as far back as 1947, and in Chicago where she sang the Female Chorus in Britten's *The Rape of Lucretia*.

The 1947-8 season at the Metropolitan saw two more important events for her—Ellen Orford in the first Metropolitan performance of *Peter Grimes* and her first Donna Anna. Then came Mistress Ford, Sieglinde (which Bayreuth heard in 1953), Gutrune, Rosalinde in *Fledermaus*, Chrysothemis, Musetta, Venus and Eboli. By the end of the 1954 season she had a repertory of some forty soprano roles, but was already singing such mezzo parts as Eboli and Carmen. Then as she herself has put it 'I came to find myself more comfortable in the darker, more dramatic qualities of the soprano voice . . . the centre or pivot of my voice became the notes A and B, the true mezzo centre'.

It was in 1955 that she decided to make a complete break with the soprano repertory, and so Amneris, Marina in *Boris*, Laura in *Gioconda*, Herodias in *Salome* and the old Countess in the première of Barber's *Vanessa* were added to her repertory.

Resnik's European career can be said to have begun at Covent Garden in the autumn of 1957 when she made her début as Carmen, when her interpretation was hailed as one of the best for many years. She has returned to London regularly since, being heard as Amneris, Marina in *Boris*, the Old Prioress in *The Carmelites*, Mistress Quickly in *Falstaff*, and Ulrica in *Un Ballo in Maschera*. To all her roles she brings not only her warm vibrant voice, firm and strong at the top, but also a deep musical and dramatic understanding. Her acting is full of subtle details and she is a vital figure on the stage.

There is still much for Regina Resnik to do for she is in her early forties and her voice is in magnificent condition. Vienna has already heard her in Carmen, and will undoubtedly hear her in other roles; Salzburg her Eboli; Stuttgart her Clytemnestra and Herodias; Venice her Kundry; and Milan her Fricka and Waltraute. She herself wants to sing Dido in *The Trojans* and Jocasta in Stravinsky's *Oedipus Rex*.

ELENA RIZZIERI

ONE of the most attractive Susannas and Despinas at post-war Glyndebourne has been the Italian soprano Elena Rizzieri, one of the small group of Italian artists who really know how to sing Mozart, and who are also something of specialists in the *opere buffe* of the eighteenth and early nineteenth centuries.

Rizzieri was born in Rovigo in October, 1922. She studied in Venice at the Conservatorio Benedetto Marcello with the famous soprano Gilda Dalla Rizza. Her début took place on January 26, 1946 at the Teatro La Fenice, Venice, as Marguerite in *Faust*. Her success was immediate, and she was soon singing all over Italy including La Scala, where her first role was Liù, Rome where she was heard as Mimi, and Marina in *I Quatro Rusteghi*, and Naples as Eurydice.

Her first Mozart success was as Susanna in Rome in 1952 in a cast that included Tebaldi as the Countess and

Simionato as Cherubino. The conductor on that occasion was Vittorio Gui, who brought her to Glyndebourne in 1955. Andrew Porter writing in *Opera* found her 'a vivacious and pretty actress, with a voice attractive in timbre, forward and delicately controlled'. And the following summer she was a delicious Despina.

Her repertory numbers some sixty roles, and includes roles of widely differing character both vocally and dramatically—Eva in *Meistersinger* and the Snow Maiden, Violetta and Galuppi's *La Diavolessa*, Anaide in Rossini's *Mosè* and Caterina in Pizzetti's *Vanna Lupa* (a role she created), Clementina in Boccherini's work of that name and Parasia in *The Fair at Sorotchins*. Rizzieri's Puccini roles include the rarely-performed *La Rondine*, which her teacher Dalla Rizza created, and Butterfly. In this latter role she has been much praised, and following a performance of it in Rome in 1952 she was specially presented by the Japanese Ambassador with a special set of costumes designed by the Japanese painter Nakahara. In addition, the Italian magazine *Oggi* included her in its list of best singers in 1953, nominating her as the best Puccini soprano.

Besides appearing at Glyndebourne, Rizzieri has sung with great success in Barcelona, Brussels, Lisbon, in Germany, and at the Théâtre des Nations Paris, where she was heard in 1957 as Serpina in *La Serva Padrona* and Lesbina in *Il Filosofo di Campagna*. She was heard in these two parts in London when the Virtuosi di Roma gave two delightful double bills of Italian eighteenth century opera after successful performances in Rome and Paris.

Perhaps one of the funniest things ever seen or heard in London during the last ten or fifteen years however was this soprano's performance in Fioravanti's *La Cantatrice Villane* in which she sang the part of the young uncouth country wench who fancied herself as an operatic soprano. She and two other young ladies take part in a 'performance' of Metastasio's *Ezio* set to music by the local composer Don Marco. When the opera was revived in Paris in 1842 Persiani and Frezzolini sang the rival prima donnas. Rizzieri in the Persiani role brought down the house with a bravura performance of the 'Grand aria' from *Ezio*.

NICOLA ROSSI-LEMENI

THE post-war opera scene has been lucky with its supply of fine singing-actors—Christoff, Gobbi, Hotter, Uhde, and the Italo-Russian bass Nicola Rossi-Lemeni.

He was born in Constantinople on November 7, 1920; his father was a Colonel in the Italian army, his mother a Russian, whose maiden name was Xenia Lemeni Macadon —she had been a teacher of singing at the Odessa Conservatory. His interest in singing began in his boyhood, and when he was thirteen he began to study music; he was inspired by the songs of Chaliapin, and was for the most part self taught, using gramophone records as models. During the war he was in the Italian army, and in 1946 was ready to make his début.

This occurred at the Teatro Fenice, Venice in May of that year, as Vaarlam in *Boris Godounov*. In the summer of the same year he was heard at the Verona Arena as Ramfis in *Aida* and in the autumn season at the Scala that year, he was heard as Varlaam in *Boris* with Pasero in the title part. His first great personal triumph was in the part of Philip in *Don Carlos* at the Teatro Giuseppe Verdi, Trieste, in December, 1946, with Barbieri as Eboli.

In the summer of 1947 Rossi-Lemeni returned to the Verona Arena to sing on the opening night of the season, as Alvise in *La Gioconda*; this was the memorable performance when Callas and Richard Tucker made their Italian débuts; Serafin was the conductor. During that season he also sang Méphistophélès in *Faust* with Tebaldi as Marguerite, Serafin again conducting. The 1947-48 season was a busy one for this artist, he added to his repertory the parts of the Landgrave (*Tannhäuser*), Archibaldo (*L'amore dei tre Re*), Khovanski (*Khovanshchina*), Marke (*Tristan*), Silva (*Ernani*), and Boito's Mefistofele singing at Bologna, Trieste, Naples, Genoa, Venice, Florence and the Terme di Caracalla, Rome.

Rossi-Lemeni opened the 1948-9 season at the Rome Opera in the title part of Rossini's *Mosè* and later that season (also in Rome) sang his first Boris, a part in which he has made a great success both in Europe and America. Serafin was again the conductor and it is to him that he owes a great deal, for not only did the eminent conductor help him in the early stages of his career, but Rossi-Lemeni married Serafin's daughter, Vittoria, in December,

1949; they had first met in Buenos Aires in the summer of that year, when Rossi-Lemeni was singing at the Teatro Colonas as Ramfis, Il Padre Guardiano, Oroveso and Méphistophélès.

During the 1950-1 season the bass returned to La Scala to sing the Verdi *Requiem* under De Sabata and in *Lucrezia Borgia*; and the following season was heard as Oroveso, Basilio, Mefistofele, and King Philip. At Rome he sang as Zaccaria in *Nabucco* and the title-roles in Bloch's *Macbeth* and Gruenberg's *The Emperor Jones*. His American and English débuts were both made in the title role of *Boris* in 1951 and 1953 respectively.

Writing of his American début, the late Cecil Smith said 'Mr. Rossi-Lemeni is the most commanding Boris we have heard since Chaliapin.... he projected the character in an unbroken line of mounting intensity, capping the climax with a corkscrew fall from his raised throne that sent a gasp through the audience. His visual portrayal was accompanied by vocalism that was Slavic in timbre and absorbing in its range of colour and volume.'

The bass was also heard in San Francisco as Il Padre Guardiano in *Forza del Destino* in 1951, and as Mefistofele in Boito's opera in 1952 and 1953. It was as Gounod's Méphistophélès that he made his Metropolitan début on the opening night of the 1953-4 season in Peter Brook's controversial production of the opera, which transferred the period from the fifteenth to nineteenth century. He was also heard in New York as Don Giovanni, and Boris (which he sang in English).

During the next two or three seasons, Rossi-Lemeni seemed to go through a vocal crisis, his voice losing some of its volume and roundness. Yet he was still able to dominate the stage and scored yet more successes in Italy, America and Monte Carlo. Some of the roles in which he was specially successful at this time were Caspar in *Freischütz*, Selim in *Il Turco in Italia*, Kovanski in *Khovanshchina*, and Archibaldo in *L'Amore dei tre Re*, all parts which gave admirable scope to his dramatic talents.

Two more roles in which he was successful were added to his repertory in the 1956-7 season, the title role in Handel's *Giulio Cesare* and Henry VIII in Donizetti's *Anna Bolena*. Shortly after this he returned to London to sing Don Giovanni at the Stoll Theatre, an interpretation which he acted up to the hilt, reaching a stupendous climax in the supper scene. At this time too, he was divorced from Vittoria Serafin, and shortly after he married the attractive Rumanian soprano Virginia Zeani, with whom he has often appeared.

In March, 1958 Rossi-Lemeni scored another great individual personal success at La Scala as Thomas à Becket in the première of Pizzetti's *Murder in the Cathedral*, in which he was, according to the Milan critic Sartori 'unrivalled in the perfection of his performance and in his skill in creating the character'. He has repeated the role elsewhere in Italy and in New York. In complete contrast, during the same season he sang a 'vivacious Dulcamara (*Elisir d'Amore*), irresistible in ripeness and comedy'.

Some other aspect of this remarkable singer must be mentioned. Not only does he speak six languages, but he also writes poetry—three volumes have been published. He has designed many of his own costumes, and has also produced some performances of opera. In fact he would seem to possess many of those qualities which would suit him to the management of an opera house, when he decides to give up singing.

LEONIE RYSANEK

When the great soprano Lotte Lehmann returned to London in the autumn of 1957 to give a series of masterclasses, she held a press conference at Covent Garden, the scene of many of her greatest triumphs between 1924 and 1938. Among the many questions asked her was one about the post-war generation of singers. She spoke about the performances she had heard in Vienna at the re-opening of the State Opera, and singled out Leonie Rysanek as possessing potentially the greatest talent among the younger generation of sopranos.

Rysanek was born in Vienna in November, 1926. She studied singing at the Conservatory there with Alfred Jerger (the first Mandryka in *Arabella*), and in 1948 was heard in a concert singing arias from *Alceste* and *Un Ballo in Maschera*. The following year she was engaged for the Innsbruck Opera where she made her début as Agathe in *Freischütz*. There she met the baritone Rudolf Grossmann with whom she continued her vocal studies, and whom she later married.

From Innsbruck Rysanek went to Saarbrücken where she sang for two years (1950-2) during which time she sang Sieglinde in the first post-war Bayreuth *Ring* (1951). At Saarbrücken she increased her repertory to include Arabella, Donna Anna and Elvira, Tosca, Desdemona, Senta, and Leonora in *La Forza del Destino*. In Vienna she appeared as a guest singing Tatiana in *Eugene Onegin*. But it was to be a few more years before she became a member of the Staatsoper.

In 1952 she began her engagement at Munich, where for four years she was greatly admired in the German and Italian repertory, singing many new roles, including Lady Macbeth, Desdemona, Santuzza, Turandot, and three Strauss roles in which she has few if any equals to-day— The Kaiserin in *Die Frau ohne Schätten*, Danae in *Die Liebe der Danae*, and the title-role in *Die Aegyptische Helena*.

It was as Danae that she was first heard in London, when she sang in two of the four performances of Strauss's last opera which were given in the short season by the Munich Opera at Covent Garden. 'A vocally ravishing performance especially in the last act with the voice going up to a C sharp *in alt* in the last "Midas"' wrote William Mann in *Opera*. The following summer she sang Chrysothemis in London; in 1955 Sieglinde, in 1959 Tosca, and in 1963 Elsa and the Marschallin.

In the 1954-5 season Rysanek was heard with the Berlin and Vienna Operas regularly, as well as in Munich. In Berlin in 1955 she sang Reiza in *Oberon*, and was accorded an ovation, which according to Desmond Shawe-Taylor would not have disgraced Lotte Lehmann or Maria Müller. 'I see why,' he wrote, 'she has a naturally full and warm timbre; and there is excitement and drama in her singing'. In Berlin too in 1956 she scored a great personal triumph as Elecra in *Idomeneo*.

When the present writer heard her as Helena in Munich in the summer of 1956 he wrote 'Leonie Rysanek in the title role displayed her full vocal powers admirably. Including the wonderful Tosca of Milanov, this was the greatest display of soprano singing I heard this year. The voice is sumptuous, beautiful, full and vibrant; the stage presence radiant—what more could one want?'

A few weeks later the soprano made her American début with the San Francisco Opera as Sieglinde, also singing Senta and Aida. The following year she was heard as Lady Macbeth, Amelia, Turandot, and Ariadne, and she has returned there again in 1958 and 1959; as well as singing with the Chicago Opera.

Perhaps her greatest challenge came when she was asked by Rudolf Bing to take over the role of Lady Macbeth at the Metropolitan in 1959 in place of Callas. She sang with almost too much beauty of tone for the role, one is told. She then went on to sing Elisabeth de Valois and Aida.

Having returned to Bayreuth in 1958 after an absence of seven years, to sing Elsa and Sieglinde, she was announced for Senta in the new *Fliegende Holländer* there in 1959, as well as Ariadne in a new production of Strauss's opera, at the Cuvilliéstheater in Munich at the same time.

According to *Time* magazine Miss Rysanek was forty pounds lighter than in 1958, when she made her Metropolitan début. 'It's a concession to the American public' she said. When asked what it was like to follow Callas she replied, 'there is no fight, no following in anyone's footsteps. We need a Callas and a Tebaldi and a Milanov —and a Rysanek'. How right she is.

PAUL SCHOEFFLER

PAUL SCHOEFFLER is one of the best examples in the world of opera of the advantages of the German operatic system; a system in which a young artist can begin in small roles graduate slowly to larger ones, and finally become one of the most sought after singers in the world.

Schoeffler was born in Dresden in 1897 and brought up in a musical household. He often attended performances at the Dresden Opera, and sang as a boy alto in a local church. He then went to the local conservatory where he studied the violin, organ and composition; and then when his voice broke, he began to take singing lessons. When he was twenty-four, he went to Milan to study with the famous baritone Sammarco, and he also studied in Berlin with Grenzebach, and Dresden with Staegemann. His début was made at the Dresden Staatsoper in 1927 as the Herald in *Lohengrin*.

He was soon singing Marcello in *Bohème*, Papageno, and

roles in the Lortzing operas. In 1930 he sang the title-role in Weinberger's *Schwanda* in its first Dresden performance; in 1931 he was heard as Posa in *Don Carlos*; in 1933 as Iagos and Mandryka in *Arabella*; in 1934 in Handel's *Giulio Cesare* and Mozart's *Figaro*. In 1934 too, came the first step towards Schoeffler's international career, his Covent Garden début as Donner, followed a few weeks later by Schwanda in the opera's English première. Schoeffler has always had a great affection for London; his wife is English, the sister of Mark Lubbock, and he has often returned to sing at Covent Garden.

Between 1935 and 1939 he was heard in London as Kurwenal, Gunther, Jochanaan, Wotan in *Rheingold*, Scarpia, Galitzky in *Prince Igor*, Schlemil in *Hoffmann*, and as Figaro and Don Giovanni with the Dresden State Opera, when that company visited Covent Garden in the autumn of 1936.

In 1938 Schoeffler made his first guest appearances at the Vienna Opera as Pizarro, Hans Sachs, and Figaro. After the *Meistersinger* performance the director of the Staatsoper went to see Schoeffler in his dressing-room, and told him that there would be a permanent contract for him in Vienna whenever he wanted to come. And the following season he became a permanent member of the company, and is still (1964) one of the most valued and popular singers in Vienna.

Schoeffler first appeared at Salzburg in 1938 as Pizarro. The following year he was heard there as Wolfram, and since the war he has sung Alfonso in *Così fan tutte*, Don Giovanni, La Roche in *Capriccio*, the title role in Einem's *Dantons Tod* (which he created in 1947), Jupiter in the world première of Strauss's *Der Liebe der Danae* (1952), and the Music Master in *Ariadne auf Naxos*. Writing in *Opera* in October, 1952 about the *Liebe der Danae*, Andrew Porter said 'It is hard to imagine a better performance of the role (Jupiter) than he gave: noble, tender, humorous, passionate by turns, a fully rounded and vocally splendid impersonation'.

Schoeffler has been back at Covent Garden several times since the end of the war; first with the Vienna Company in 1947 when he sang Don Giovanni, Alfonso, and Pizarro; and then as Gunther, Kurwenal, Sachs and Wotan between 1949 and 1955.

He joined the Metropolitan, New York in 1949, and in addition to his Mozart and Wagner roles, sang there as Scarpia, the Grand Inquisitor in *Don Carlos*, Pizarro, and Jochanaan in *Salome* in which role he made his début. The late Cecil Smith writing about this event in *Musical America* said 'Mr. Schoeffler's Jokanaan was magnificent. . . . His superb baritone voice possessed a deeply sympathetic quality, and his musical expression achieved the utmost loftiness and nobility. It was profoundly moving, the finest portrayal of Jokanaan in my experience with the opera'. His Don Giovanni a week later earned similar praise.

To list all this singer's roles would require much space, but mention should be made of his Boccanegra. Cardinal Borromeo in *Palestrina*, King Philip in *Don Carlos*, Ivan Tarassenko in Salmhofer's opera of that name, and his Mathis, in Hindemith's *Mathis der Maler*. Space also makes it impossible to include the names of all the theatres in which Schoeffler has sung. It can safely be said however that there is no important operatic stage on which Schoeffler has not appeared. His warm voice, good humour, and serious approach to his art make him welcome the world over.

ELISABETH SCHWARZKOPF

IF ever an artist has reached the top of her profession by dint of long study, hard work, and the most searching self-criticism, that artist is Elisabeth Schwarzkopf. She has established herself as one of the finest singers to have emerged from Germany in the post-war period, and is equally at home in lieder as in opera. She is as popular at the Scala, Milan as at Salzburg or San Francisco, and has endeared herself to the British public as few other singers of our time have.

Schwarzkopf was born in Posen in 1915. She received her early musical training at the Berlin Hochschule für Musik, where her first teacher was the contralto and lieder singer; Lula Mysz-Gmeiner; she decided that Schwarzkopf was also a contralto and trained her accordingly. After two and a half years with this teacher she transferred to Dr. Egenolf, through whom she got her first engagement at the Städtische Oper in Berlin. In 1938 she made her début as a Flower-Maiden in *Parsifal*, and during her first two seasons in Berlin she sang many small roles, including the First Boy in *Die Zauberflöte*, Esmeralda in *The Bartered Bride*, the Wood Bird in *Siegfried* and Valencienne in *Die lustige Witwe*. From 1941 she began to assume larger roles; Oscar (*Un Ballo in Maschera*), Musetta, Lauretta (*Gianni Schicchi*) and Zerbinetta (*Ariadne auf Naxos*). Schwarzkopf's singing of this last role brought her to the attention of Maria Ivogün, the Hungarian coloratura soprano, who had herself been the outstanding Zerbinetta of the 1920's, and she took on Schwarzkopf as her pupil. Ivogün's husband, Michel Raucheisen, one of the finest accompanists in Germany, played a great part in Schwarzkopf's development as a lieder singer.

In 1942 she was invited to appear as a guest artist with the Vienna State Opera, and in 1944 she was engaged as leading coloratura soprano in Vienna. There she sang Rosina, Blöndchen (*Die Entführung aus dem Serail*), Zerbinetta and Musetta. After the liberation of Vienna, Schwarzkopf sang with the State Opera until the end of the 1949 season. Besides the roles already mentioned, she was heard as Constanze, Donna Elvira, Pamina, Violetta, Gilda, Mimi, Liù, and Sophie.

London first heard her on the opening night of the Vienna Opera's autumn season at Covent Garden in 1947, when her aristocratic and beautifully sung Donna Elvira, showed that Germany could still produce first-rate operatic artists. A few days later she was heard as Marzelline in *Fidelio*. Summing the season up in *The Observer* Charles Stuart wrote, 'Most of all, in and out of my dreams, I shall remember Schwarzkopf's Elvira, every platinum note of it'.

The following year Schwarzkopf was persuaded to join the Covent Garden company and for four seasons, until the summer of 1951, she sang all her roles in English (very clear English too one remembers). This meant that, in addition to studying new roles, she had to re-learn those she already knew in German. Between 1948 and 1951 London heard her as Pamina, Sophie, Violetta, Susanna, Mimi, Manon, Gilda, Cio-Cio-San, and Marzelline, all of which she sang in English; Eva she sang in German.

Some of Schwarzkopf's finest work has been in collaboration with Herbert von Karajan, with whom she first sang at the Salzburg Festival of 1948 as the Countess in *Figaro*. Karajan, who both produced and conducted the work, took the Salzburg cast to the Scala in Milan the following winter, and since then both he and Schwarzkopf have appeared regularly at the leading Italian opera house. There she has sung Elisabeth in *Tannhäuser*, Donna Elvira, the Marschallin, Elsa in *Lohengrin*, Mélisande (under De Sabata), Marguerite (*Faust*), Pamina, Mistress Ford, and Fiordiligi. At the Venice Festival of 1951 Schwarzkopf created the part of Anne Trulove in the first performance of Stravinsky's *The Rake's Progress*.

It was in 1951 that Bayreuth re-opened its doors with a performance of the Choral Symphony under Furtwängler. Schwarzkopf was the soprano soloist. In addition she was heard there as Eva and the First Rhinemaiden. Since then Schwarzkopf has not been attached to any one opera company, though since Karajan became director of the Vienna Opera, she always arranges to give the Vienna Opera several evenings each season.

Schwarzkopf's American début was not in opera, but in a recital at the Town Hall, New York, in 1953. Two years later she made her American operatic début; this was at San Francisco as the Marschallin and Donna Elvira. In 1956 she was heard as Fiordiligi and Mistress Ford; in 1957 as the Marschallin and Fiordiligi, and in 1958 as Countess Almaviva, Marenka (which she sang in English). Her scheduled appearances in 1959 both in San Francisco and Chicago had to be cancelled owing to ill health. But fortunately she was able to return to Covent Garden as the Marschallin in the first performances there of *Rosenkavalier* in German since 1938.

It is perhaps no mere coincidence that Schwarzkopf and Callas are not only admirers of each other's art, but also friends. For they both are aristocrats of vocal style, and both relentless seekers after perfection. In Vienna Schwarzkopf has been called 'the star among stars'. A recent Fiordiligi there was said by Joseph Wechsberg to have been 'a stunning exhibition of vocal technique, impeccable style, musical taste, of charm and drama and art'. What more could one want from any singer?

GRAZIELLA SCIUTTI

GABRIEL DUSURGET, the remarkable artistic director of the

Aix-en-Provence Festival has many vocal discoveries to his credit, among them the attractive soubrette, Graziella Sciutti, whose first stage appearances were at the 1951 Aix festival as Lucy in Menotti's *The Telephone*.

She was born in Turin in 1932 and studied in Rome at the Academy of Santa Cecilia. She made her concert début in Venice in the Italian Prize Contest, and then was heard, again in concerts, in Rome, Turin, Genoa, and Naples. In addition to singing Lucy in the 1951 Aix festival, she was heard as Elisetta in *Il Matrimonio Segreto*. In the autumn that year she sang at the Venice Festival in Boccherini's *La Clementina* under Issay Dobrowen. The next summer saw her back at Aix as Susanna; a performance that the Earl of Harewood found 'Remarkable and delightful, acted with charm, and sung with exemplary musical feeling and accuracy, achieving a triumph of delicacy in "Deh vieni non tardar".'

The following summer she was again at Aix, this time as Despina as well as Susanna. Then she went to Paris, where she sang the name part in Sacha Guitry's and Reynaldo Hahn's *Mozart*. This was followed by Polly in Kurt Weills's *Die Dreigroschenoper* in Monte Carlo and also in Paris. Then in the summer of 1954 Sciutti came to Glyndebourne for the first time as Rosina in *Il Barbiere*. She would not cause a riot with the audience that demanded a brilliant coloratura; but her enchanting performance, excellent musicianship and charming personality soon endeared her to British audiences.

After the 1954 Glyndebourne Festival Sciutti returned to Aix to create the role of Marianne in the première of Henri Sauguet's *Les Caprices de Marianne*. This was her first tragic role, and she brought it off with complete success. To quote Lord Harewood again, 'her dignified acting was as delightfully accomplished as her singing.'

With the re-opening of the Teatro di Corte in Naples in November, 1954, and the opening of the Piccola Scala in Milan the following year, Sciutti came into her own in Italy. In revivals of works by Paisiello, Rossini, Cimarosa, Piccinni, etc., as well as in new Italian works she became a great public favourite. Indeed in Milan she was christened La Regina della Piccola Scala (in contrast to Callas who was La Regina della Scala). She sang in the first two operas at La Piccola Scala, *Il Matrimonio Segreto* and *Così fan tutte*, she created the part of the Dwarf in Ghedini's *L'Ipocrita Felice*, and also sang in Malipiero's *La Donna è Mobile* there.

In 1956 Sciutti made her Covent Garden début as Oscar in *Un Ballo in Maschera*. Artistically she stood head and shoulders above the rest of the cast on this occasion, displaying style, elegance and charm to rare degree, and singing in very clear English. The following summer she was heard at Edinburgh as Carolina in *Il Matrimonio Segreto* with the Piccola Scala Company, in which role she won all hearts. She had a busy summer that year, for at the Holland Festival she sang Anne Trulove in *The Rake's Progress* and at Aix she was again Susanna.

In the autumn of 1957 Sciutti sang another new role, that of Marie in Donizetti's *La Fille du Régiment* at the Wexford Festival. Desmond Shawe-Taylor writing in *Opera* said, 'she made a delightfully spirited and attractive vivandière; in her bearing and manner there was something suggestive of an Italian Irmgard Seefried, a saucy hoydenish quality which the audience found irresistible.' Back she was at Glyndebourne the following summer; this time as Nannetta and Susanna.

More recently she has appeared at Salzburg as Despina (the sauciest and most adorable interpreter of the role) in Rennert's production of *Così fan tutte*, as Norina in *Don Pasquale* at La Piccola Scala, as Bellina in a revival of Cimarosa's *Le Astuzie Femminili* and Rachelina in Paisiello's *La Molinara*, both these at the Teatro di Corte in Naples. Sciutti's American début took place during the 1961 San Francisco season, when she sang Oscar and Susanna.

IRMGARD SEEFRIED

THE famous 1947 autumn visit to London by the Vienna Opera has already been quoted more than once in these pages. It is not easily forgotten, for after having been cut off from the continent for nine years, London heard for the first time many new young artists who had grown up in Germany and Austria during the war years: Schwarzkopf, Jurinac, Welitsch, and Seefried were indeed worth waiting for. Seefried made her début on the season's second night as Fiordiligi in *Così fan tutte*, following it a week later with Susanna.

Like Elisabeth Schumann, Seefried has come to be associated with Vienna, although not of Viennese birth. She was born in the Bavarian town of Koengetried, in October, 1919. Her father was a school-teacher, and taught her the rudiments of music from the age of five, but when she was seventeen he unfortunately died. Her family was hit by a double tragedy, for her only sister also died, and her mother was not willing for her other daughter to follow a musical career. However, young Irmgard Seefried had been able to complete a six-months course of study at the Augsburg Conservatory. 'At that time everyone was against me', she says. 'I could hardly read a note of music; I could play the violin by ear, but had no immediate hope of earning my living by singing.' However her teacher, Professor Meyer, had faith in her, and she was able to continue her studies under his guidance without her mother's knowledge. She was able to earn a little money by singing at parties and receptions, and finally was chosen to sing a solo part at a student concert. She did not know that her mother was in the audience, and was surprised when after the concert she found her among those who had come to congratulate her.

After leaving the Conservatory in 1938 she obtained an engagement at the Opera House at Aachen, where another young artist was beginning his career. This was the conductor Herbert von Karajan. She made her début as the Priestess in *Aida*, following it by Nuri in d'Albert's *Tiefland*. She remained at Aachen for three years, working with Karajan and singing Agathe (*Der Freischütz*), Nannetta (*Falstaff*), Marenka, Pamina and Susanna. An invitation to Dresden followed in 1943, but at the same time the offer of a full contract with the Vienna State Opera was forthcoming, and she joined that company, making her début there as Eva under Karl Böhm, with Paul Schoeffler as Hans Sachs.

During her second season in Vienna Seefried was chosen to sing the role of the Composer in *Ariadne auf Naxos* during the eightieth birthday celebrations of Richard Strauss. By the end of the 1946 season her repertory had grown to include Fiordiligi, Susanna, Marzelline, the three soprano roles in *Hoffmann*, Nedda and Cio-Cio-San. In 1946, too, she married the violinist Wolfgang Schneiderhan, who was at that time the leader of the Vienna Philharmonic Orchestra. The following year, as already mentioned, she came to London with the Vienna Opera.

Seefried has a particular affection for the Salzburg Festival, and has sung there regularly since the festival was resumed after the war. Fiordiligi, Pamina, Zerlina, and the Composer in *Ariadne auf Naxos* have been among the roles she has sung there.

Because Seefried is attached to her home and family, she has not returned to the Metropolitan since her initial season there in 1953; and because she likes the concert platform as much as the opera stage, she has only added three new roles to her repertory in the last six years—Cleopatra in Handel's *Giulio Cesare*, Blanche in Poulenc's *Carmelites* and in *Cardilluc*. She has however returned to a role she sang in her early days, Marenka in the *Bartered Bride*, and she has recently scored a great success as Octavian, in which role she returned to Covent Garden in 1962.

Seefried's obvious enjoyment in singing is apparent in her work. She sings, she says, because she likes it. She dislikes the term prima donna, and certainly does not like it being used about herself. Proud possessor of the Lilli Lehmann medal awarded to her by the Mozart Association of Salzburg, which she prizes more than any ovation she receives from an audience, she, like that great artist after whom the medal is named, has dedicated her life to music. Happy herself, she makes her listeners happy too.

AMY SHUARD

'This performance of *Faust* had the added pleasure, indeed thrill, of introducing to this listener a young soprano in the role of Marguerite who should, if carefully nurtured, become in the next five years or so the finest dramatic soprano in England since Eva Turner. This gold-mine is Amy Shuard, a twenty-five year old girl whose only previous operatic experience was in South Africa. She possesses a truly thrilling voice of the kind that becomes fuller and more powerful in its upper reaches; the tone is round and vibrant, and the stronger support which the lower portion of the voice still needs will no doubt soon come. In addition she has a charming stage presence and a natural acting ability.'

LEONIE RYSANEK

as *Abigaille* in 'Nabucco'

as *Helena* in 'Die Aegyptische Helena'

as *Lady Macbeth* in Verdi's 'Macbeth'

PAUL SCHOEFFLER

as *King Philip* in 'Don Carlos'

as *Hans Sachs* in 'Die Meistersinger'

ELISABETH SCHWARZKOPF

as *Mistress Ford* in 'Falstaff'

as *Despina* in 'Così fan tutte'

as *Rosina* in Paisiello's 'Il Barbiere di Siviglia'

as *Nannetta* in 'Falstaff'

GRAZIELLA SCIUTTI

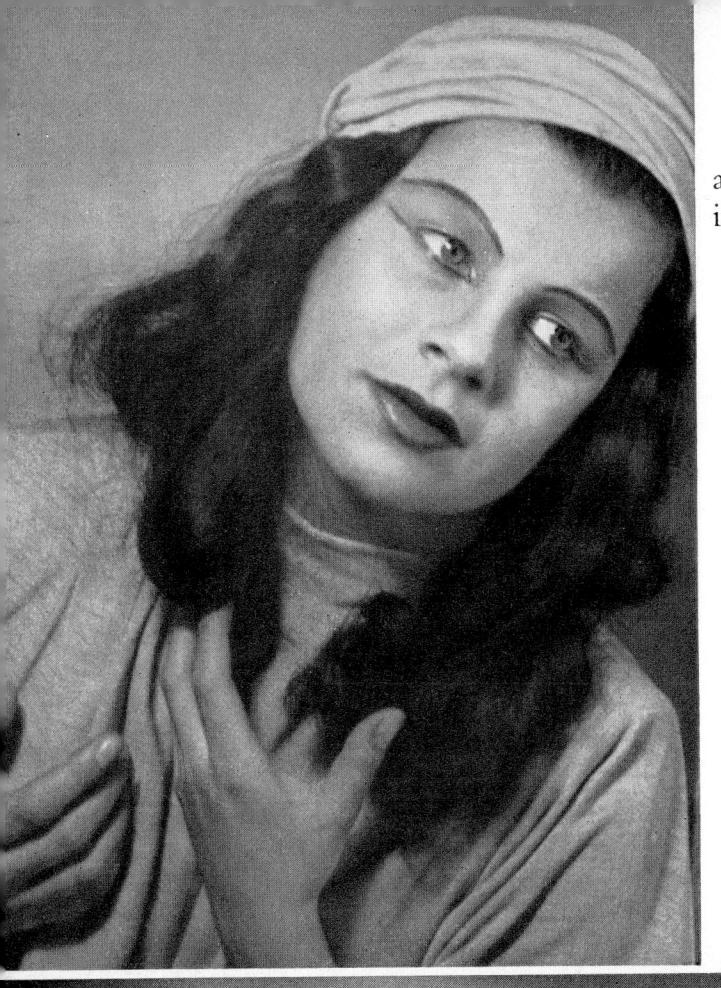

as *Liù* in 'Turandot'

as *Pamina* in 'Die Zauberflöte'

IRMGARD SEEFRIED

as *the Composer* in 'Ariadne auf Naxos'

CONSTANCE SHACKLOCK

as *Amneris* in 'Aïda'

as *Brangaene* in 'Tristan und Isolde'

as *Gutrune* in 'Götterdämmerung'

AMY SHUARD

as *Princess Turandot*

CESARE SIEPI

as himself

as *Don Basilio* in 'Il Barbiere di Siviglia'

as *Don Giovanni*

These words by the present writer appeared in *Opera* in April, 1950. Six years later she became a member of the Covent Garden Company, and was soon heard as Aida, Amelia, Butterfly, Giulietta in *Hoffmann*, and Freia and Gerhilde in the *Ring*. At Sadler's Wells she had been acclaimed for her powerfully sung and acted Katya Kabanova and Magda Sorel. Back at Covent Garden between December, 1956, and the autumn of 1959, she was acclaimed as Jenufa, as Cassandra in *Les Troyens*, as the finest Turandot since Eva Turner, and as an outstanding Sieglinde and Gutrune. In other words *Opera's* prophecy had come true.

Amy Shuard was born in London in July, 1924. Her musical education was at the Trinity College of Music, where she studied voice under Ivor Warren. In 1948 she won the medal awarded by the Worshipful Company of Musicians, and then went to South Africa to represent the college in a lecture and concert tour. The result of this was so successful that she was invited back to South Africa the following summer to sing with a company that was touring the Union, as Aida, Venus in *Tannhäuser* and Giulietta in *Hoffmann*. While in South Africa she met a young medical student, Peter Asher, who subsequently came to this country, and in 1954 they were married.

On her return from South Africa Shuard gave an audition at Sadler's Wells, and was immediately engaged. Her début was made there in November, 1949, as Musetta. During her first season she also sang Marguerite, Santuzza and, during the Company's provincial tour, Carmen.

It was during the following season that she really showed her mettle, when she sang the role of the Princess Eboli in *Don Carlos*, Sadler's Wells's contribution to the 1951 Verdi celebrations. This role is generally sung by a mezzo-soprano like Stignani, but Shuard gave the most exciting vocal and dramatic performance on the stage in that production; in 'O don fatale' she displayed the real grand manner which earned her an ovation.

During the same season she was heard in another Verdi role, Amelia Boccanegra, and in the title role of Janacek's *Katya Kabanova* which, as the Earl of Harewood pointed out, needs both intensity and experience; the former she provided but the latter at that stage of her career she naturally did not possess.

In the course of the next two seasons she added the roles of Nedda, Giorgetta (*Il Tabarro*) and Butterfly to her repertory. Then, at the end of the 1953-54 season, she went to Milan for a period of study.

Her return in January, 1954, when she sang Butterfly at Sadler's Wells found her voice fuller, more vibrant and more thrilling than before, though one noticed a lack of support in the middle of her voice, and an inability to project her soft notes so that they carried.

One of Amy Shuard's greatest assets is that she is never satisfied with herself, and she is always ready to listen to advice and criticism. And so she knew that she still had some hard work to put in before her vocal production became all it should be. And work she did, so that when she sang Katya Kabanova under Kubelik in the Sadler's Wells revival during the 1953-4 season, she gave the finest performance of her career up to that time: a wholly integrated study, in which singing and acting were all of a piece. In the following year she scored a similar triumph as Magda Sorel in *The Consul*.

At Covent Garden she greatly benefited from singing Butterfly and Aida under the baton of Rudolf Kempe. But her greatest triumph was as Turandot in December, 1958. Philip Hope-Wallace wrote in *Opera*: 'Not only did she look regal, but sang with her pristine radiance of tone and her superb suggestion of limitless reserve. I have never heard her to better advantage, and cannot really think I have heard a more splendidly assured Turandot since Eva Turner. The support of the voice in the climaxes was marvellous, and most consoling after the yowling one has heard in this testing role'.

This was only the beginning. In September, 1959, Covent Garden took another calculated risk, and cast Shuard as Sieglinde and Gutrune in its annual *Ring*. The word 'radiant' was used by many critics to describe her singing and interpretation of Sieglinde (she had with advantage coached the role with Hilde Konetzni, and later worked with Eva Turner); while her Gutrune really made sense of the character. Reverting to her Sieglinde, Neville Cardus writing in the *Manchester Guardian* said 'I have heard most of the Sieglindes of the past thirty or forty years, and not many have had a more poetic distinction than Miss Shuard's after only one or two efforts at the most endearing of Wagner parts . . . . Had she arrived here fresh from Darmstadt all the fashionable places in town would now be raving about her'. This is one of the things native British artists have to fight against. But already there are signs that not only are our native artists being invited abroad, but they are also being accepted in their own country. Indeed the 1961-2 season saw Shuard triumphing in Vienna as Turandot and Aida and at the Colon, Buenos Aires as Lady Macbeth. At Covent Garden she has added Leonore in *Fidelio*, Schoenberg's *Erwartung* and Brünnhilde and Elektra to her repertory. The future looks bright for her, and there is little doubt that she will be the next British Isolde and Salome.

CONSTANCE SHACKLOCK

AMONG the British singers who have emerged at Covent Garden in the post-war period, Constance Shacklock is one of the few who was a foundation member of the Covent Garden Company in 1947.

She was born in 1913 near Nottingham—on a farm which belonged to her father in Sherwood Forest. She sang a good deal locally, and took lessons with Roy Henderson. Before the war she was a member of the Nottingham Operatic Society, participating in performances of Gilbert and Sullivan. From 1939 to 1944 she studied at the Royal Academy of Music in London by which institution she was awarded a scholarship. Her teacher was the famous baritone Frederick Austin. While at the Academy she won all the prizes there were for the contralto voice.

From 1943 until the end of the war she toured the country with C.E.M.A. Then in 1946 she sang the role of Sabrina in *Comus* with the International Ballet. An audition for Covent Garden followed, and she was engaged for the newly-formed opera company, making her début on December 12, 1947 in Purcell's *Fairy Queen*. Her first wholly operatic role was Mercedes in *Carmen* a month later. And during the company's initial season she was heard as Rosette in *Manon*, Third Lady in *The Magic Flute*, Annina in *Rosenkavalier*. In November 1947, in the company's second season she took over the part of Azucena in *Il Trovatore* at very short notice, and was also heard as Mrs. Sedley in *Peter Grimes*, Carmen, Marina in *Boris Godunov*, Magdalene in *Meistersinger*, and Brangaene in *Tristan und Isolde* when it was revived for Flagstad. This was the role in which she really established herself as a fine artist. 'Constance Shacklock sang the exacting Brangaene music excellently; she seems to have the making of a first rate Wagnerian singer', wrote Ernest Newman.

During the 1948-9 season, Constance Shacklock added two roles to her repertory with which she has been very much identified since—Octavian in *Der Rosenkavalier* and Amneris in *Aida*. In the following year she added Fricka to her Wagnerian repertory and was also heard as Herodias in the controversial Dali-Peter Brook *Salome* production with Welitsch.

Two memorable events occurred during the 1950-1 Covent Garden season, and in both of these Constance Shacklock participated; the farewell of Kirsten Flagstad, and the arrival of Erich Kleiber. Flagstad decided to sing her last Wagner on the stage at Covent Garden during the 1951 Festival of Britain season, and after having been heard as the *Götterdämmerung* Brünnhilde and Sieglinde in an extra *Walküre* performance, she bid farewell to the London Wagner public as Isolde, and once again it was Shacklock who sang Brangaene. Kleiber's engagement as guest conductor at Covent Garden marked the beginning of Shacklock's international career. This great German conductor was so impressed by her work, which benefited from his inspiring presence in the pit and from working with him generally, that he invited her to Berlin the following season to sing Brangaene at the State Opera (this in fact had not been this singer's foreign operatic début for she had sung the same role in Holland opposite Flagstad in 1949).

In 1953 the mezzo-soprano was heard as Elisabeth in Britten's coronation opera, *Gloriana* sharing the role with Joan Cross, and singing it with the company during their visit to Rhodesia. Two other foreign appearances should be chronicled, Octavian at the famous Teatro Colon, Buenos Aires in 1956, and her series of appearances in Russia during the 1956-7 season, including some at the Bolshoi in Moscow, as Carmen and Amneris. In 1958 she visited Australia, and at the end of that year returned to Covent Garden as Amneris, Octavian, and Herodias. The first weeks of 1959-60 season saw her back again at the opera house in her old part of Marina in *Boris Godunov* which she sang on that occasion in Russian.

Constance Shacklock was married to Eric Mitchell, a pianist and organist on the musical staff at Covent Garden, and much of her success must be due to their many hours of musical study together.

CESARE SIEPI

OUTSTANDING among the low-voiced singers who have emerged in post-war Italy is the handsome young bass, Cesare Siepi. He was born in Milan in February 1923. He studied singing privately and made his début at the early age of eighteen at Schio as Sparafucile. His career was interrupted by the war during which he became an active anti-fascist, and in September 1943 he was forced to take refuge in Switzerland.

In August 1945, Siepi returned to Italy and resumed his career at the Fenice Theatre where he made his second début as Zaccaria in Verdi's *Nabucco*. In the following year he sang during a summer season organized by the Scala at the Palazzo del Sport in Milan, where he was heard as Sparafucile, Il Padre Guardiano, and Ramfis. His success in these performances led to his engagement for the first season at the rebuilt Scala, and he was heard there on the opening night of the 1946-7 season, again as Zaccaria, under Serafin. From then until 1950 he was La Scala's leading bass, and sang in many operas each season. His repertory at that time included Baldassare in *La Favorita*, Lothario in *Mignon*, Raimondo in *Lucia di Lammermoor*, Pogner, Colline, the Count in *La Sonnambula*, and Méphistophélès in both Gounod's *Faust* and Boito's *Mefistofele*. He was chosen to appear in the latter work by Toscanini during the 1948 Boito celebrations at La Scala, when he was also heard as Simon Mago in *Nerone*.

Siepi first came to Great Britain with the Scala Company in the summer of 1950 when he sang in the Verdi *Requiem* at the Edinburgh Festival, and then a week or so later was heard as Pistol in *Falstaff*, and again in the *Requiem* at Covent Garden. A few weeks later he left for New York, where he had been engaged by Rudolf Bing as a last minute replacement at the Metropolitan, making his début on the opening night of the 1950-1 season, which was also the opening night of the Bing régime at the Metropolitan. His début role was that of King Philip in *Don Carlos*. Cecil Smith praised his first performance in *Musical America* in these words: 'He is a fine singer, a capable actor, a real artist, and a valuable addition to the company.'

During Siepi's first New York season he also sang Don Basilio, Méphistophélès, and Colline. Early in his second season he was heard as Figaro in the Mozart opera, and a year later he sang the title-role in *Don Giovanni*. His Mozart interpretations have also been heard at Salzburg where many consider him to be the successor of the late Ezio Pinza, the finest basso-cantante of his day. His strikingly handsome physique, and his exuberant acting, fit him for the role of the Don.

Of his first Figaro, *Musical America* wrote, 'His was a superior Figaro, with the makings of a memorable one'; while his first Don Giovanni was similarly praised. In March 1953 he sang his first role in English, and a large one at that, the title part in *Boris Godunov*, and roused his audience to a great demonstration after the death scene.

During the 1956-7 season at the Metropolitan, Siepi was heard as Silva in the revival of Verdi's *Ernani* in which, according to Ronald Eyer, 'he gave the most fully developed dramatic performance of the evening ... and was warmly applauded for his singing of "Infelice" '—and this despite a cast that also included Milanov, Del Monaco and Warren. Later in the same season when he repeated his King Philip in *Don Carlos*, the same critic wrote, 'Mr. Siepi has always sung Philip's music with a fabulously beautiful tone, but his characterization, vocally and dramatically has never before suggested with such rich detail, the monarch's troubled, lonely, yet tyrannical spirit. It seemed like one of the major achievements of to-day's operatic stage'.

It would seem therefore that by the beginning of the 1957-8 season that Siepi had reached the height of his powers both vocally and dramatically. His next new Verdi role in New York was Fiesco in the new production of *Simon Boccanegra* during the 1959-60 season, his tenth consecutive one at the Metropolitan. His return to Covent Garden during 1961-2 season as Don Giovanni and Philip in *Don Carlos* was most welcome.

GIULIETTA SIMIONATO

THE Italian mezzo-soprano, Giulietta Simionato, is one of the most admired and exciting artists in present-day Italian opera. She can be said to have succeeded to the place held during the last twenty-five or more years by the great Ebe Stignani, and is considered the leading Italian mezzo-soprano, and an exponent of the art of *bel-canto*.

Simionato was born in Forli in 1910. She spent her childhood in Sardinia, and began her musical studies at Rovigo with Ettore Lucatello. In 1933 she gained first prize in a *bel-canto* competition in Florence, and during the next few years she sang small roles in Florence, Padua, and at La Scala, Milan, while at the same time she continued her studies. In 1938 she made what she likes to regard as her official début at the Teatro Comunale in Florence, as the Young Mother in Pizzetti's *L'Orseolo*.

During the 1939-40 season at La Scala she sang Beppe in *L'Amico Fritz* and during the next few seasons there was heard as Hansel, Berthe, Emilia and in a number of minor roles. In the 1943-4 season she was heard as Rosina in a revival of *Il Barbiere di Siviglia* which she sang in the original key; and during the same season also sang Cherubino, Meg in *Falstaff*. Dorabella and Mignon soon followed; and in 1948 she was chosen by Toscanini to sing Asteria in Boito's *Nerone*.

In the summer of 1948 Simionato came to Edinburgh to sing Cherubino. London first heard her quite unheralded in the summer of 1953 when she sang Adalgisa, Azucena, and Amneris, all opposite Callas. Of her Amneris Andrew Porter wrote in *Opera*: 'To someone who had heard Giulietta Simionato only in various Rossini roles, her Amneris came as a surprise (though of course it had been much praised in Italy). One knew her for a coloraturo mezzo of agility and finish with fascinating seductive timbres in the lower part of her voice. Now one discovered that she is also mistress of a strong, even, dramatic mezzo, remarkable throughout its range for the emotion it can carry. One did not regret Stignani or Barbieri with Simionato there, acting with superb authority . . .'

Simionato's American début took place in 1953 at San Francisco, when she sang Charlotte in *Werther*, Marina in *Boris*, and Carmen. The following year she sang in Chicago as Adalgisa, Rosina and Carmen. She has returned there regularly since, being heard also as Azucena, Preziosilla, Amneris, Mistress Quickly, Mignon, Laura in *La Gioconda*, and the Principessa di Bouillon in *Adriana Lecouvreur*.

In 1954 Bellini's rarely performed *I Capuletti ed I Montecchi* was specially revived for her. This is a version of the Romeo and Juliet story (with happy ending!) in which Simionato plays the role of Romeo. She has sung this role also in a concert performance of the opera in New York. Amsterdam, Salzburg, and Vienna are other operatic centres where Simionato is a welcome visitor.

She first sang in Holland in 1954 in the Scala, Milan production of *La Cenerentola*. The following year she was heard as another Rossini heroine, again in a Scala production, Isabella in *L'Italiana in Algeri*. In this latter role she demonstrated that she is a born comedienne; the chuckles, the wealth of expression both vocal and facial that she displayed in the role were a joy; and her singing was delightful.

Salzburg has heard her as Eboli, Azucena, and Orfeo in Gluck's opera: Vienna in several of her most famous roles including Santuzza. Her repertory knows no bounds. One of her greatest successes was Jane Seymour in the revival of Donizetti's *Anna Bolena* at La Scala with Callas. 'It would be difficult to find a more striking representative of the role than Simionato, who looked superb and whose upper register is particularly rich and free', wrote Desmond Shawe-Taylor in *Opera à propos* Simionato in this opera. Of her Leonora in the same composer's *La Favorita* at Verona in 1958, the same critic wrote, 'Giulietta Simionato delighted the audience by the sheer assurance and skill, both vocal and dramatic of her performance'. She is truly one of the most gifted of contemporary singers.

LEOPOLD SIMONEAU

IN July 1950, a few days before I went to Glyndebourne to hear *Così fan tutte*, I had tuned in the wireless to a French station to hear *Don Giovanni* from the Aix-en-Provence Festival. In the course of the evening I heard

Mozart tenor-singing of a calibre I had only previously heard in the opera house from Richard Tauber, and on gramophone records of John McCormack. I was not the only one who was impressed with this broadcast, for when I spoke to Mr. Moran Caplat, Glyndebourne's General Manager, I found that the good news of this Mozart tenor had already reached Glyndebourne. And the following summer he made his British début as Don Ottavio and Idamante in *Idomeneo*.

Simoneau was born in a suburb of Montreal. He was the tenth child of Joseph Simoneau, a choir master and Olivine Boucher, a singer. All the family was musical, and when only eight years old, Leopold began his formal musical studies, first at Rhode Island where he lived with an aunt, his mother having died when he was still an infant, then in Montreal, where he returned when he was thirteen. In his early teens he sang in the choir of St. Patrick's Cathedral in Montreal, and when he was seventeen he took part in a performance of *La Chanson de Fortunio*, an Offenbach operetta, at Laval University where he was studying. A few years later he sang on the local radio, and was paid three dollars, which he immediately spent on an opera score.

In 1943 he began his concert and operatic appearances singing Don Basilio in *Figaro* under Beecham in Montreal, and then appearing seven times in eleven days as Wilhelm Meister in *Mignon* at the Varietès Lyriques, also in Montreal.

In 1945 Simoneau went to New York for a further period of study with the tenor Paul Althouse and the producer Herbert Graf. The following year there were operatic appearances in Philadelphia, New Orleans, and Central City. In the latter centre he sang fourteen performances of Lionel in *Martha* under Emil Cooper. The final stage in his initial period of development was his engagement to sing Belmonte under Sir Thomas Beecham in a Montreal production of *Die Entführung aus dem Serail*. (It is interesting to note that Beecham again engaged Simoneau for this role when he recorded the complete opera in London in 1958.)

In 1949 Simoneau joined the company of the Paris Opéra and Opéra-Comique, where he remained for two seasons. Singing with him was his wife, Pierrette Alarie, whom he had met in the studio of his Montreal singing teacher, and who has sung with him on many occasions. She is a coloratura soprano, and her roles include Zerlina, Blondchen, Lakmé, Oscar, and Olympia.

After Simoneau's French and British débuts, he was heard at La Scala, Milan, under Karajan in *Don Giovanni* when he was compared to Tito Schipa. A typical press comment was this: 'One of the revelations so far this season was Leopold Simoneau, here for the first time as Ottavio. His *mezzo-voce* is of a beauty rarely heard these days, reminiscent of some of the old *tenori leggieri*. He has an outstanding musical intelligence and voice control, coupled with a natural dignity that was in perfect keeping with his part.'

In June 1953 he sang Tom Rakewell in the French première of *The Rake's Progress*. One leading French critic thought that his performance in the role 'could hardly be excelled in vocal agility, accuracy of intonation and understanding of the music.' He then made his usual appearances at Aix, and was heard as Ottavio at the Munich Festival. He sang the same role in the spring of 1955 in the two performances of *Don Giovanni* which launched the Lyric Theatre of Chicago. He has sung in Chicago fairly regularly since in Mozart, as Wilhelm in *Mignon*, Alfredo, Nemorino and Cavaradossi.

Simoneau's London début took place in the autumn of 1954 at the Royal Festival Hall when he sang Ottavio and Ferrando in *Così fan tutte*; in the latter his singing of 'Un Aura Amorosa' was so meltingly beautiful that one regretted that the second Ferrando aria was omitted in that performance.

Not unnaturally Mozart is Simoneau's favourite composer. 'I've found that the best approach for me', Simoneau has said, 'is simply to listen to Mozart. I've sung the role of Ottavio nearly a hundred times. And each time I find myself actually listening and discovering new facets of his music. . . . . . To me Mozart is the most exact of all composers: you sing his music his way or you don't sing it at all. I try to sing it in what I think is his way. And I am constantly being surprised by how marvellous and human his way is.'

ELEANOR STEBER

FOR many years the Sherman-Williams Company of America sponsored a series of broadcasts over the N.B.C. network, known as 'The Metropolitan Auditions of the Air'. In this series the winners each year were offered contracts at the Metropolitan, and since the inception of these auditions the world of opera has discovered many talented young artists, including Arthur Carron, Leonard Warren, Margaret Harshaw and Eleanor Steber, who have since achieved international fame.

Eleanor Steber was born in July, 1916, in Wheeling, West Virginia. Determined since her youngest days to become an opera singer, she gained a scholarship to the New England Conservatory at Boston, where she worked very hard, earning a few dollars by playing the piano at a dancing school and singing in oratorio performances in Boston and the surrounding district. Each year the Metropolitan Opera visited Boston on its spring tour, and on one of these visits she was signed on to appear as a super in one production. When she arrived at the stage door on the evening of the performance, to her dismay she discovered that another, unknown young lady had signed in as Eleanor Steber, and so her eagerly awaited début with the Metropolitan while still studying never came off!

In 1940 she settled in New York, and prepared for the radio audition in the spring of that year. As a result of it she won a contract for the 1940-1 season at the Metropolitan, and made her début on 8th December, 1940, as Sophie in *Der Rosenkavalier*. She received 'rave' notices in the New York press; here is a typical one from *The New York Times*: '.... a Sophie, fresh and delicate. She sang all Sophie's high notes in the "Presentation of the silver rose" scene without a tremor or a deviation from pitch.' Her only other role in her début year was Micaela in *Carmen*. During the next few seasons her repertory slowly grew, and by the end of the war it included the Countess Almaviva, Donna Elvira, Marguerite, Antonia and Giulietta in *The Tales of Hoffmann*, Violetta, Alice Ford in *Falstaff* and Eva in *Die Meistersinger*. In less than ten years after her début as Sophie in *Der Rosenkavalier* she was singing the role of the Marschallin in the same opera.

Gradually giving up her lighter roles, she assumed such parts as Elisabeth de Valois in *Don Carlos*, Desdemona in *Otello* and Fiordiligi in *Così fan tutte*. On one occasion at the Metropolitan she sang these last two roles on the very same day—Desdemona at a matinée and Fiordiligi in the evening. As one critic remarked: 'It is doubtful whether any prima donna has ever sung in one day two roles so taxing and so utterly different in their requirements of vocal technique and voice placement.'

Eleanor Steber's European début was at the 1947 Edinburgh Festival, when she was heard as the Countess in *Figaro*. Six years later she appeared at another European festival—Bayreuth—where she sang Elsa in *Lohengrin*. On that occasion there were two American artists in the cast, for Astrid Varnay was the Ortrud. One of her greatest successes was at the Florence Festival in 1954, when she sang Minnie in *La Fanciulla del West*. For this opera she specially learned to ride a horse.

During the 1954-5 Metropolitan season Steber sang the role of Arabella in the first performance in New York of Strauss's opera. This role she sang in English and it was a part that both appealed to her personally and admirably suited her personality. 'Eleanor Steber was at the height of her best vocal style and managed the high *tessitura* of her music with complete security' wrote Ronald Eyer in *Musical America*. During this season too she sang her first Donna Anna which critics found a most exciting portrayal.

After her 1954-5 New York season, Steber embarked on a tour of Yugoslavia singing Violetta, Tosca and Marguerite; and later in the summer of 1955 she sang Ilia in *Idomeneo* in the first International Festival of Music and Drama to be held in Athens.

During the 1957-8 Metropolitan season, Steber created the title role in Samuel Barber's *Vanessa*—a part she repeated later at Salzburg. Ronald Eyer, reporting the event in *Opera* noted that she sang beautifully in the title role 'which with its generally high *tessitura* and emotional intensity is a formidable assignment'. In the following season she sang Marie in *Wozzeck* in the first performance of that opera at the Metropolitan. Like Simoneau however, it is as a Mozart singer that Steber is pre-eminent—Constanze, Fiordiligi, Donna Anna, Elvira, Ilia, the Countess and Pamina.

In an interview for the *Musical Courier* Steber had some interesting things to say about Mozart style, which for her is 'not a question of vocal exercises, but of singing with controlled emotion, which in turn is projected with the full blooded Italian bel-canto'. As a soprano who has sung both Anna and Elvira in *Don Giovanni*, she is of the opinion that Anna is a *lirico spinto* role, and Elvira a dramatic soprano part—which is surely historically correct.

Steber has spent the greater part of her career in the United States, and one regrets that she found so little time to sing more in Europe, where her voice and temperament would undoubtedly be appreciated.

ANTONIETTA STELLA

IT is quite surprising how many present day singers owe their careers to voice competitions organized by national or municipal authorities or even by commercial undertakings in both Europe and America. In this book alone, the names of several such singers appear—Licia Albanese, Lucine Amara, Anita Cerquetti, Margaret Harshaw, Jean Madeira, Eleanor Steber, Leonard Warren are among those that immediately spring to mind. Antonietta Stella is another such artist.

She was born in Perugia in 1930, and began to take singing lessons when still a child. She then went to the local conservatory where her teacher was Francesco Morlacchi with whom she studied for six years. After winning prizes in contests organized by Enal at Bologna in 1949, and at the Concorso at Spoleto in 1950 where she appeared as Leonora in *La Forza del Destino*, she was engaged for the Rome Opera for the 1950-51 season; there she made her début, again as Leonora, and was also heard in a modern opera by Rigacci called *Ecuba*, and in Respighi's *La Fiamma*.

Stella's success was immediate, for she possessed at the very outset a most beautiful soprano voice, with an exquisite upper register. Engagements came pouring in from Bergamo, Bologna, Palermo, Genoa, and elsewhere in Italy, and also from Lisbon, and various German centres. Between the autumn of 1951 and the summer of 1953 she sang Aida, Desdemona, Maria Boccanegra, Leonora in *Trovatore*, Elisabeth in *Tannhäuser*, Sieglinde, Senta, Mathilde in *William Tell*, the title role in Respighi's *Lucrezia*, and other roles. Early in the 1953-4 season she made her Scala début as Desdemona, earning the highest praise from the demanding Milan public and critics; this was followed by her Venice début as Elisabeth de Valois in *Don Carlos*.

The soprano first crossed the Atlantic to sing in Rio in 1954; she also appeared in Havana, San Paõlo (where she sang in Gomez's *Lo Schiavo*) and Puerto Ricco before going on to the Colon, Buenos Aires. Her repertory too was slowly expanding, and now included Elena in *Vespri Siciliani*, Amelia in *Ballo*, Violetta (which she recorded at La Scala under Serafin), and Tosca.

Stella's Covent Garden début was in the summer of 1955 as Aida with Gino Penno as Radames, Ebe Stignani as Amneris, and Gobbi as Amonasro. Although her make-up and costuming aroused some adverse comment, her singing did not. Philip Hope-Wallace writing in *Opera* commented 'She had presence, acting ability, and warmth of personality, as well as a naturally gorgeous dramatic voice, full, strong, and of lovely quality.'

The Metropolitan, New York, first heard Stella during the 1956-7 season, and she became one of the company's most popular contemporary sopranos. Her début was in November 1956 as Aida. Ronald Eyer writing in *Musical America* said: 'There seemed almost no limit to the sheer decibel strength of the vocal organ, and it possesses that phenomenal kind of projective power that sends the tone, full-bodied into the farthest reaches of the auditorium and easily rides the crest of any ensemble of voices and instruments pitted against it. This is not the whole story however, Miss Stella also has a lovely *mezzo-voce*, which she clearly knows how to control.' She repeated her success a few days later in *Trovatore*; and in her first season was also heard as Tosca. During the 1957-8 season she sang in the new production of *Madama Butterfly* which one leading New York critic wrote: 'Miss Stella, a lovable and radiant artist like Tebaldi, had the beauty and power of voice and the dramatic instinct to make Cio-Cio-San wholly a creature of flesh and blood.'

The 1958-9 season saw Stella opening the San Carlo season in Naples as Madeleine de Coigny in *Andrea Chénier*, and making several appearances in other Italian houses as well as returning to the Metropolitan. She was chosen to open the 1959-60 Metropolitan season as Leonora in a new production of *Il Trovatore*. If not one of the very greatest of the sopranos of this century, she is certainly one of the hardest working and conscientious, and is continually refining her art and winning new admirers by her carefully schooled vocalism.

RISË STEVENS

ONE of the most colourful personalities at the Metropolitan Opera for the last twenty-five years has been the mezzo-soprano Risë Stevens. She was born in New York in 1913 of a Norwegian father and Austrian mother. She sang on the radio when she was ten, and when seventeen joined an operetta company's chorus. She made her début in the small role of Kathinka in *The Bartered Bride* at the Hechscher Theatre in New York, and when she was nineteen began having lessons with Mme. Schoen-René, a pupil of the great Pauline Viardot. For three years she attended the Juilliard School, and while still a student there sang the title-role in Gluck's *Orfeo*. In 1935 she went to Salzburg to study with Gutheil-Schoder, and the following year she was offered a contract at the Metropolitan Opera, which she turned down as she felt she lacked experience. Instead she decided on Europe and auditioned for the Prague Opera, where she made her début during the 1936-7 season singing Octavian, Mignon and Orfeo with much success.

Risë Stevens's second Prague season found her singing Amneris, Carmen, Cherubino and Hänsel. She then was invited to sing as a guest in Vienna and Cairo, and in the summer of 1938 sang at the Colon, Buenos Aires, as Octavian and Erda. The next step was an engagement at the Metropolitan, where she made her début in a revival of *Mignon* in December 1938, in a cast that included Richard Crooks and Pinza. 'A well cultivated voice of moderate power and compass and velvety in quality was disclosed as her first asset' wrote Oscar Thompson, and then continued, 'But she went beyond routine good singing and in her delineation of the role, has an illusion and an appeal to place this Mignon beside the cherished impersonations of the character by Lucrezia Bori and Geraldine Farrar'.

Two nights later she sang her first New York Octavian and 'confirmed and deepened the impression she had made at her début'. A Fricka and Erda however seemed to confirm that Wagner was not for her.

In the summer of 1939 she sang Cherubino and Dorabella at Glyndebourne under Fritz Busch. The late Richard Capell wrote 'Risë Stevens with her youth and graceful gawkiness, leaves us saying that there is small likelihood of our ever seeing another so effectively Cherubino-like'; while the *Observer* commented 'This year they have found a Cherubino whose charm and skill are such that any producer could be forgiven for attempting feats of virtuosity when she is on the stage'. Her Dorabella was no less successful, and plans for the 1940 Glyndebourne season went ahead with a proposed *Carmen* with Risë Stevens in the title role. It was to be another sixteen years however before this artist returned to Glyndebourne, for the second world-war put an end to Glyndebourne's plans for 1940—and it was during the war years that this artist scored her greatest American successes.

In the 1940-1 season she added Delilah in Saint-Saëns's opera to her Metropolitan repertory, and she repeated her Glyndebourne triumph as Cherubino in New York. In the 1945-6 season she sang Laura in *La Gioconda;* and other roles she assumed in New York included Marina in *Boris Godunov*, Marfa in *Khovanshchina*, Hänsel, Orlofsky in *Fledermaus* and Orfeo. She returned to the Colon, Buenos Aires in 1939 and 1940, and sang with the Chicago, San Francisco and Cincinatti Opera companies.

Stevens sang her first American Carmen at Cincinatti, in 1943; she repeated it the following year at San Francisco; and in the 1945-6 season sang the role at the Metropolitan. She has repeated the part on many occasions since, especially in the controversial Tyrone Guthrie production of the work which was first seen in New York in January 1952.

During the war years, Risë Stevens made some successful musicals for Metro-Goldwyn-Mayer including *The Chocolate Soldier* and *Going My Way*. She is also a popular television personality, and appears frequently in long coast to coast concert tours in the United States.

Her European appearances in the post-war period have been few in number; Octavian at the Paris Opéra in 1949; Cherubino at Glyndebourne in 1955 (which was recorded); and Erodiade in Mortari's *La Figlia del Diavolo* which she created at La Scala, Milan in 1954.

LEOPOLD SIMONEAU

as *Alfredo* in 'La Traviata'

as *Don Ottavio* in 'Don Giovanni'

as *Jane Seymour* in 'Anna Bolena'

as *Rosina* in 'Il Barbiere di Siviglia'

GIULIETTA SIMIONATO

as *Azucena* in 'Il Trovatore'

GIULIETTA SIMIONATO
as *Princess Eboli* in 'Don Carlos'

ELEANOR STEBER

as *Minnie* in 'La Fanciulla del West'

as *Marie* in 'Wozzeck'

ANTONIETTA STELLA

as *Aida*

as *Elisabetta* in 'Don Carlos' and as *Madama Butterfly*

TERESA STICH-RANDALL

as herself

as *Fiordiligi* in 'Così fan tutte'

EBE STIGNANI

as *Laura Adorno* in 'La Gioconda'

as *Adalgisa* in 'Norma'

RISË STEVENS

as *Carmen*

as *Orfeo*

as *Octavian* in 'Der Rosenkavalier'

TERESA STICH-RANDALL

THOSE opera enthusiasts who possess the famous Toscanini recordings of *Aida* and *Falstaff* will know that Teresa Stich-Randall sang the small role of the Priestess in the first, and the more important part of Nannetta in the second. In both recordings however she displays a beautiful fresh young voice, and sings with that great purity of style that has ever since become the hall-mark of her performances. The *Aida* was recorded in April 1949, the *Falstaff* the following year, when the singer was twenty-two and twenty-three years old respectively.

How did it come about that this young American soprano was chosen by Toscanini for these two Verdi performances? As is so often the case luck had a good deal to do with it. Teresa Stich-Randall, who was born in New Hartford, Connecticut in 1927, has been singing in public ever since she was five, taking part in church socials. When she was ten she entered the Hartford School of Music, and five years later became a music student at Columbia University in New York. While there she sang the role of Gertrude Stein in the Virgil Thomson-Stein opera, *The Mother of Us All* in 1947, and the title-role in Otto Luening's *Evangeline* the following year. She then took part in some performances given by the New Lyric Stage touring company, and also sang in several concerts broadcast by the National Broadcasting Company. It was after one of these, in which she had sung Violetta's aria from *La Traviata* that she was summoned to the studio telephone and heard a strange voice ask her in a heavy Italian accent, 'Are you the young lady who has just sung the aria from *La Traviata* on the N.B.C?' When she said that she was, the voice asked her whether she was interested in singing the role of the Priestess in *Aida* the following day in place of the soprano originally engaged who had fallen ill. The young singer thought this was some kind of joke and asked the 'voice' whether he was serious. The speaker at the other end of the telephone became annoyed, and told her that if she was interested in in his proposal she had better decide within the next two hours, and left a telephone number.

Stich-Randall was interested, and still not knowing to whom she had been speaking, telephoned the number she had been given. A voice answered 'Maestro Toscanini's residence'. Thus began one of the most successful careers in opera today.

Toscanini was much impressed by the soprano's voice, musicianship and seriousness of purpose, that he invited her to sing Nannetta in the *Falstaff* broadcast with him. In this role she created a great impression which resulted in an invitation from the Metropolitan for her to join the company. At the same time she was offered a Fulbright award to go and study in Europe. She was at a loss at what to do, and not un-naturally she consulted Toscanini, who advised her to go to Europe—'The Met. can wait' he said. And so with an introduction from the Italian conductor and a Fulbright award the young soprano crossed the Atlantic.

In January 1951 Stich-Randall won first prize in the Concours International for opera singers at Lausanne, and in October the same year, she won a further award at the Geneva Competition. These two prizes led to appearances at the Basle Opera, and concerts and radio engagements in Switzerland and Italy. Indeed between the two competitions, she was engaged to sing the part of the Mermaid in Weber's *Oberon* in the open-air performance of Weber's opera at the 1951 Florence Festival, which entailed her swimming across the lake of the Boboli Gardens as well as singing!

The following year she returned to Florence to sing Amenaide in Rossini's *Tancredi*, and then she made her first appearance in Austria at the 1952 Salzburg Festival under Paumgartner. This resulted in an engagement at the Vienna State Opera, where she made her début in October that year as Violetta. She has been one of the leading members of the Vienna Opera ever since where her roles have included Micaela, Giulietta in *Les Contes d'Hoffmann*, Constanze, Pamina, the Countess, Fiordiligi, Sophie in *Der Rosenkavalier*, and Titania in Britten's *A Midsummer Night's Dream*.

It is perhaps as a Mozart singer that Stich-Randall has earned for herself a special place in post-war opera—and it has been rather at the yearly Aix-en-Provence Festival than in Vienna that her Mozart singing has been most appreciated. 'Teresa Stich-Randall is certainly one of the best Countesses today; beauty of vocal colour, musical sensitivity, elegant phrasing, and also her fine bearing, give great distinction to her assumption of the role', wrote

Jacques Bourgeois one of France's leading critics in *Opera* in 1953. And five years later Andrew Porter wrote of her Pamina, 'Teresa Stich-Randall, regular primadonna of the Aix company, sang Pamina with limpid full tone, and delicately studied phrasing. Her imaginative handling of the G minor aria was exquisite'. The soprano's singing of the same role at the Rome Opera during the 1958-9 season created a sensation, as did her Fiordiligi at Naples and Ariadne at Lisbon.

With the exception of a Gilda at the Chicago Opera in 1955, the American soprano's career was entirely confined to Europe until 1961 when she made a highly successful début as the Countess in Mexico City, following it up with a Sophie in *Rosenkavalier* (a role she sings exquisitely as can be heard on the complete HMV recording with Elizabeth Schwarzkopf and Christa Ludwig, under Karajan). She then returned to the States to make her Metropolitan début as Fiordiligi and to sing again in Chicago as Donna Anna. It surely cannot be long before she is heard at either Covent Garden or Glyndebourne —she is already well known in England as a concert artist.

Off-stage the soprano is as attractive as she is on. The sense of humour and high spirits which break through her Fiordiligi are much in evidence, and she is a brilliant conversationalist. She loves good food, good company and hot, sunny weather. Yet never far below the surface is that seriousness of purpose that has always characterized her approach to music, especially to that of Mozart.

EBE STIGNANI

EBE STIGNANI, like most great artists of the day, has been hailed with superlatives and catch-phrases: 'the Flagstad of Italy', 'the greatest living exponent of the art of *bel canto*', 'one of the greatest voices now before the public'. The great difference in the case of Stignani however, is that these claims happen to be true.

Ebe Stignani was born in Naples in July 1904. Her parents had come to Naples from Rome, where her father was a salesman of machinery, and Ebe was their only child. When she was ten she entered the Naples Conservatory of San Pietro a Maiella as a student of the piano. Her course of studies included choral singing which she began at the age of fifteen, and it was then that her unusual voice was heard for the first time.

Her voice teacher at the Conservatory was Agostino Roche; and it was he who recognised the phenomenal range and extraordinary sensitivity of Stignani's voice. He advised her against singing dramatic and lyric-soprano parts, and to take full advantage of the natural colouring of the voice and sing mezzo-soprano and contralto parts. It seems hardly necessary to add that she followed his advice.

In July 1925 she graduated with a degree for voice and piano, having also studied harmony and counterpoint. At the graduation concert she was heard by the director of the San Carlo Opera House who immediately offered her a contract which she accepted. Her début was made later the same year in the part of Amneris under the direction of Gino Marinuzzi. She remained at the San Carlo for the whole of the 1925-6 season, making fifty-four appearances.

After her Naples season she went to Venice and there she was heard by one of the directors of the Scala who invited her to Milan for an audition with Toscanini. At the conclusion of the audition Toscanini merely nodded his head, and the young Ebe was left in doubt as to its outcome; she did not have to worry for long, for the next morning's post brought her the Scala contract for the 1926-7 season.

Her Scala début took place on 22nd December, 1926 as Eboli in *Don Carlos*. This was the eighth and last performance of the opera for the season, and she took over her part from Giuseppina Cobelli. Her colleagues on that occasion were Bianca Scacciati as Elisabeth de Valois, Antonin Trantoul as Don Carlos, Carlo Galeffi as Posa and Tancredi Pasero as Philip; the conductor was the young Antonino Votto, who took over the performance which had been prepared by Toscanini. The critic of the *Corriere della Sera* wrote: 'Mme. Stignani displayed a sweetness of voice and precision of technique which fully merited the unanimous applause with which she was acclaimed.'

During her first season at the Scala she also sang Aennchen in *Der Freischütz*, Gutrune, Amneris, and Laura in *La Gioconda*, a part that was to become one of her greatest. The *Gioconda* performance was conducted by Toscanini and the title part was sung by Giannina Arangi-Lombardi. In the next season she repeated the parts of Aennchen and Eboli and added that of Meg in *Falstaff*. She had the added satisfaction however of being the only Eboli for the *Don Carlos* performances, and of having Toscanini to conduct the opera for her. As season succeeded season at the Scala her repertory expanded and by the end of the 1933-4 season she had added Preziosilla, Azucena, Fenena (*Nabucco*), Adalgisa, Rubria (*Nerone*), Ortrud, Brangaene, Leonora (*Favorita*), Marina (*Boris*), and Cathos (*Le Preziose Ridicole*) to her earlier parts.

After the departure of Toscanini from the Scala, there was a sad lowering of standards, which continued until De Sabata became one of the theatre's regular conductors, and it was under his baton that many of Stignani's greatest triumphs of the 1930's took place. The 1934-5 season opened with a revival of Ponchielli's seldom heard *Il figliuol prodigo* (*The Prodigal Son*); this was part of the centenary celebrations for the composer's birth that were held all over Italy during the 1934-5 season. Stignani sang the part of Nefte, and the rest of the cast included Gina Cigna, Antonio Melandri, Carlo Tagliabue and Tancredi Pasero; Victor De Sabata was again the conductor. During the same season she was heard as Eudosia in Respighi's *La Fiamma* and as Music and Silvia in Monteverdi's *Orfeo*.

It was during the 1935-6 season at the Scala, that Stignani sang, under De Sabata, the part of Delilah, a part she herself describes as her favourite role, 'combining as it does the operatic and oratorio styles. Delilah is a noble enchantress and a woman of dignity who sacrifices herself for the good of her people' says Mme. Stignani. One of the leading Italian critics of her first Scala Delilah wrote that 'she offered a glowing interpretation of the part, an unforgettable portrayal'.

During this period Ebe Stignani was heard not only in every Italian opera house of importance, but in South America, Switzerland, Spain, Germany, and elsewhere in Europe. Her repertory was still growing and included Maria (*Mosè*), Arsace (*Semiramide*), La grande vestale (*Vestale*), Isabella (*L'Italiana in Algeri*), Orfeo (Gluck), Ulrica, Mistress Quickly, Principessa di Bouillon (*Adriana Lecouvreur*), Madélon (*Andrea Chénier*), La Voce (*Lucrezia*: Respighi), Santuzza, Carmen, Marta (*Khovanshchina*), and Hänsel.

Stignani was not heard at Covent Garden until 1937—she was to have come to sing Eboli in Beecham's *Don Carlos* revival of 1933, but was prevented from so doing by previous commitments in South America. Her Covent Garden début took place on 7 May, 1937 as Amneris in an *Aida* performance whose cast included Gina Cigna in the title-role, Martinelli as Radames and Cesare Formichi as Amonasro; Francesco Salfi was the conductor. She returned to Covent Garden in 1939 and was heard as Azucena in the last *Trovatore* performance that season conducted by Gui, with Cigna, Jussi Björling and Armando Borgioli, and once again as Amneris in a superb *Aida* with Caniglia, Gigli and Borgioli and conducted by Beecham. Although the *cognoscenti* among the audience recognised her great vocal achievements, the critics, with one or two noteworthy exceptions like Francis Toye and Dyneley Hussey, were not exactly enthusiastic. Indeed the doyen of our English critics could only describe her as 'an efficient workwoman of the ordinary Italian opera type'! It was left to Hussey writing in the *Spectator* in June 1939 to show a true understanding of her art as far as London was concerned: 'Mme. Stignani's Amneris is one of those rare performances that provide a pattern of how a particular part should be sung. Her voice is of great power and beauty, with its dramatic excitement in every tone that makes the great Verdi singer—I heard part of her broadcast in *Il Trovatore*, and though the radio is a searching test to operatic singers, what I heard was faultless and I cannot imagine "Ai nostri monti" sung better.'

She made her American début with the San Francisco opera in 1938, and although engaged by Edward Johnson for the Metropolitan in the 1939-40 season, was unable to leave Europe because of the war. Not until 1948 did she make her début in New York, and that was in concert and not opera. Virgil Thomson, that most demanding of American critics, said of her début, 'her reputation as an artist was completely justified—there is no questioning the perfection of her style.' While Howard Taubman was able to write in the *New York Times*: 'It may be that the art of *bel canto* is dying as the gloomy ones say, but you couldn't tell it last night at Carnegie Hall where Ebe Stignani made her New York début.'

New York opera-lovers made pilgrimages to Philadelphia to hear her sing in *Gioconda* and *Trovatore*. Cecil Smith writing in *Musical America* after witnessing her performance as Laura said: 'In this reviewer's opinion, her excessive weight does not constitute a satisfactory reason for the Metropolitan's failure to engage so supreme an Italian singer, if indeed this is the reason for a neglect that nobody who has heard Stignani will be able to understand.' I personally am not surprised, for I have seen a letter from a certain agent to the pre-war Covent Garden management recommending another mezzo-soprano for the part of Amneris on the grounds that although Stignani was vocally unrivalled in that part, her figure was against her!

London audiences are faithful to their favourites, and when Stignani returned in the summer of 1952 to sing Azucena, she was given a rapturous welcome. She certainly deserved it, for her singing was a model of the Italian *bel-canto* style. And when she came back again a few months later to sing Adalgisa to Callas's Norma, enthusiasm knew no bounds. She repeated her Amneris at Covent Garden in 1955, her Adalgisa in 1957, and her Azucena at Drury Lane in 1958.

In Italy she continued to delight audiences at La Scala and elsewhere until recently as Eboli, Adalgisa, and Orfeo. Her voice extending from low F to high C has retained its youthfulness. She uses her wonderful chest register to great dramatic effect, and never indulges in those vulgarities which characterize the efforts of her less tasteful compatriots.

Like most great artists she is extremely modest, and she feels that there is always something new to learn. 'I have never had to struggle to succeed, but I have felt sharply the responsibility to do always a little better than last time'. And that she has always done. She is certainly assured of an honoured place in operatic history.

RITA STREICH

ONE of the most popular coloratura sopranos and soubrettes in post-war opera is the German soprano Rita Streich. She was born in Barnaul in Russia of Russian and German parentage in December 1920. Soon after her birth her family returned to Germany, living first in Essen and then in Jena. While still at school her piano teacher, charmed by her pretty voice, persuaded her to take up singing. She began her voice studies at Augsburg, her first voice teacher being a pupil of the famous Maria Ivogün, still considered the greatest of Zerbinettas. Later she studied with Ivogün herself. She then moved to Berlin where she continued her studies with another great coloratura soprano, Erna Berger, who took her on as her only pupil.

At the end of the war, Rita Streich concluded her stage training, and made her début at the East Berlin State Opera in the 1945-6 season singing Amor in *Orfeo*, Blöndchen in *Die Entführung aus dem Serail*, and Olympia in *Hoffmann*. She remained at the State Opera for six seasons, adding Zerlina, Sophie, Gilda, Adina and other roles to her repertory. She was invited to make guest appearances at a number of western German opera houses, and in 1951 became a permanent member of the Städtische Oper in west Berlin. During the next few seasons she extended her repertory still further to include Zerbinetta, Queen of Night and Susanna. In 1952 and 1953 she sang the Woodbird at Bayreuth; and began to make appearances outside Germany: in Paris as Susanna, Vienna as Gilda, Rosina, Zerlina, and Rome as Queen of Night.

It was not long before she was heard at the Salzburg and Aix-en-Provence festivals; at Salzburg she sang Aennchen in *Freischütz* under Furtwängler in 1954 and the following summer at Aix she sang Despina and Susanna. Her London début followed her 1954 Salzburg appearances; this was with the Vienna Opera in its second post-war visit to London when she sang Susanna and Zerlina, without indulging in the usual gush to which so many German and Austrian Mozart soubrettes are prone.

Streich returned to Salzburg in the summer of 1956, and the following year was to have made her Glyndebourne début, but unfortunately was prevented from doing so by a virus infection that she contracted during rehearsals. She eventually came to Glyndebourne in 1958. Before this however she made her successful American début at San Francisco in September 1957 as Sophie, following it a week later with Zerbinetta in the local première of Strauss's *Ariadne auf Naxos*: 'her voice was sweet and agile in her fiendishly difficult aria, and her characterization had great personal charm' wrote the critic of *Musical America*. Her third role that season was Despina. The soprano returned to San Francisco in 1958 to sing Zerbinetta which was also the role of her postponed Glyndebourne début; and in 1960 she made her Chicago début as Suzanna.

It is in a small opera house that Rita Streich makes her best effect, for truth to tell her exquisite art and voice is lost in the vaster reaches of large theatres. The gramophone however is a perfect medium for her art, and her Queen of Night, Zerbinetta, and especially her Sophie, are the best modern interpretations and performances of these roles on disc.

JOAN SUTHERLAND

ONE of the most amazing and at the same time gratifying leaps into stardom in recent years has been achieved by the Australian soprano, Joan Sutherland, who has been one of the members of the Covent Garden Opera Company since 1952. Not since the days of Melba has there been a British soprano capable of sustaining the great lyric-coloratura roles in the Italian repertory—and the comparison with Melba is made even more valid, as Sutherland, like her great predecessor, is an Australian.

She was born in Sydney, New South Wales in November 1926. When she left school she took a secretarial post and studied singing in her spare time. In 1947 she had advanced far enough to sing in a concert performance of *Dido and Aeneas* and in 1950 she entered for the 'Sun' aria competition—which she won, and also received a Mobil Quest award which included a £1000 scholarship. During this year she sang in oratorios and concerts in Australia, and also sang the title-role in Eugene Goossens's *Judith* at the Sydney Conservatory.

In 1951 Joan Sutherland came to London to study at the Royal College of Music with Clive Carey, and in 1952 sang Giorgetta in *Il Tabarro* in the College's summer opera production. Her potentialities were immediately recognised—typical of the press comments on this student performance were those of Arthur Jacobs who wrote in *Opera*: 'The most arresting portrayal came from Joan Sutherland; here is a dramatic soprano of high quality and well-controlled power. Doubtless Clive Carey has assisted Miss Sutherland to develop her considerable stage presence; and one may confidently look forward to hearing more of her'.

Meanwhile Joan Sutherland had given three Covent Garden auditions—for already her large flexible voice was capable of singing 'Ritorna vincitor' from *Aida* and 'Qui la voce' from *I Puritani*, to say nothing of Elisabeth's Greeting from *Tannhäuser*! Altogether she sang thirteen different arias in her three Covent Garden auditions before she was given a contract for the 1952-3 season.

Her Covent Garden début was on October 28, 1952 as the First Lady in *The Magic Flute*; this was followed with Clothilde in the famous Callas-Stignani *Norma*, an Amelia in *Un Ballo in Maschera*, the Countess in *Figaro*, the Overseer in *Elektra*, and some performances of Lady Penelope Rich in Britten's Coronation opera, *Gloriana*.

Sutherland opened her second Covent Garden season by singing Helmwige in *Die Walküre*, Frasquita in a new production of *Carmen*, the off-stage Priestess in *Aida*, and then on May 13, 1954, Agathe in *Freischütz*. Cecil Smith wrote in *Opera*: 'With a competence as impressive as it was modest, she established herself as one of the whitest hopes of the soprano department. Her voice is a true operatic lyric soprano. It is large enough to carry across the orchestra all the time in all registers. It is round and rich, yet pure and clear. Her A flats in "Und ob die Wolke" were as enchanting in texture as any tones we have heard all year. As yet she has not quite the flexibility to take all of Agathe's earlier scena at the desirable pace, but there is nothing about her basic method of singing that should keep her from developing all the flexibility in the world..... Naturally she needs to acquire and perfect a repertoire. Once she has done this she should become and remain an important asset to the company'.

And this of course is what she has done and has become since those words were first written. During the remainder of the 1953-4 season she was heard again as Penelope Rich, the Overseer, Helmwige, a most mellifluous Rhinemaiden (Woglinde), and as the Woodbird. In this year too she sang the title role in Weber's *Euryanthe* for the B.B.C. and she married her childhood friend from Australia, Richard Bonynge, who has been so valuable to her as a coach and in musical problems connected with

Italian vocal writing of the nineteenth century.

The 1954-5 season saw her creating Jenifer in the world première of Tippett's *The Midsummer Marriage*, a role that had some of the most fiendishly difficult vocal music to sing, and which she coped with in a breath-taking fashion. She also sang during the course of the season all three soprano roles in *Les Contes d'Hoffmann*. During the following two years she added Micaela, Pamina, Eva, and Gilda to her repertory, and in the summer of 1956 sang the *Figaro* Countess and the First Lady at Glyndebourne. In March 1957 she took a great step forward when she sang the title role in Handel's *Alcina* in a production by the Handel Society. On this occasion she displayed a beauty of tone, technique, control, that surprised even her warmest admirers, and sang with an ease and assurance that she had rarely displayed up to that time in public. A few weeks later at Covent Garden she sang her first Gilda, and gave a foretaste of what was to come two years later when she tackled Lucia.

At Glyndebourne in the summer of 1957 she sang Mme. Herz in Mozart's *Der Schauspeildirektor* and gave a finely accomplished display of singing. In December the same year she sang Desdemona at Covent Garden with a purity and simplicity that were quite disarming. In the English première of Poulenc's *The Carmelites* a fortnight later her beautifully sung Madame Lidoine was much admired. Then in the summer of 1958 she went to Vancouver where she scored a great success as Donna Anna in Rennert's production of *Don Giovanni*.

It was the 1958-59 season that finally set the seal on her career, with her triumphant Lucia. She had already scored a great success in Covent Garden's contribution to the Handel celebrations when she sang the Israelite Woman in *Samson*. 'It was worth waiting three hours', wrote W. S. Mann 'to hear the liquid gold, and springing mercury of her voice in this great aria' [Let the Bright Seraphim].

To prepare Lucia, Covent Garden sent her to Italy to study the role with the great Tullio Serafin, who had been engaged to conduct the work, and then when she returned to London, she was produced by that young genius of the Italian opera houses, Franco Zeffirelli. He helped her to turn Lucia into a flesh and blood creature.

Vocally she was able to colour words and phrases with poignancy and great meaning; and her singing of the coloratura made it sound child's play. Her runs, trills and ornamentations were both marvellous and breath-taking. In the morning she awoke to find herself famous, and invitations began to arrive from foreign opera houses. In Vienna she has sung Donna Anna and Desdemona; in Venice, Alcina; and her Lucia was heard in Paris, Palermo and elsewhere before the end of the 1959-60 season. She opened the 1960 Glyndebourne season as Elvira in a revival of *I Puritani*, and then began the 1960-61 Covent Garden season as Amina in a new production of *La Sonnambula*.

Sutherland's Scala début was in the title role of *Beatrice di Tenda* during the 1960-61 season, and inevitably she sang her Lucia there. Indeed 1961 was a Lucia year for her with performances in Edinburgh, Paris, London, Dallas, San Francisco, Chicago and New York. She returned to La Scala in 1962 to sing the title role in Rossini's *Semiramide*, in its first performance there since the 1880s.

She has many plans for the future: Norma, Anna Bolena, Lucrezia Borgia, Cleopatra, and Elena in Rossini's *La Donna del Lago*. These of course are serious roles, but Sutherland also has hankerings after lighter parts—Norina in *Don Pasquale* and Adina in *L'Elisir d'Amore*. As off-stage the soprano has a marvellous sense of humour and is full of good spirits, there is no reason why she should not tackle lighter parts. With her heaven-sent voice and great musical gifts there are boundless possibilities for her future, always provided she does not become too pianured in her singing and pays attention to her diction.

SET SVANHOLM

WAGNERIAN *heldentenors*, as any operatic impresario will tell one, are hard to come by; the great ones of this century can be counted on the fingers of one hand—Jean de Reszke (he just gets in, he sang his last Wagner roles in 1901), Peter Cornelius, Lauritz Melchior, Max Lorenz, and Set Svanholm. Like two of his distinguished predecessors, Cornelius and Melchior, Svanholm is a Scandinavian; and like de Reszke and Melchior, he began his career as a baritone.

Set Karl Viktor Svanholm, to give him his full name,

was born in Västerås, the eighth city of Sweden, on September 2, 1904. His Father was the pastor of the Lutheran Church, his mother a school teacher. The young Set began his musical training under the guidance of his father, who taught him to play the organ; not only did he play for the services in his father's church, but he also became choirmaster and conductor.

While still at school, he sang as a boy-soprano in the school choir; and he recalls that one member of his class, writing a criticism of the boys' performance wrote, 'One of the boys made a false entry, the boy's name is Svanholm'; that must have been the first written musical criticism he received!

Even before matriculating, Svanholm began his career at Tillberga, where in 1922 he was appointed organist; then at Säby, where from 1924 to 1927, he was both organist and school-teacher. By 1927 he had been able to save enough money to enrol as a student at the Stockholm Conservatory, where he remained until 1929. There he underwent a very thorough musical training; he became a more than competent pianist, and studied composition and counterpoint; these accomplishments go a long way to explain Svanholm's great musicality. After his two years at the Conservatory, he was appointed choir master at St. James's Church in Stockholm, a position he held for twenty years.

At the Conservatory, Svanholm became one of the four pupils of John Forsell, a famous baritone and the director of the Stockholm Opera. In his audition for Forsell, he sang Wolfram's 'O du mein holder Abendstern'; Forsell is said to have remarked that if Svanholm made a success it would not be as a Wagnerian! The other three pupils of Forsell at that time were a tenor called Jussi Björling, a bass-baritone called Joel Berglund, and a soprano called Nini Högstedt, who gave up her ideas of becoming an opera singer, and became Mrs. Svanholm instead.

In the autumn of 1930 Svanholm made his operatic début at the Royal Opera, as Silvio in *Pagliacci*, following it up a year later with Figaro in *Il Barbiere di Siviglia*, with Jussi Björling as Almaviva.

Svanholm says that he imitated Forsell in all he did; indeed, so similar was the timbre of both their voices, that once Forsell suggested to Svanholm that he should sing the off-stage measures that prelude Figaro's first entrance in *Il Barbiere* at an actual performance at the Stockholm Opera; Forsell did this, and no one in the theatre, artist or audience, noticed!

It was not long however before Svanholm came to the conclusion that he was not a baritone, but a tenor; he had only sung baritone as a young man he declares, because he considered it more manly, and all the time he was studying, he was able to emit high B's. So, encouraged by his wife, he embarked on a further period of vocal study, this time on his own. He did not find the transition difficult, and soon his voice was becoming fuller and freer. When he felt he was ready to sing a tenor role, he went to Forsell and told him that he had discovered a new tenor. 'Who is it?' asked his teacher; 'It's me,' replied Svanholm —and then sang 'Celeste Aida' for him.

On September 22, 1936, came Svanholm's second Stockholm début; this time as Radames in *Aida*. Then followed Max in *Freischütz*, and Don José, which he learned in ten days; and in 1937, Lohengrin and Siegmund, which were both his first Wagnerian roles, and the first parts he sang in German.

He was, at this time, heard by Bruno Walter, who invited him to come to Vienna in 1938. This was the beginning of Svanholm's international career, and soon engagements followed at Berlin, Munich, Prague and Budapest. At the last mentioned city he was a special favourite, singing often opposite Maria Müller; he made a great success as Otello, and as Manrico in *Il Trovatore*, and on one occasion he had to sing 'Di quella pira' three times. In the summer of 1938 he sang Walther and Tannhäuser at Salzburg. In 1940 he was offered a contract by the Metropolitan Opera in New York, but was prevented from going to America by the war. In 1942 he sang Tannhäuser at the Scala, in Italian, and Erik and Siegfried at Bayreuth.

During the war years Svanholm had the great advantage of being able to work with Leo Blech, who had made his home in Sweden, and conducted regularly at the Stockholm Opera; Svanholm feels that he owes a lot artistically to Blech. By the end of the war he had increased his repertory enormously, and it then included Florestan, Bacchus, Vasco da Gama in *L'Africaine*, Samson, Canio, Otello, Calaf, Laca in *Jenufa*, Vladimir in *Prince Igor*, most of the Wagnerian four parts, and roles in Swedish opera such as Dudley in Fried Walter's *Queen Elizabeth*, Martin Skarp in Kurt Attenberg's *Fanal*, and Tord in Oskar Lindberg's *Fredlös*.

1946 was an important year for Svanholm; in Stockholm he sang the title role in the first performance outside England of Britten's *Peter Grimes*; he crossed the Atlantic for the first time, singing Tristan and Siegmund in South America at Rio; he made his North American début, singing Lohengrin at San Francisco, and finally on November 15, made his Metropolitan début as the young Siegfried.

'He is not only an exceptionally gifted singer,' wrote Olin Downes in the *New York Times*, 'but also, it appears, a sound musician who sings his part accurately as it is written'.

During his first season in New York, Svanholm was also heard as Tristan, Siegmund, Walther, Parsifal and Radames. He sang in New York regularly from 1946 to 1956, and besides his Wagnerian roles has been heard as Florestan, Herod in *Salome*, Aegisth in *Elektra*, Admète in *Alceste*, Einstein in *Fledermaus*, and Otello.

Svanholm's London popularity dates from November 11, 1948, when he made his Covent Garden début in *Siegfried*, with Astrid Varnay as Brünnhilde, Hans Hotter as the Wanderer and Peter Klein as Mime. 'In Mr. Svanholm, a Swedish tenor, a successor has at last been found to Mr. Melchior, a Siegfried indeed, who with all respect to Mr. Melchior looks more like a young stripling. Indeed this Siegfried was almost too attractive a character, hardly showing those Nazi symptoms which young Siegfrieds were apt to display even before the days of the Hitler Youth. Mr. Svanholm looked well, sang well and acted well!' So wrote *The Times*; while Desmond Shawe-Taylor, writing in *The New Statesman*, remarked that Svanholm was a thorough musician of a type unfamiliar in the world of opera.

Svanholm became a regular visitor to Covent Garden, where he has sung Loge, Siegmund, both Siegfrieds, Walther, Lohengrin and Tristan. He has also sung with great success in other European opera houses and at the Teatro Colon in Buenos Aires, where he sang the part of Apollo in the first non-European performance of Strauss's *Daphne* in 1948.

Svanholm's musicianship has been mentioned more than once in this biography. This, plus his great intelligence, two virtues which are not possessed by many tenors, make him an ideal Wagnerian; for in Wagner's operas, perhaps above all others the treatment of text is of the utmost importance. Several critics including Ernest Newman, have pointed out how scrupulous Svanholm is in adhering to the note values, unlike his famous predecessor at Covent Garden and in New York; how precise is his rhythm, and how he gauges each phrase to a nicety as a musical-verbal entity.

It is not easy to cite individual examples of Svanholm's art; but perhaps I can give two: a specific one from *Siegfried*, and a more general one from *Götterdämmerung*. His young Siegfried has always been praised, and when he is at the top of his form, as he was during the London *Ring* cycles 1955, he will suddenly illuminate a phrase with a beauty of tone and a display of *legato* which even his best friends will admit he too rarely uses, as in the pianissimo on 'In schlafe liegt eine Frau', in the awakening scene in the last act. Then there is the wonderful mass of detail with which he invests the older Siegfried, especially in the last act of *Götterdämmerung*; first in the scene with the Rhinemaidens then in the narration to the Vassals, and lastly in his very moving death scene.

In 1955 Svanholm was appointed artistic director of the Stockholm Opera in succession to another singer, Joel Berglund, who had held the position since 1949. This meant the end of Svanholm's international career, so after two appearances as Parsifal at the Metropolitan in the spring of 1956, and an unscheduled but highly successful *Götterdämmerung* at Covent Garden opposite Birgit Nilsson, in the autumn of that year, he has confined his operatic appearances to a few each season with his own company at Stockholm. It was with the Stockholm Opera that he sang again in Great Britain in the summer of 1959, when the ensemble visited Edinburgh. As Siegmund he showed that he had lost little if any of his artistry, and his voice sounded better than on many occasions in previous years.

Ill-health forced Svanholm to resign his post at the Stockholm Opera in May 1963, and his death in October 1964 came as a severe blow to the world of opera.

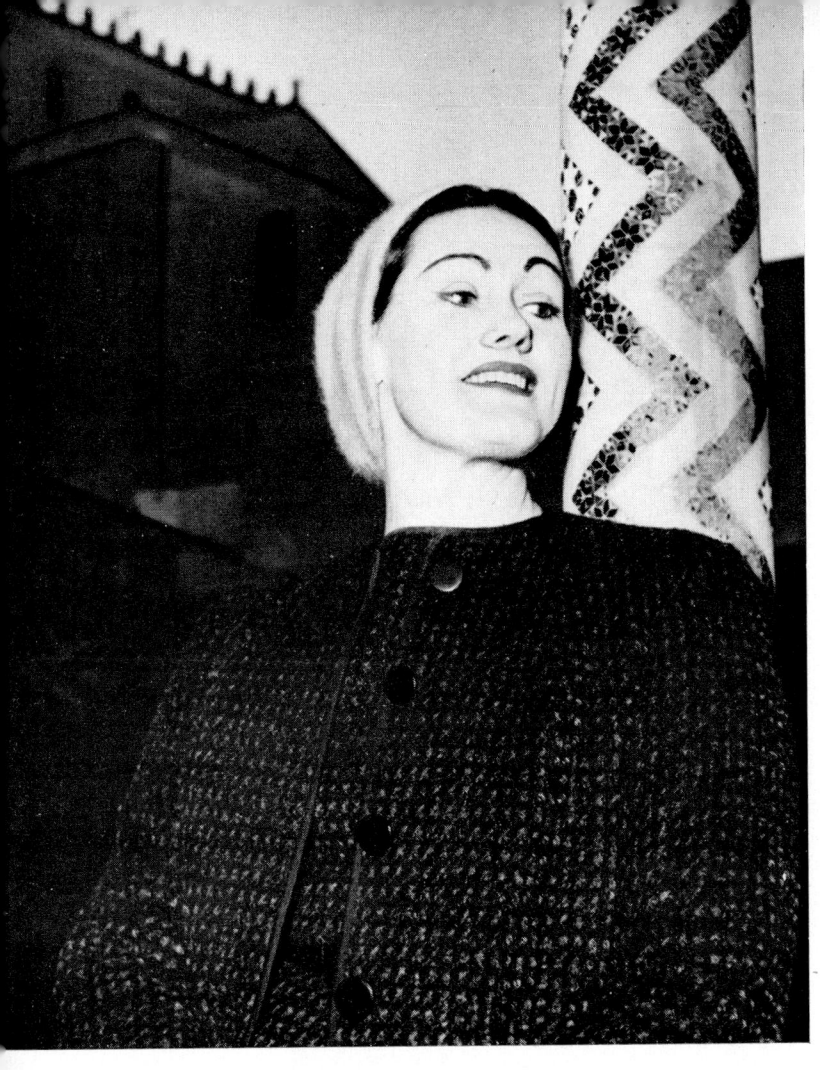

JOAN SUTHERLAND

as herself

as *Alcina* in 'Handel's Opera'

as *Lucia*

JOAN SUTHERLAND
as *Elvira* in 'I Puritani'

SET SVANHOLM

as *Siegfried*

as *Tristan*

FERRUCCIO TAGLIAVINI
as *Werther*

RITA STREICH
as *Zerbinetta* with

HEINZ BLANKENBURG
as *Harlequin* in 'Ariadne auf Naxos'

RENATA TEBALDI

as *Olimpia* in Spontini's opera of that name

as *Tosca*

RENATA TEBALDI

as herself

BLANCHE THEBOM

as *Amneris* in 'Aïda'

as *Dido* in 'The Trojans'   as *Dalila*

RICHARD TUCKER

as *Andrea Chénier*

as *Don Alvaro* in 'La Forza del Destino'

HERMANN UHDE

as *Mandryka* in 'Arabella'

as *Gunther* in 'Götterdämmerung'

as *Wozzeck*

ASTRID VARNAY

as *Elektra*

as *Brünnhilde* in 'Götterdämmerung'

as *Count Almaviva* in 'Il Barbiere di Siviglia'

CESARE VALLETTI

as *Des Grieux* in 'Manon'

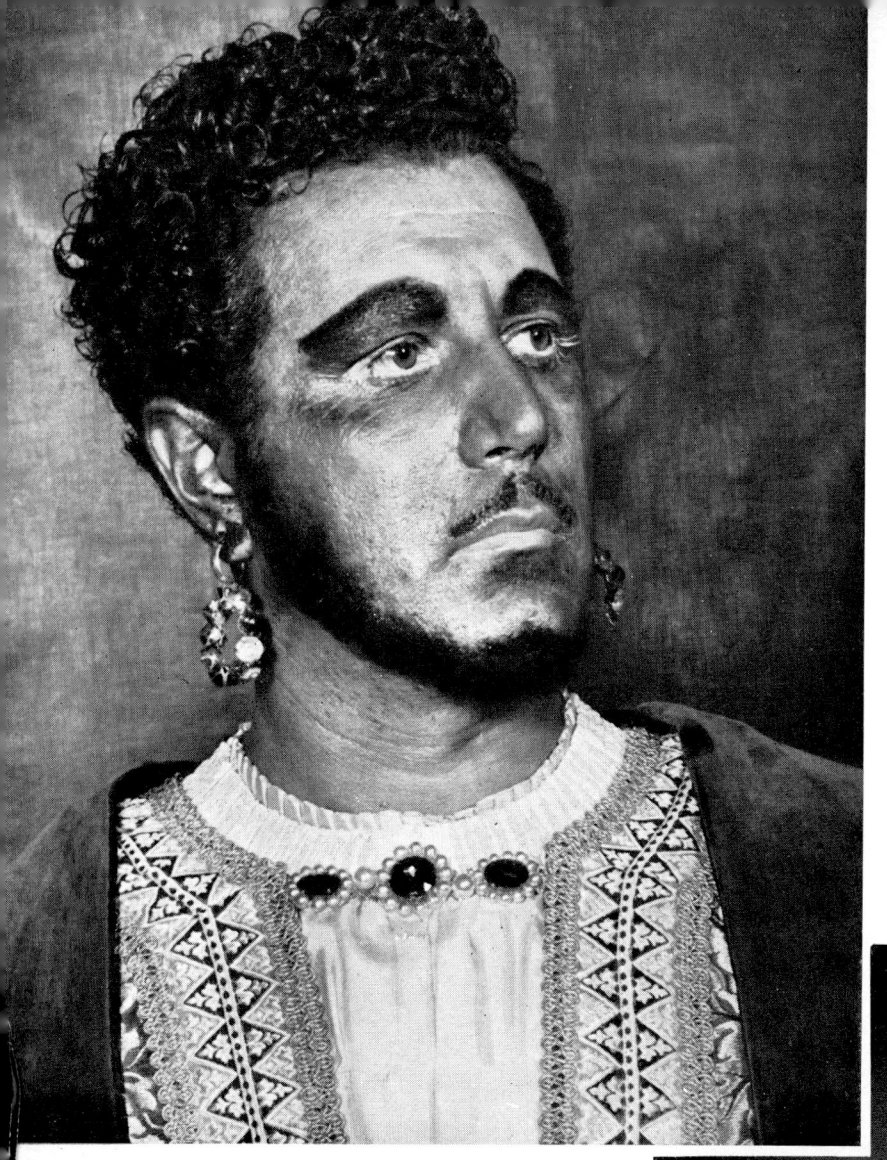

RAMON VINAY

as *Tristan*

as *Otello*

FERRUCCIO TAGLIAVINI

THE story of the favourite tenor seems always to read more like a novel than do the lives of the soprano or baritone, and with Tagliavini, no less than his predecessor Gigli, the story of how he became Italy's leading tenor in a very short time, is no exception to this rule.

He was born in Reggio Emilia in 1913, and like many boys before him sang in the local church choir. He received no formal education, being taught with the children of a wealthy gentleman for whom his father worked as an overseer. In his early teens however he did attend a local school, and while there made his first public appearance in an operetta called *La Gran Via* in which he was cast in the part of a policemen! Of course the leading singer fell ill, and Tagliavini had to replace him, earning for himself the nickname of 'Il piccolo Caruso'.

Tagliavini soon abandoned any pretensions he might have for making a career in singing, and instead entered the engineering and mechanics business. He served his term of military service in the army and then resumed his business career. He still sang for pleasure, and his father even tried to persuade him to take up singing—a welcome change from those parents who have tried to prevent their children from pursuing a musical career. At length he was persuaded to spend a few hours a week studying under Brancucci.

In 1938 he entered for the Concorso Nazional Italiano in the lowest grade. He won the local, regional and finally the national competition, singing 'O Paradiso' from *L'Africana* on each occasion. The national 'bel-canto' prize took him to Florence where he undertook a seven months' course with the famous tenor Amadeo Bassi, and on October 28, 1939, he made his début at the Teatro Comunale of Florence as Rodolfo in *La Bohème*.

There was no slow progress through provincial houses for Tagliavini, for immediately engagements began to flow in. The Florence Festival, La Scala, Milan, and the Teatro Reale dell' Opera, Rome, all heard him during the first two or three years of his career. His roles at this time included Tamino, Duca di Mantova, Almaviva, Elvino, Fritz, Nemorino, Edgardo, Federico in *L'Arlesiana*, Des Grieux and Werther. His partner in many of these operas was the soprano Pia Tassinari, and the story of how he met her, sang with her, and finally proposed to her in an air-raid shelter also reads like a novel.

The war had naturally delayed Tagliavini's international career, but his reputation had spread across the Atlantic during the 1940s, and in the summer of 1946 he was heard at the Teatro Colon, Buenos Aires, as Cavaradossi and Rodolfo; at Rio de Janeiro in the same two roles and as Werther; and in Mexico City as Edgardo and Cavaradossi. In the autumn of 1946 he made his United States début in Chicago as Rodolfo. Claudia Cassidy, writing in the *Chicago Tribune* said: 'He has the full tenor range, and a quality, that may, when knowledge of it gets around, have devastating effect in the box office'. He also sang Cavaradossi and Pinkerton in this season before moving to New York, where he made his Metropolitan début on January 10, 1947, again as Rodolfo. 'He sings like a young man who enjoys singing', wrote Virgil Thomson in the *New York Herald Tribune*. . . . 'He makes no attempt to sing like a baritone, and neither does he croon. He even at one point sang a genuine open-throated pianissimo, the first I have heard in Thirty-ninth Street, since I started reviewing opera there six years ago'. He remained at the Metropolitan until the end of the 1953-4 season singing Puccini and Verdi, and was also heard as Edgardo, Nemorino, and Don Ottavio.

Tagliavini's London début was with La Scala Company at Covent Garden in September 1950, when he sang Nemorino in *L'Elisir d'Amore* opposite Margherita Carosio, with Tito Gobbi and Italo Tajo. He scored an enormous triumph, as much with his charming enactment of Donizetti's country bumpkin, as with his singing. 'His "Una furtiva lagrima"', wrote Lord Harewood, 'was a triumph of pure singing and musicianship, and the cadenza, a model of its kind, effective without being blatant, and in style and scale with the rest of the aria'.

He returned to Covent Garden in 1955 and 1956 to sing Cavaradossi opposite Tebaldi and Milanov, and has also appeared with Italian touring companies in London as Nemorino, and there is no denying that in recent years his earlier golden tones, and exquisite pianissimo, are not all they were. Yet at his best Tagliavini's voice, style, and warm golden tone, mark him as one of the truly great lyric tenors in Italian operatic history.

RENATA TEBALDI

It is always gratifying when one's personal 'hunch' about a singer proves right; and let me hasten to add, with as much modesty as possible, that during the last ten to fifteen years I have had not a few of these, most of which have turned out as I had hoped.

I first heard the voice of Renata Tebaldi in the famous broadcast of May 11, 1946, when the Scala reopened, and she sang under Toscanini in the 'Preghiera' from Rossini's *Mosè*, and Verdi's *Te Deum*; on that occasion I noted that 'Tebaldi possesses a young and exciting voice, and is someone obviously to watch.' A few months later, I heard her as Elsa in a performance of *Lohengrin* from the Teatro Comunale, Bologna, when the beauty and purity of tone, and the musicality she displayed, sent tingles down my spine. Then during the 1947-8 season, I can still recollect her perfectly melting Desdemona, with Francesco Merli, from Rome, a moving Margherita in *Mefistofele* from Parma, and her ecstatic Elisabeth in *Tannhäuser* from Naples.

In the very first article I contributed to *Opera's* predecessor, *Ballet and Opera*, in January 1949, I wrote: 'The protagonist in this opera [Casavola's *Salambo* in Rome] was the young Italian *lirico-spinto* soprano, Renata Tebaldi, whose most beautiful voice I have greatly admired in such roles as Desdemona, Margherita and Elsa, and who should be heard in London.'

A few months later, Lord Harewood heard her as Pamira, in a revival of Rossini's *L'Assedio di Corinto* at the Florence Festival, and he wrote, also in *Ballet and Opera*, 'The music is dominated by the soprano, superbly sung at this performance by Renata Tebaldi. I have mentioned her before (as Desdemona at the Scala earlier that season), and there seems no point in disguising a conviction that she is probably the foremost lirico-dramatic soprano in the world. This is one of the singers whose every part seems to lie exactly in the middle of the voice. Not a note either time I heard her was out of place, and she negotiated Rossini's dramatic coloratura firmly and exactly throughout the long role. Here was the *mezza-voce* of a lyric soprano, the attack of a dramatic; here was the phrasing of an artist; here the grand manner. Italy has at least one great singer in her midst.'

Tebaldi was born in Pesaro on February 1, 1922. She was brought up in Parma, and studied at the conservatory with the intention of becoming a pianist. In those days, she says, nothing was further from her mind than being a singer; but she was in the habit of singing aloud the themes of pieces she was studying. Her piano teacher, Signora Passani, noticed that her voice had a considerable range, and without saying anything, arranged for a singing teacher to hear her. When she was eighteen she gave her first audition, and sang 'Un bel dì' from *Butterfly;* she made a deep impression on her teacher Maestro Campogagliani; and then later became the pupil of Carmen Melis, a famous soprano of the 1920s who sang at Covent Garden as Tosca and Musetta.

In 1944 Tebaldi left the Conservatory before obtaining her diploma, owing to the bombing; and on May 23 of the same year made her début as Elena in Boito's *Mefistofele* at Rovigo. This was followed by appearances in the Italian provinces, and a Desdemona at Trieste in 1946. Then, she was invited by Toscanini to take part in the reopening of the Scala, as already mentioned.

During the summer of 1946, the Scala organized a season at the Palazzo del Sport, Milan, and Tebaldi was heard as Elena and then as Margherita in *Mefistofele*, and Elsa in *Lohengrin*. In the first winter season at the reopened Scala she sang Mimi and Eva, and during that winter she was also heard at the Fenice Theatre, Venice, as Tosca and at Parma as Violetta. In the summer of 1947 she sang at Verona as Marguerite in *Faust*, reappearing there during the next three summers as Desdemona, Elsa and Margherita.

For the 1947-8 season her engagements included appearances in Rome as Desdemona, Violetta and Salambo, and at the San Carlo, Naples, as Elisabeth and Violetta. In the autumn of 1948 she returned to the Scala to sing Madeleine de Coigny in *Andrea Chénier*, and in the 1948-9 season she was chosen to sing the same role in the Giordano commemoration performance at the Scala on March 6, 1949, under De Sabata, with Del Monaco and Silveri. During the same season she sang her first Scala Desdemona, and for the last ten years she rarely missed a Scala season, where besides the parts already mentioned she has sung Alice Ford, Violetta, Adriana Lecouvreur, Tosca, La Wally, Tatiana (*Onegin*) and Leonora (*Forza*).

At the 1950 Florence Festival, Tebaldi sang the title-role

in Spontini's *Olimpia*, and has also sung there as Aida, Leonora and Desdemona. Later in 1950 she sang the part of Cleopatra in Handel's *Giulio Cesare* in the ruins of the Teatro Grande, Pompei.

In August 1950, Tebaldi made her British début, singing in the Verdi *Requiem* with the Scala Orchestra and Chorus both at the Edinburgh Festival and at Covent Garden, and as Desdemona with Vinay and Bechi at Covent Garden.

During the Verdi celebrations of 1951, the San Carlo, Naples, revived for her *Giovanna d'Arco*; this was the first performance of the opera for something like a hundred years, and the company was invited to give two performances of it in Paris. Tebaldi's other contributions to the Verdi year included appearances as Desdemona, Alice Ford, Aida, and in the *Requiem*.

Since then Tebaldi has had few free months, for she is constantly engaged in Italy, America, and more recently appears each season in Vienna. Her only appearances in London, other than those of 1950, were in the summer of 1955 when she sang Tosca with Tagliavini and Gobbi. New York however hears her every season. She made her Metropolitan début in January 1955 as Desdemona, and in her first season sang Mimi, Madeleine de Coigney, and Tosca. During her second and third New York seasons she added Aida, and Violetta (in Guthrie's controversial production of this opera) to her Metropolitan roles; and between 1958 and 1960 was heard as Butterfly, Manon Lescaut, and Maria Boccanegra, as well as her usual roles. In addition, Chicago audiences have heard her as Adriana Lecouvreur, Alice Ford, and Leonora in *La Forza del Destino*.

The soprano's return to La Scala in December 1959 after several seasons absence was the occasion of almost hysterical demonstrations. She was greeted with endless ovations, and flowers were showered on to the stage from all parts of the house.

What is this busy person like off-stage? When does she find the time to relax, and what does she do with the little spare time she has between appearances and recordings?

She is, she says, a great home-lover; and her flat in Milan is full of antiques, and valuable pieces of porcelain; she also confesses to a love of cooking, and enjoys, or rather enjoyed, for now she says she must be careful what she eats, risotto with parmisan cheese and mushrooms.

'I adore cars,' she adds; 'I have bought myself a green streamlined one. I have a licence, but haven't yet mustered sufficient courage to face the hellish traffic of Milan by myself! And then I enjoy reading, especially adventure stories; but I avoid thrillers, for they make me sleep badly! I love flowers too, and my flat is always full of them; on the balcony I have planted hydrangeas'.

That is a brief off-stage picture of Tebaldi painted by herself. Now what of the art, and that wonderful golden voice?

Let me quote one of Italy's leading critics, A. Procida, writing in the *Giornale di Napoli* about her Violetta a year or two ago: 'The Miracle of a dramatic voice, which at the same time is exquisitely pure, whatever the volume of sound, which can display the virtuosity of a sopranoleggiero, and yet has an elegance and an ethereal-like quality, is not something that happens every day. It is necessary to go back to Muzio before we meet such a phenomenon. In short Tebaldi is a great singer, and an actress who lives and suffers spiritually the character she portrays. This was demonstrated in an unforgettable manner in the great Act II duet with Giorgio Germont.'

This comparison with Muzio has been a feature of the reviews Tebaldi received in both Rio de Janeiro and Buenos Aires, where that great singer was a favourite in the 1920's and early 1930's. In New York it was Rethberg's name that sprang to many people's minds.

What else can one add? I personally find the voice one of the most beautiful to have come out of Italy in the last quarter of a century. Most of the Italian sopranos we heard at Covent Garden between the wars either sang too loudly or too softly and generally with a superabundance of chest-notes; and none displayed the beautiful *mezza-voce* of this artist. A year or two back, when she was singing too frequently, the voice went through a period of strain, and lost some of its beauty and steadiness; fortunately that was only temporary. To-day the voice is once again as lovely as it ever was. A generation that can boast both a Tebaldi and a Callas can indeed count itself fortunate.

BLANCHE THEBOM

BLANCHE THEBOM, the tall handsome American mezzo-soprano of Swedish parentage, was born in Monessen, Pennsylvania, shortly after the end of the first world war. Her parents were both born in Sweden but had emigrated to America; and it was on their first return visit to their native country in 1938 that their daughter's vocal potentialities were discovered—or rather on the way to Sweden on board the ship the *Kungsholm*. She sang at one of the ship's concerts; at this time she had never had a singing lesson, but she so impressed Kosti Vehanen, Marian Anderson's accompanist, that he encouraged her to think of a vocal career, suggesting she go to New York to study.

When the Thebom family returned to America from Sweden, Blanche, who was the secretary of a prominent Canton business man, Alvin Gibbs, wondered how she could follow Vehanen's advice and go to New York to study. Her problem was solved when her employer heard about it, for he and his wife offered to underwrite Blanche Thebom's musical education, and so in the spring of 1939 she went to New York, where she began her vocal studies with the great Edyth Walker, and later she was coached in stage work by Lothar Wallerstein.

In November 1941, Thebom made her début, in concert, singing Brahms's *Alto Rhapsody* under Eugene Ormandy in Philadelphia. Other orchestral concerts and vocal recitals followed; and in January 1944, she gave a highly successful Town Hall recital in New York. By then she was known to Edward Johnson at the Metropolitan, who invited her to join the company for the 1944-5 season. Before this, however, in the summer of 1944, she appeared in the film *When Irish Eyes Are Smiling*, in which she was joined by the baritone Leonard Warren.

Thebom's début with the Metropolitan was as Brangaene at Philadelphia in November; then on December 14 came her New York début as Fricka. Ronald Eyer wrote in *Musical America*: 'Stepping forth, abrupt, and unannounced, as Wagner requires in the second act, Miss Thebom made the audience sit up and take notice .... she came well equipped, with a big colourful and beautifully controlled voice. She presents an attractive Junoesque yet youthful figure. And she possesses a poise and stage-wisdom seldom encountered among newcomers to the lyric theatre.'

Brangaene followed in February 1945, and the *Rheingold* Fricka a month later; and on the company's spring tour, she sang Laura in *La Gioconda*. This last role, Giulietta in *Hoffmann*, and Venus in *Tannhäuser*, were added to her New York roles during her second Metropolitan season. And gradually her repertory expanded to include Amneris, Delilah, Marina in *Boris*, Erda, Ortrud, and Marfa in *Khovanshchina* during the last years of Johnson's régime. In addition she was heard in Chicago, Montreal, and San Francisco. Then in 1950 came her European début with Dorabella at Glyndebourne, and Delilah and Brangaene at Stockholm.

With the opening of the Bing régime at the Metropolitan, Thebom added yet more roles to her repertory. Eboli in *Don Carlos*, Azucena, Orlofsky, Dorabella, Waltraute, Baba the Turk in *The Rake's Progress*, Adalgisa, Herodias, Adelaide in *Arabella*, and Carmen. Meanwhile she continued to sing many of her other roles, especially Fricka, Brangaene, and Amneris, with her usual success. Her Orlofsky in November 1951 earned for her a particular success. *Musical America* wrote: 'Another strengthening of the cast was the Orlofsky of Blanche Thebom. The handsome mezzo-soprano moved, spoke, and made gestures more like a man that others have done in the role, and managed to convey the utter boredom of the part without alienating the audience. She sang with full smooth tone, and got her songs across the footlights with conviction and wit'. Later in the season her first Waltraute won her high praise from the critics.

In the summer of 1957 Thebom participated in one of the most historic events in the history of Covent Garden, London, the first full stage production in Great Britain of Berlioz's *Les Troyens* in which she sang Dido. It took several performances before she got the measure of this demanding role, but when she returned to London to repeat it the following summer, she made the closing scene immensely moving. She also gave London audiences cause to regret that they had been unable to hear her when she was in her vocal prime some few years earlier. She was honoured at Covent Garden's centenary Gala by being chosen to sing the love-duet from *The Trojans* with Jon Vickers, sharing the evening's honours with Maria Callas, Margot Fonteyn, Amy Shuard, Joan Sutherland, and Irene Dalis.

RICHARD TUCKER

RICHARD TUCKER must be one of the few opera singers who pursues two careers. Not only is he one of the leading tenors at the Metropolitan Opera House in New York, but one of the most highly paid synagogue Cantors in the United States. In the same week he might sing the leading tenor role in *Simon Boccanegra* or *Tosca*, and then take part in the Jewish Holy Day services at the Chicago Austrian Galician Synagogue.

Tucker was born in Brooklyn in 1914. His father who had emigrated to America from Roumania, was a furrier, and sometimes sang as a cantor in his local New York Synagogue. His son Reuben (Richard) began singing in the synagogue's choir when he was six, and soon was receiving singing lessons from the synagogue's cantor, J. S. Weiser. When he had reached his mid-teens, Tucker had developed a fine tenor voice, but instead of pursuing his studies and entering the Jewish ministry, he went into the garment trade.

In 1936 he married the sister of Jan Peerce, and his brother-in-law's growing operatic successes fired Tucker with an ambition he had secretly nurtured, to become an opera singer himself. He began to take lessons with Martino, then Borghetti, and finally with the famous tenor Paul Althouse. He succeeded in getting an engagement for a Chicago radio programme called 'The Chicago Theatre of the Air', in which he sang arias from *Cavalleria Rusticana* and *La Bohème;* then followed some concerts in the New York Town Hall, and then in 1942 he scored a success in the Metropolitan Auditions of the Air singing 'De' miei bollenti spiriti' from *La Traviata*. He did not win first prize however, only second. This was followed by an engagement to sing Alfredo with a small Italian group that appeared in New York, called the Salmaggi Company.

In July 1943 Tucker asked for and obtained a full stage audition at the Metropolitan. A second one followed in 1944 and on this occasion he was asked by Edward Johnson to study the role of Enzo in *La Gioconda*, and then come back. And so on January 25, 1945 he made his début at the Metropolitan in this part with Stella Roman, Bruna Castagna, Richard Bonelli, and Nicola Moscona. Although he did not find himself famous overnight, and the critics were not over-enthusiastic, his potentialities were recognised. 'He has a voice of purest tenor quality, rich in colour, vibrant in top tones, and able to give entirely convincing emotional expression. If he emits no gallery-rousing volume, it is because he has too much taste to force'—so wrote one of New York's more discerning critics

Enzo was his only role in his first Metropolitan season. He followed it with Alfredo in December 1945, taking it over from his indisposed brother-in-law, Dimitri in *Boris* almost a year later; and the Duke of Mantua, Pinkerton, Rodolfo, and Riccardo in *Ballo in Maschera* during 1947; Edgardo, Gabriele Adorno, and Des Grieux followed in 1949; Cavaradossi, Tamino, and Don Carlos in 1950. From then on his repertory increased by leaps and bounds and now includes, in addition to the roles already mentioned, Faust, Don José, Alfred (*Fledermaus*), Ferrando in *Così*, Don Alvaro, Turiddu, Chénier, Dick Johnson in *La Fanciulla del West* and Calaf, —and on records he has sung Radames.

It was during Bing's régime in New York that Tucker really came into his own, for then he had the advantage of working with producers of the first rank, who made him act. Of his Alfred in *Fledermaus*, Cecil Smith was able to write: 'Mr. Tucker sang opulently and with melting phrasing, and his acting revealed unwonted flexibility, and a real sense of humour'. While of his Don José the same critic wrote: 'But the candour and honesty of purpose that characterize his acting nowadays induced the audience to believe in him'.

By this time Tucker had sung elsewhere in the United States, in Chicago, San Francisco, and Cincinnati. He had also appeared in the Verona Arena in 1947 as Enzo in *La Gioconda*, on the occasion of Maria Callas's Italian début. He recalled that after his singing of 'Cielo e Mar' the audience began shouting 'Bis, Bis!' but Mr. Tucker says he was terrified, thinking they were calling 'Beast, Beast!'

But the tenor has not pursued an international career— though he did sing Cavaradossi at Covent Garden in January 1958— preferring to spend most of his time with his family and in the orthodox Jewish atmosphere which he values so much.

He has found time however to record in Europe, and has sung Radames and Alvaro in *La Forza del Destino* opposite Callas for the Columbia-Angel Scala recordings. He had sung his first Radames as far back as 1949 when Toscanini chose him to sing this role in his famous N.B.C. broadcast of the opera, and is one of the few tenors on record, in more than one sense, to end 'Celeste Aida' as the composer intended. Perhaps we may yet hear Tucker sing this role on the stage. It certainly should be a vocal treat.

HERMANN UHDE

HERMANN UHDE is one of the most popular artists to have established himself internationally since the war. Always welcome in Covent Garden and the Metropolitan, well-known to visitors to Bayreuth, Munich and Vienna, he rarely has a free moment.

He was born in Bremen in 1914 of an American mother (his English is excellent) and a German father. He was educated in his native city, and embarked on his vocal studies when he was eighteen with the baritone, Philip Kraus. He was a member of Kraus's vocal school for six years, and sang bass roles in hospitals, old people's homes etc. In fact his first stage appearance was as Sarastro in a mental hospital!

Uhde's first professional engagement was at Bremen in 1936 as Titurel in *Parsifal*. He remained in Bremen for two seasons, and then moved on to Freiburg (1938-40) and Munich (1940-2). By this time he was tiring of singing old men and priests, and began to develop the top part of his voice. He began his baritone career in 1942 as a member of the German Opera Company in Holland, singing Figaro, Don Giovanni, Scarpia, and Escamillo. In 1944 he was conscripted into the army, and the following year was captured by the Americans in France, and spent the next two years in a prisoner of war camp.

Released in 1947, Uhde took up his operatic career again, and obtained a guest contract in Hanover, where he sang Scarpia, Escamillo, and Wolfram. He then moved on to Hamburg where he sang among other roles Rigoletto and Pizarro. While at Hamburg he received an invitation to sing at the 1949 Salzburg Festival, where he created the role of Kreon in the world première of Orff's *Antigonae*.

The following year at Salzburg he was heard as Tarquinius in Britten's *The Rape of Lucretia*, of which Lord Harewood wrote in *Opera*: 'Hermann Uhde quickly established Tarquinius as a spoilt adolescent, graced by an indescribably horrible grin of anticipation. His well-controlled and intelligent vocal colouring was a notable asset'.

There followed a season in Vienna, and then in 1951 he joined the Munich State Opera and has sung there regularly ever since, though in recent seasons he has had to ration his time there, as he has a joint contract with Vienna, and also gives Stuttgart and Düsseldorf a certain number of evenings every season.

At the first post-war Bayreuth Festival of 1951 Uhde created a sensation with his performances of Klingsor and Gunther, roles he repeated in 1952 and 1953, adding to them the *Rheingold* Wotan and Melot in 1952, Telramund in 1953, and the Dutchman in 1955. Uhde's great intelligence and musical sensitivity, and his highly-strung temperament, were just the kind of material for Wieland Wagner's new Bayreuth approach; and indeed, like Mödl, Varnay and other post-war Bayreuth singers, Uhde's highly personal and emotional style of acting has provided some of the most exciting moments in post-war opera. Of his first Telramund at Bayreuth, Andrew Porter wrote: 'Hermann Uhde as Telramund gave a most remarkable study—one implicit in Wagner's score, but seldom seen on the stage. No crooked dark villain, but a nobleman young, impetuous, ambitious,—half-consentingly, half-unconsciously being led astray by his wife . . . Uhde's voice rings out, strong, clean and forward, the words are sharply formed. We should have him at Covent Garden.' And to Covent Garden he came to sing his Telramund in admirably clear English a few months later.

Uhde's actual Covent Garden début however was on the opening night of the Strauss season by the Munich Opera, when he sang Mandryka in *Arabella* opposite Lisa della Casa. He has returned to London on several occasions to sing and act his unsurpassed Gunther in *Götterdämmerung*; he also made nothing less than a sensation by appearing in four roles—Lindorf, Coppelius, Dappertutto, and Dr. Miracle in Rennert's production of *Les Contes d'Hoffmann*, again sung in impeccable English.

Uhde's New York début at the Metropolitan was in the first week of the 1955-6 season as Telramund. In ensuing years he has been heard there as Wotan in both *Rheingold* and *Walküre*, Gunther, Amfortas, the Grand Inquisitor in *Don Carlos* ('Mr. Uhde was a wonderously thin, ascetic Inquisitor, with a will of iron'), Pizarro, and Wozzeck in the Metropolitan première of that work. This latter role must be counted as the crown of his career. Typical of the many wonderful notices Uhde received is this written by Ronald Eyer in *Musical America*: 'As soldier Wozzeck, Hermann Uhde achieved the kind of perfection that characterizes a prototype. There were the closed countenance and catatonic moods of deep mental disturbance, the dogged servility and automatic reflexes of stance and movement induced by long military routine, and, beneath it all, a fascination with death as the ultimate release from his smouldering anger and frustration. It was a masterful performance.'

Few artists can have enjoyed such rapturous notices as Uhde regularly receives; yet he remains quite unspoilt by it all—a completely dedicated artist in the full sense of the word.

CESARE VALLETTI

ONE of the most admired artists at the Metropolitan Opera, New York, has been the Italian tenor, Cesare Valletti, generally considered one of the most intelligent and musicianly singers before the public today. He was born in Rome in 1922, and came of a cultured family; his father was a doctor, his mother, a gifted musician who had been trained at the Academy of Santa Cecilia.

Valletti was not intended for a musicial career, and it was decided that he would join the Italian navy. He had become a boy chorister in one of Rome's leading churches and when he was seventeen, and his voice had broken, he often took part in the musical evenings which were part of his family life. He was heard at one of these by the famous baritone, Riccardo Stracciari, who recommended him to study singing seriously. Five years of hard work with Lidia Bucci-Brunacci followed. By 1947 he was ready for his début which was at Bari, as Alfredo in *La Traviata*, and he was acclaimed by the local critics as a tenor of high promise. An engagement at the Rome Opera as Almaviva in *Il Barbiere di Siviglia* followed soon after and it was not long before he had been heard in most of the leading Italian opera houses, in Cairo, Barcelona and Lisbon.

In the autumn of 1950, when the Scala Company visited Covent Garden, Valletti was chosen to sing Fenton in *Falstaff* under De Sabata. This appearance anticipated his actual Scala début, which occurred during the 1950-51 season as Nemorino in *L'Elisir d'Amore*. 'His voice is limpid and even throughout its range', wrote a leading Italian critic. He continued 'above all he knows how to sing, and phrase in perfect style. His Nemorino is modelled on Schipa and Gigli . . . . a fine acquisition for the Scala'. During his first Scala season he also sang Fenton, and Vladimir in *Prince Igor*. His Scala début had been preceded by appearances in Rome at the Teatro Elisio as Don Narciso in the famous revival of *Il Turco in Italia* with Callas and Stabile; and later that season he made his first appearances in America, singing in Mexico, Montevideo and São Paolo. By now his repertory included, in addition to the roles already mentioned, Paolino in *Il Matrimonio Segreto*, Elvino in *La Sonnambula*, Ernesto in *Don Pasquale*, Don Ottavio, Des Grieux (Massenet), Fritz in *L'Amico Fritz*, Werther, Federico in *L'Arlesiana*, Don Ramiro in *La Cenerentola* and Lindoro in *L'Italiana in Algeri*.

It was in September 1953 that Valletti made his United States début; this was with the San Francisco Company in the title-role of *Werther*, followed by Almaviva. Of the latter role, the critic of the San Francisco Chronicle went so far as to write 'Valletti's light, firm, beautiful tone, elegent musicianship and clever acting produced an Almaviva without parallel in our operatic history'. A few weeks later came his Metropolitan début as Don Ottavio, always a difficult role for a new singer. Again he triumphed, and the critics were enthusiastic. 'A beautiful style . . . . fine taste . . . . He even looked like a man, not a "ham" ', wrote the late Olin Downes in the *New York Times*. Later that season his Almaviva was described by the same critic as being 'unsurpassed in elegance, finish and spirit'.

From 1953 to 1960 Valletti sang regularly at the Metropolitan. He is one of the few contemporary Italian tenors moreover, who gives an annual song recital in New York, in which lieder and art songs predominate. He can sing in English too, and his Ferrando in the Metropolitan's English *Così fan tutte* earned him much praise.

Valletti has returned to Italy on numerous occasions since his American début, and has been heard with the Scala Company at the Holland Festival. In the summer of 1958 he sang again at Covent Garden in *La Traviata* opposite Callas. He has also taken part in many complete opera recordings including *La Cenerentola*, *L'Italiana*, *La Fille du Régiment*, *Traviata*, *Manon*, and *Butterfly*.

Valletti is an advocate of opera in English, at least as far as comic opera is concerned. 'What is the point in a comic opera if the audience doesn't understand the fun? Some flavour is lost, of course, without the original language, but an excellent translator ought to be able to capture a lot of it'.

ASTRID VARNAY

THERE cannot have been many sopranos in operatic history who made their débuts at a few hours' notice in the role of Sieglinde, never having appeared before on any operatic stage. If that were not nerve-racking enough, to know that one was substituting for the indisposed Lotte Lehmann could not have made things really easy. That was on 6th December, 1941, at the Metropolitan Opera House in New York. The performance was broadcast throughout America and the singer appeared naturally without a rehearsal of any kind. Six days later the same artist was called on to sing the role of Brünnhilde, again at a few hours' notice, this time as a substitute for Helen Traubel. Americans call this 'pinch-hitting', and Madame Varnay was a 'pinch-hitter' on quite a number of occasions in the first years of her operatic career.

Like so many Wagnerian singers, Astrid Varnay is a Scandinavian. She was born in Stockholm on April 25, 1918. Her mother, Maria Yavor, was a coloratura soprano, and her father, a stage director and producer who helped to launch the first opera company in Oslo. From the time she was five Astrid Varnay spent most of her time in America. Her musical studies were at first directed towards becoming a pianist, and for eight years she attended the New Jersey Musical College. In 1937 she took a non-muscial job as a stenographer, and devoted her spare time to taking singing lessons with her mother. Deciding that she wanted to make singing her full-time career, she wrote to Herman Weigert, then one of the musical staff at the Metropolitan, asking him for an audition. Weigert, a former professor of music at the Berlin Hochschule, was impressed by what he heard and suggested she sing for Georg Szell, who was just as impressed. She then sang for Edward Johnson, who urged her to continue to study with Weigert and then apply for a formal audition at the Metropolitan.

In May 1941 Varnay signed her contract with the Metropolitan, and in 1944 she married Herman Weigert. Her first scheduled appearance was to have been in January 1942, but on December 6, 1941, at a few hours notice, she was asked to replace an indisposed Lotte Lehmann as Sieglinde, in a Saturday matinée performance of *Die Walküre* which was also being broadcast. Six days later she was again called to sing in the same opera, this time as a substitute for Helen Traubel, as Brünnhilde. In addition to these two roles she sang during her first season Elsa, Elisabeth and Telea in the world première of Menotti's *The Island God*.

The *New York Times* writing about her unannounced début commented: 'The exceedingly comely Swedish-American soprano acted with a skill and grace only possible to those with an inborn talent for the theatre ..... Miss Varnay is a valuable addition to the Metropolitan roster'.

Of her Brünnhilde a few days later the critic of *Musical America* wrote: 'Her Brünnhilde had the style of a veteran. She is unquestionably one of the most brilliantly gifted singers of the day, at twenty-three. If she will husband her voice it may confidently be predicted that she will become one of the leading Wagnerian sopranos of our time'.

During the next five years Varnay was heard in most of the Wagnerian repertory adding the roles of Kundry, Ortrud, Gutrune, and Isolde to her repertory. At the same time she was studying the Italian repertory, and in May 1948 was heard as La Gioconda, Aida, Tosca, and Santuzza in Mexico. Two years later she was heard as Maria in a revival of *Simone Boccanegra* at the Metropolitan.

The reports and criticisms that had reached London about her were enthusiastic, but knowledge of this artist was confined to those few people who read American

JON VICKERS

as *Florestan* in 'Fidelio'

as *Aenas* in 'The Trojans'

as *Siegmund* in 'Die Walküre'

LEONARD WARREN

as *Barnaba* in 'La Gioconda'

as *Rigoletto*

WOLFGANG WINDGASSEN

as *Rienzi*

as *Siegfried*

as herself

VIRGINIA ZEANI

as *Violetta* in 'La Traviata'

musical papers, and to the various concert agents. So it was with much pleasure that one heard her name announced at a press conference at the Royal Opera House in the autumn of 1948, as being the Brünnhilde and Isolde for a series of Wagnerian performances due to take place in November of that year. To sing Isolde at Covent Garden after Flagstad was yet another challenge to this young artist, but one which she faced with courage, because the great Norwegian soprano had always been a source of inspiration to her.

In 1951 she returned to Europe to sing Lady Macbeth at the Florence Festival, after which she came back to Covent Garden to sing the title-roles in *Salome* and *Aida*, and Leonora in *Il Trovatore*. She also took part in an unforgettable performance of *Die Walküre*, in which she sang Brünnhilde to Flagstad's Sieglinde. A month or two later saw her at Bayreuth, where she has shared the leading soprano roles with Martha Mödl ever since. Munich is another European centre for which Varnay has a special affection, for it was there that she sang her first *Fidelio* in 1952.

During the 1951-2 season she also added the role of Elektra to her repertory. Cecil Smith wrote about her thus: 'Her comprehension of the text in its relation to the music, and consequently her inflection and colouration of both words and music, made her performance absorbing; and her ability at all times to sing as high or as low, as loudly or as softly as the occasion required, and always to come across the biggest orchestra sonority, made her singing a really imposing feat'.

The following year she sang her first Marschallin; and her Bayreuth Ortrud and Isolde were counted among the best performances of her career. In the summer of 1955, again at Bayreuth, she scored one of the greatest successes of her career as Senta.

Since the death of her husband in the spring of 1955, Varnay has spent most of her time in Europe, and is a valued member of the Deutsche Oper am Rhein, Düsseldorf/Duisburg. She also sings regularly at Hamburg and Stuttgart, where in 1959 she created the part of Jocasta in Orff's *Oedipus*. She returned to Covent Garden in 1958 and 1959 for the *Ring*, repeated her wonderful Isolde at Edinburgh in 1958 in Wieland Wagner's production of *Tristan* with the Stuttgart Company, and sang her unrivalled Ortrud with the Hamburg Opera at Sadler's Wells (again in Wieland Wagner's production) in 1962—so exciting was her invocation to the gods in act 2, that the audience burst into applause in the midst of a Wagner opera!

Like her German colleagues, Varnay's approach to her roles is most serious. She too is one of those artists who insists on reading as much background literature as possible before attempting a new part. She considers the words as important as the music, and this was especially noticeable in her reading of the roles of Brünnhilde and Isolde. Of the latter Ernest Newman wrote that 'it was all in all one of the best sung and acted Isoldes that I have ever seen'. Indeed Varnay's acting is a perfect example of what operatic acting should be. She does not employ meaningless gestures, but lets her actions grow from the meaning of the words she is singing. Naturally graceful, and moving on the stage with great ease, I doubt whether any *Siegfried* Brünnhilde has ever awoken so beautifully to greet the sun.

JON VICKERS

NEARLY every generation appears to suffer from a shortage of first-rate tenors, and in our time the number of real *heldentenors* has been infinitesimal. Indeed until the advent of Jon Vickers, our Siegmunds and Parsifals were sung by lyric tenors, who in the days of Melchior or Peter Cornelius would never have been heard in such roles.

Vickers was born in Prince Albert, Saskatchewan in Canada in 1926. As a boy he sang in his local church choir, but he had at that time no ideas of becoming a professional singer, indeed his ambition was to become a doctor. At the time he was ready to enter university the war was just ending, and it was exceedingly difficult for a young civilian to get a place in medical school with the return of many demobilised soldiers; so the young Vickers went into business, working in a grocery store in Winnipeg, and eventually managing a local Woolworths. At the same time he sang in clubs and amateur productions including one of *Naughty Marietta* in which the soprano, a professional from New York, was so impressed by his singing that she advised him to study seriously. Then followed eight years at the Royal Conservatory of Toronto, where his voice teacher was George Lambert.

During the eight years that Vickers was a student, he was able to take professional engagements in Canada, and use the money he thus earned to help support him—his tuition was paid for by a scholarship. Thus he sang at the Toronto Opera Festival under Hans Geiger as Don Ottavio, the Duke in *Rigoletto*, Don José, and in other roles.

In November 1955 he auditioned for David Webster, Covent Garden's General Administrator, who was on a visit to Canada, but heard nothing from London for eight months. During that time he sang Florestan opposite Inge Borkh in a concert performance of *Fidelio* in New York, and in several concerts on the Canadian Radio in which he was heard in excerpts from Wagner. Then in May 1956 he received a cable from London asking him to come for a Covent Garden audition. He put this off until he had completed a period of five weeks' musical coaching he had arranged in New York, and then flew to London, where he was offered a full contract for the 1956-7 season. Before he joined the Covent Garden company however, he sang the Male Chorus in Britten's *Rape of Lucretia* with great success at the second festival of music at Stratford, Ontario. The correspondent of *Opera* magazine reported 'The greatest success was scored by the tenor, Jon Vickers, as the Male Chorus. His fine singing and acting marked him out as an artist with a fine future'.

Jon Vickers' European career began in the spring of 1957, when he sang Gustavus (as the role of Riccardo was known in Covent Garden's production of Verdi's *Ballo in Maschera*) on the company's spring tour. When the company returned to London at the end of April, he repeated the role, and then a few days later was heard as Don José in *Carmen*. Philip Hope-Wallace commented: 'Here was an admirable Don José, with a handsome and virile assurance and plenty of acting ability, as his last desperate encounter with the siren showed'.

At the beginning of June came the now famous Covent Garden production of Berlioz's *Les Troyens* in which Vickers sang Aeneas with an assurance and heroic ring in the voice that immediately marked him out as a future Siegmund, a role he sang with enormous success at Bayreuth in the summer of 1958 and which he repeated at Covent Garden a few weeks later. Meanwhile he had added Radames to his Covent Garden repertory—the best Radames London had heard since Martinelli—and then another Verdi role, that of Don Carlos in the opera of the same name, in the splendid production of that work during the theatre's centenary season; in the same cast were Gré Brouwenstijn, Fedora Barbieri, Tito Gobbi, and Boris Christoff; Giulini was the conductor and Visconti the producer.

In November 1958 Vickers was heard as Jason in Cherubini's *Medée* opposite Callas at the Dallas Civic Opera, a role he repeated in London, again with Callas, the following summer. He was also heard as Samson in a stage production of Handel's oratorio, in which his singing of 'Total Eclipse' was especially notable.

Early in 1959, Vickers went to Vienna where he sang Siegmund, José, Radames and Canio; and then in the summer of the same year he sang his first Parsifal at Covent Garden in which he vocally reminded many listeners of Melchior, and which was movingly and sincerely acted. The autumn of 1959 saw his San Francisco début; then came his Canio in Zeffirelli's production of *Pagliacci* at Covent Garden, and during the same period, one of the greatest performances of Don José seen or heard in London in living memory. In January 1960 came his Metropolitan début. During his first New York season he sang Canio, Siegmund, and Florestan in a new production of *Fidelio*. In the last two roles especially he was highly acclaimed.

London did not have to wait long to hear Vickers as Florestan, for he took part in the already historical Klemperer *Fidelio* with Jurinac, Hotter and Frick in February 1961. His searing performance and the sincerity with which he invested the role was most moving.

The tenor's future is an exciting one. A return to Bayreuth cannot be long delayed, and we eagerly await the first British Siegfried, Tristan and Otello for many years.

RAMON VINAY

To have sung nearly two hundred and fifty performances of *Otello*, twenty-five of them with the Covent Garden Company; to have appeared at the Scala for seven seasons and at Bayreuth every year between 1952 and 1958 is a record of which any tenor might be proud—especially when that tenor happens to be neither Italian nor German by birth. Yet like most great artists, Ramon Vinay is singularly modest about his achievements. Of course he enjoys talking about them once he can be persuaded, but he would much rather chat about astrology, carpentry, hi-fi equipment or amateur cinematography; at all of these hobbies he is no less adept than as an interpreter of some of the most exacting tenor roles in the operatic repertory.

Vinay was born in the agricultural town of Chillán in Chile—also the birthplace of Claudio Arrau—during the first world war. His parents were French-Italian, and Ramon was educated at the local Ecole Normale before being taken to France by his father to complete his education. At his school in France he played the violin in the school orchestra, but did not study singing.

Shortly before the war he went to New Mexico to gain experience in one of his father's businesses (Jean Vinay operated a saddlery and harness factory); it was then that he first became interested in singing, and was persuaded by his friends to enter for an amateur radio competition sponsored by Coca-Cola. He was heard by a member of the Mexico City Opera, and engaged for the company. At that time he was a baritone, and his début was as Di Luna in *Il Trovatore*. Like two other great Otellos before him, Zenatello and Zanelli, Vinay found that his voice was changing, and after a period of further study emerged as as dramatic tenor (it is interesting to recollect that Zanelli too was a Chilean and that Di Luna was the second role he sang in public). Vinay's first tenor role, also in Mexico, was Don José.

In 1944 Vinay sang his first Otello in Mexico. *Musical America* reporting on this event wrote that 'the sensation of the season was Ramon Vinay's superb characterization of the difficult title role in Verdi's *Otello*'. The following summer he sang Des Grieux in Puccini's *Manon Lescaut*, Samson, José and Cavaradossi. Singing opposite him as Tosca was the American-Indian soprano, Mobley Lushanya, who later became his wife.

Some of the performances that summer were conducted by the French conductor Jean Morel, who engaged Vinay for the autumn season at the New York City Center, where he made his début as José. His success in this role led in its turn, to an engagement at the Metropolitan to sing the same part in the 1945-6 season, and then a re-engagement for the 1946-7 season as Radames and José. It was noted that as Radames 'Mr. Vinay sang with dignity and authority . . . . . and is to be commended particularly for following Verdi's directions and singing the final B flat of the aria pianissimo, rather than bellowing it forte as many tenors like to do'.

Three weeks after his first Metropolitan Radames, *Otello* was scheduled, with Torsten Ralf in the title role; this tenor fell ill, and Vinay was pressed into service at ten hours' notice to sing a part which he had only sung once before, two years previously. *Musical America* wrote that 'the result was of high artistic merit and of the greatest credit to the tenor . . . . his Otello was full-scaled both vocally and histrionically'. The most important result for Vinay of this performance was that he was approached by Toscanini, who asked him to coach the role with him in preparation for the performance he was to conduct for N.B.C. the following season. This is of course the performance that was also recorded and issued here by H.M.V. some four years ago. The result of the tenor's work with Toscanini can be heard in his wonderful interpretation of the role of the Moor. The American critic Herbert Peyser wrote, 'He sang with a plangent splendour, a dramatic fury and a heart shaking pathos one does not recall in any Otello since Slezak', and another critic described his performance as 'the epitome of vocal artistry'.

The New York *Otello* opened the doors of La Scala to Vinay, and he inaugurated the 1947-8 season at that house in *Otello* conducted by De Sabata, with Caniglia as Desdemona and Bechi as Iago. He repeated the part at the Verona Arena, Naples, and elsewhere in Italy, and again the following season at the Scala, this time with Tebaldi as Desdemona. It was in this role that London first heard him in September 1950 with the Scala Company at Covent Garden; he also sang it at Salzburg in 1951 and 1952 under Furtwängler.

Meanwhile Vinay had sung Samson at the Scala, Canio at the Metropolitan, and an entirely new kind of role for him, Tristan, which he first performed at the San Francisco Opera in the autumn of 1950.

The challenge of Wagner was one that Vinay met with

his customary success. The study of this role was all the more difficult, for at that time Vinay spoke no German. His Isolde was Flagstad, and the conductor Jonel Perlea.

Later that season he sang the role in New York opposite Helen Traubel under Fritz Reiner. 'Mr. Vinay's Tristan revealed his power as a singing actor far more profoundly than anything else he has done here' wrote one New York critic. 'His German diction was still somewhat Latin, but he knew what he was singing about every moment. His Tristan was noble, courtly, passionate and metaphysically subtle, by turns. He made the anguish of the dying knight in the third act almost unbearably keen'; and other critics were just as enthusiastic. It was little wonder that when Bayreuth was looking for its first post-war Tristan for the summer of 1952, it was to Vinay they turned. Here was an artist whose intelligence, musicianship and eagerness for hard work appealed to the Wagner brothers; and in Martha Mödl he had a wonderful Isolde to sing opposite him.

I find, looking back to what I wrote in *Opera* in 1952, that I thought his Tristan noble and poetical, but hardly real. But the following summer Andrew Porter was able to say that his Tristan was 'very good'. Writing about Vinay's Siegmund, which he was singing for the first time in 1953, the same writer noted that 'he is a serious and intelligent artist, and if his Siegmund improves as his Tristan has done, then in the future we should have a splendid interpretation'. This happened, and in the summer of 1954 Andrew Porter noted 'a vocal refinement in his Siegmund which will astonish all those who heard him sing the role only in Bayreuth'. Tannhäuser and Parsifal have been added to Vinay's Bayreuth roles. He has also sung the *Götterdammerung* Siegfried in New York, but unfortunately illness prevented him from appearing in the role in London.

Such is Vinay's versatility that he has assumed with equal success the title role in Alfano's *Cyrano de Bergerac* at the Scala and at Rome, and Lensky in *Eugene Onegin* at the Holland Festival in 1955. His dramatic insight is such that he was able to create a most moving figure of this character, and Lensky's emotional crisis in the Ball Room scene was, on that occasion, entirely credible. The beautiful aria allotted to the tenor before the duel scene as sung by Vinay was one of those rare and treasured moments in my opera-going.

Just as this generation knows every nuance and inflection in a Callas performance and will always remember it, so there are moments throughout Vinay's Otello that will always remain in the memory—'Datemi ancor l'eburnea mano', for example when Otello repeats it ironically in the third act duet with Desdemona. This is operatic artistry at its greatest; and in Vinay, I think it fair to say, we have one of the finest singing-actors of this generation. In 1961 Vinay bravely decided to give up the tenor repertory, and after a few months re-study sang Telramund at Bayreuth in 1962 and prepared Iago and Scarpia for the 1962-3 Season.

LEONARD WARREN

ONE of the most tragic events in the history of opera was that which terminated Leonard Warren's career at the Metropolitan Opera House on 4 March 1960. On that night Verdi's *La Forza del Destino* was being performed; the occasion marked the return of Renata Tebaldi after more than a year's absence. Richard Tucker was singing Alvaro, Jerome Hines the Father Guardian, Salvatore Baccaloni Fra Melitone, and Leonard Warren, one of his greatest roles, Don Carlo. The opera was well under way, and following the famous tenor-baritone duet, 'Solenne in quest 'ora', Warren was left alone on the stage. He began the recitative to the aria 'Urna fatale', a recitative that opened with the words 'Morir! Tremenda cosa' (To die! Tremendous moment). He sang the aria magnificently, and acknowledged the applause. A few more words of recitative followed, and then Warren moved to the left of the stage and was seen to fall forward, as if he had tripped. He remained motionless, and the Surgeon (Roald Reitan) entered with the words 'Lieta novella, e salvo'. There was no response from Leonard Warren, and a few seconds later Mr. Reitan ran over to him; he turned an anxious face to the conductor, Thomas Schippers, and then the curtain was lowered. Rudolf Bing announced that the performance would continue; a little later another member of the management told the audience that after a short interval the baritone Mario Sereni would complete the performance.

At 10.30 the interval bells rang and the audience returned to their seats. Mr. Bing re-appeared in front of the curtains, his face grave, and he announced: 'This is one of the saddest days in the history of opera. I will ask you please to stand in memory of one of our greatest performers who died in the middle of one of his greatest performances . . . . . I am sure you will agree with me that it would not be possible to continue with the performance'. Thus ended a career at the Metropolitan which had begun on 27 November 1938, during which the baritone had sung 408 performances in New York and 230 on tour of 26 roles.

Leonard Warren was born in the Bronx district of New York on 21 April 1911. His father was a Russian-born furrier named Varenov, and the family was originally Jewish (Warren became a Catholic in 1942). Originally it was planned that Leonard would enter the family business, but in 1935 after a visit to the Radio City Music Hall where he heard a bass soloist, he applied for an audition, and was admitted to the Radio City Music Hall chorus. He then began to study with Will J. Stone at Greenwich House Music and Sidney Dietch.

One of Warren's colleagues in the chorus dared him to enter for the Metropolitan Auditions of the Air. Wilfred Pelletier, one of the judges and a conductor at the Metropolitan was so impressed with what he heard that he persuaded Edward Johnson to try to help the young baritone by finding a backer to pay for his study in Europe. (This was George Martin of Cleveland). For seven months Warren worked in Rome under Riccardo Picozzi, and in Milan under Giuseppe Pais. He learned seven roles, and also met an ex-Juillard School student, Agathe Leifflen, whom he married in 1942.

Warren returned to New York for the 1938-9 season, and his first appearance on the Metropolitan stage was at a Sunday night concert on 27 November 1938 when he sang Germont in the Germont-Violetta scene from *La Traviata* with Marisa Morel, and Tonio in Act I of *Pagliacci* with Hilde Burke and Giovanni Martinelli. 'He disclosed a resonant voice of good quality' wrote *Musical America*. What might be termed his 'début proper' came on 13 January 1939 when he was heard as Paolo in *Simon Boccanegra* in a cast that boasted Lawrence Tibbett in the title-role, Maria Caniglia as Amelia, Martinelli as Gabriele, and Ezio Pinza as Fiesco. Oscar Thompson commented 'His voice was resonant and of dramatic timbre, adequate in compass and volume, and well used'.

During this first Metropolitan season Warren also sang Rangoni and Stechelkalov in a revival of *Boris Godunov*. In his second New York season he was heard as Valentin, the Herald in *Lohengrin*, Amonasro, and Barnaba in *La Gioconda*. Then followed Alfio, Escamillo, the High Priests in *Alceste* and *Samson et Dalila*, Ilo, in the première of Menotti's *The Island God*, and Enrico in *Lucia*.

During the summer of 1942 Warren made his South American début at the Teatro Colon, Buenos Aires, where he sang, with great success, Rento, Amonasro, and his first Boccanegra. He then went on to Rio where he repeated his Renato, and was heard as Germont and Méphistophélès. He returned to Rio for the next three seasons, and was also heard again in Buenos Aires in 1943, when he sang Germont, Rigoletto, Falstaff and Tonio, and in 1946 when he sang Renato and Boccanegra.

During the 1942-3 and 1943-4 New York seasons Warren was heard in a dozen or more roles, and firmly established himself as one of the company's most reliable and popular performers. It was as a Verdi baritone that he scored his greatest successes and will best be remembered. He first sang Iago during the 1946-7 season, and although many critics found his interpretation dramatically wanting, they all agreed that vocally it was superb. When he sang his first New York Boccanegra during the 1949-50 season, Robert Sabin wrote in *Musical America:* 'In recent years, Mr. Warren has added greatly to his stature as an actor, and his improvement has made itself felt in the refinement and emotional power of his singing. His Simon Boccanegra, like his Rigoletto and Falstaff, is a distinguished characterization.' Of his Rigoletto in the new production of that work during Bing's second New York season, 1951-2, *Musical America* wrote: 'Mr. Warren's Rigoletto always distinguished, was now enriched in numberless musical and dramatic details and sung with an even more richly coloured outpouring of tone. He has never seemed a better artist or a finer singer'. These were the two roles Warren sang at La Scala, Milan during the 1953-4 season.

There were still two more Verdi roles that he was to

add to his repertory, Carlo in the revival of *Ernani* during the 1956-7 season, and Macbeth in the first production of this opera at the Metropolitan in the 1958-9 season. Such phrases as 'impeccable vocalism', and 'master of this arduous role' appeared in reviews of the first, and 'golden tones', 'subtly inflected portrayal' of the second. Gérard in *Andrea Chénier* and Scarpia were two other roles he sang during the latter part of his Metropolitan career.

Warren's career then was primarily an American one, centred on New York, though there were appearances in Chicago and San Francisco. Likewise, although he did sing some non-Italian roles, his career was that of an Italian baritone. His voice, large and solid was of great natural beauty. His range was phenomenal, and at parties it is said he amused his guests by singing tenor arias, high C's and all! The critic Harold Schoenberg called him 'A human bellows mounted on matchsticks'.

His colleagues and musical coaches all testified to his great seriousness as an artist. He carefully studied the background to the roles he undertook and was immensely careful as to details of costume and stage business. He soaked himself in Shakespeare and Scottish history to prepare himself for *Macbeth*; and when studying Scarpia, he discovered that historically, the character should wear a pair of socks with red clocks on them. It did not matter that no one beyond the first two or three rows would see this detail, it had to be correct to satisfy Warren.

Fortunately this fine artist has left behind an enormous legacy of records—arias as well as complete operas. Among the latter one must single out *Pagliacci*, *Trovatore*, *La Forza del Destino* and *Macbeth*.

WOLFGANG WINDGASSEN

VISITORS to post-war Bayreuth need no introduction to Wolfgang Windgassen, who has been the mainstay of the tenor repertory at the Festspielhaus: Siegfried, Parsifal, Tristan, Erik, Tannhäuser, Walther. But it is not only Bayreuth that welcomes Windgassen every year; he is to be heard regularly in London, Vienna, and Stuttgart.

Windgassen was born in Annemasse, Switzerland of German parents, in 1914. His father was an opera singer, Fritz Windgassen, and his mother, also a singer, was the sister of Eva von der Osten, the famous Dresden soprano and first Octavian. Wolfgang Windgassen spent his childhood in Cassel, and then he moved to Stuttgart where his father was leading tenor from 1923-1944. He heard his first opera when he was nine, D'Albert's *Tiefland*, in which the leading roles were sung by his parents. When he was fourteen he began working in the Stuttgart Theatre on the technical staff, on a purely voluntary basis. He studied drama with his father, and then entered the local conservatory, where his teachers were Maria Ranzow and Alfons Fisher. From 1937-41 he served in the German army, but was released to accept an engagement at the small provincial house at Pforzheim, where he made his début as Alvaro in *La Forza del Destino*. In 1944 when all the German theatres were closed he was again conscripted; but as soon as the war was over he was engaged by the Stuttgart Opera, of which company he still is a member.

The tenor's first parts at Stuttgart were in the Italian repertory, and he also sang roles like Hoffmann, Max in *Freischütz*, Tamino, and Florestan. He then began to prepare the Wagnerian repertory, and in the 1950-51 season sang his first Siegmund. Meanwhile he had been heard by Wieland Wagner who engaged him to sing Parsifal and Froh in the first post-war Bayreuth Festival in 1951. His success at Bayreuth was considerable, and he repeated Parsifal there in 1952, adding Siegfried and Lohengrin in 1953, Tannhäuser in 1955, and Walther in 1956.

In the 1951-2 season he sang Florestan at La Scala, where his great aria in Act 2 'was sung with a delicacy and feeling rare among German tenors'. He returned there to sing Lohengrin, Siegmund and other roles in subsequent seasons. Of his first Bayreuth Lohengrin in 1953, Andrew Porter wrote: 'Wolfgang Windgassen is almost certainly the best Wagnerian tenor on the stage today. For the part of Siegfried he still lacks sheer vocal stamina (though almost all other qualities were his), but his Lohengrin was strong, noble, sweet and lyrical'. By the following summer's Bayreuth Festival, however, the same critic was able to write: 'Without losing any of the youthful freshness in his voice, Wolfgang Windgassen has developed new heroic resources since last year's Siegfried, and gives an eminently satisfying account of the role'.

The following December (1954), Windgassen made his Covent Garden début as Tristan, in a performance of *Tristan und Isolde* memorably conducted by Rudolf Kempe, with Sylvia Fisher. 'I doubt if a more satisfying Wagner tenor has been heard since the war—which means in effect since Lauritz Melchior', wrote Desmond Shawe-Taylor; while Philip Hope-Wallace remarked that Windgassen was 'one of those rare German *heldentenors* who sings notes instead of barking like a sea-lion'. In the Covent Garden *Ring* of 1956 Windgassen sang his first London Siegfried, a role he has sung there regularly since. Meanwhile he had become a regular member of the Vienna State Opera, dividing his appearances between there and his home opera, Stuttgart, where he still appears regularly. It is at Stuttgart that he still sings an occasional Italian role—Cavaradossi, Turiddu, Riccardo in *Ballo*, Radames, and Otello. At Stuttgart too he has been heard as Gerard in *Euryanthe*, the Kaiser in *Die Frau ohne Schatten*, Rienzi, Don José, and Pylades in *Iphigénie en Tauride*.

In between his appearances in Stuttgart and Vienna, Bayreuth and London, Windgassen finds time for guest appearances elsewhere in Germany, in Spain and Portugal, France and Italy, Belgium and Switzerland. He has only spent one season however in New York, 1956-7. Despite this heavy schedule, the tenor finds time for some relaxation, including his favourite hobby of model railways, which he shares with his young son, Peter.

VIRGINIA ZEANI

THERE have been quite a few successful husband-wife partnerships among opera singers—Grisi and Mario, Patti and Niccolini, Eva von der Osten and Friedrich Plaschke, Maria Gay and Giovanni Zenatello, Rosa Raisa and Giacomo Rimini are some of the couples that immediately spring to mind. More recently we have had Virginia Zeani and Nicola Rossi-Lemeni.

The Roumanian soprano was born in Transylvania in 1928. She studied in Bucharest, and then in Milan, where besides studying voice with Lidia Lypkowska, she pursued a course of literature and philosophy at the university. Her début was at the Teatro Duse in Bologna in 1948 as Marguerite in *Faust*, followed shortly after by Violetta at Turin. Appearances at most of the smaller Italian theatres followed, and there were also visits to San Sebastiano in 1949 where she sang Micaela and Nedda, and to Cairo in 1950 where she was heard as Adina. During the next three years her repertory expanded and she added Lucia, Manon, Elvira in *Puritani*, Gilda and Mimi to her roles.

London first heard Zeani in the summer of 1953 when she sang Violetta in an Italian season at the Stoll Theatre. The following year she sang Amina in *La Sonnambula* at Catania, and Adele in *Comte Ory* at Florence; and then during the 1955-6 season scored a great success in Rome as Elvira in *I Puritani*. This led to a Scala engagement the following year where she made her début as Cleopatra in Handel's *Giulio Cesare* with her future husband, Nicola Rossi-Lemeni in the title role. During her first Scala season she was chosen to create the part of Blanche in Poulenc's *Dialogues des Carmélites*. Shortly afterwards she sang at the Paris Opéra, in Vienna, and returned to London to sing the first Lucia heard there since 1925, in a season at the Stoll organized by S. A. Gorlinsky. Unlike previous Italian seasons by *ad hoc* companies in London, this one had the benefit of fine orchestral playing from the Royal Philharmonic and the London Symphony Orchestras under Vincenzo Bellezza and Manno Wolf-Ferrari. Philip Hope-Wallace in the *Manchester Guardian* wrote: 'If Mme. Zeani has not quite Mme. Callas's electrifying personality, she acted and sang with real dramatic and musical sense—very much the opposite of vain canary vocalist who often inhabited this role in the past. Her florid singing is effortful, but the beautiful line she once exhibited here in *Traviata* in a previous season is surer now and the performance is both pleasant to see and hear with very few of those piercing "tutta forza" top notes so much beloved in Italy'.

Since 1957 Zeani has been in much demand all over Italy. She has also appeared in Dublin and Madrid, Mexico and Zurich, Rio de Janeiro and Lisbon. In 1959 she added the role of Olga in *Ivan the Terrible* to her repertory, singing this part at Palermo; and in the 1959-60 season she sang her first Thais at the San Carlo, Naples. Early in 1960 she was summoned from Vienna to Covent Garden at twenty-four hours notice to replace a sick Joan Sutherland as Violetta, returning to the Austrian capital the next day to sing Micaela in French, and Violetta again a few days later. During 1959-60 season she sang all three soprano roles in *Les Contes d'Hoffmann* at the Rome Opera with her husband as the various evil spirits. Since 1960, Zeani has added three more roles to her repertory: Maria de Rohan in Donizetti's opera of that name, which she has sung at the San Carlo, Naples, Mariella in Mascagni's *Il Piccolo Marat*, which she has also sung at Naples and in other Italian theatres, and Desdemona, which she sang for the first time at the Rome Opera under Serafin, in December 1962. So far this versatile artist has not sung in the United States, but her début there cannot be long delayed.

AUTHOR'S POSTSCRIPT

To choose the names of a hundred singers of the post-war period to include in this book has been no easy task. Everyone, including the author, can think of another hundred names that deserve to have been included—that they are omitted does not mean that they too are not worthy of the title 'Great Singers'. It has been a difficult task to keep the right balance between the voices, and also to ensure that both British and American artists, some of whom perhaps have not made great international careers, but who have contributed to the enjoyment of operagoers on either side of the Atlantic, have been included in the correct ratio.

Biographies of singers are notoriously difficult things to compile; some artists are naturally reluctant to disclose the correct years of their birth, and others have somewhat hazy memories about the early days of their careers—and it has not always proved possible to check every fact from source (*i.e.* in the programmes of the opera houses or in the relevant newspaper reviews). Further, a biography is out of date as soon as the facts are typed, and the fact that this book has been several years in the course of production, explains why some biographies seem somewhat briefer and more out-of-date than others.

I also wish it had been possible to have written exhaustive critical biographies of every singer in this book—but this has not been the case; and so if this book falls between two stools (*i.e.* a book of reference and a book of critical studies) I can only ask my readers' indulgence.

H. D. R.